BORDERS OF QUALITATIVE RESEARCH

Navigating the Spaces Where Therapy, Education, Art, and Science Connect

Jennifer Leigh

First published in Great Britain in 2024 by

Policy Press, an imprint of
Bristol University Press
University of Bristol
1–9 Old Park Hill
Bristol
BS2 8BB
UK
t: +44 (0)117 374 6645
e: bup-info@bristol.ac.uk

Details of international sales and distribution partners are available at policy.bristoluniversitypress.co.uk

British Library Cataloguing in Publication Data
A catalogue record for this book is available from the British Library

ISBN 978-1-4473-5562-5 hardcover
ISBN 978-1-4473-5563-2 paperback
ISBN 978-1-4473-5565-6 ePub
ISBN 978-1-4473-5564-9 ePdf

Cover design: Lyn Davies Design
Front cover image: James Breslaw
Bristol University Press and Policy Press use environmentally responsible print partners.
Printed and bound in Great Britain by CPI Group (UK) Ltd, Croydon, CR0 4YY

FSC
www.fsc.org
MIX
Paper | Supporting responsible forestry
FSC® C013604

This book is dedicated to my parents, Anne and Jon, my husband Jimmy, and our children, Lincoln, Lucas, Summer, and Kira. I love you all so much.

Contents

List of figures

About the author

Jennifer Leigh is a Reader in Creative Practices for Social Justice in the School of Sociology, Social Policy, and Social Science Research, which is part of the Division for the study of Law, Society, and Social Justice at the University of Kent. She initially trained as a chemist, somatic movement therapist, and yoga teacher before completing her doctorate in education at the University of Birmingham. She has a particular interest in using embodied, reflective, and creative practices for social justice, impact, and public engagement. Her current work includes addressing and highlighting experiences of marginalisation in academia, health, and science due to intersectional factors including disability, gender, race, and caring responsibilities.

At Kent she co-leads the Future Human Signature Research Theme, is co-chair of the Visual and Sensory Research Cluster, and co-chair of the Staff Disability Network. Jennifer developed and leads the Summer Vacation Research Competition for postdoctoral researchers and undergraduates. Outside of Kent she leads research for WISC, an international network for Women in Supramolecular Chemistry, is co-lead of the National Association for Disabled Staff Networks' STEMM Action Group, is the Disability Champion for The Athena Forum, and is part of the #WIASN (Women in Academia Support Network)'s research working group. She also sits on the Wellcome Trust Inclusive Research Practice and Design Expert Advisory group, VITAE's Policy Advisory Group, and the strategy group for Empowering Female Minds in STEM (EFeMS).

Her recent books are *Women in Supramolecular Chemistry: Collectively crafting the rhythms of our work and lives in STEM* (2022, Policy Press), *Embodied Inquiry: Research methods* (2021, Bloomsbury), *Ableism in Academia: Theorising lived experiences of disability and chronic illness in higher education* (2020, UCL Press), and *Conversations on Embodiment across Higher Education: Teaching, practice, and research* (2019, Routledge). Her next book *How to Thrive in Laboratory Life: A toolkit* will be published by Routledge in 2024. Her email is j.s.leigh@kent.ac.uk, and her socials are @DrSchniff, @SupraChem, and @SupraLab1.

Acknowledgements

Much of this book develops the work and research that has formed the basis of my academic career to date, and I would like to thank and acknowledge all the publishers and presses in which my articles, papers, and chapters have appeared. Please note that all of the images in the book are my own with the exception of Figure 5 which was taken by Phaedra Petsilas.

I would like to thank and acknowledge all the people who have helped, supported, and believed in me. As well as the people I am dedicating this book to, this includes Sheila and Jeffrey who may not have understood exactly what I did but were still proud of me. My brother Dan and the amazingly wonderful Viv who have always made sure I have my feet on the ground, and all the rest of my wider family. I want to give a big shout out to my doctoral supervisor and friend Richard Bailey, who took a punt on me way back and has been there ever since. To Ellie who I met as a trainee yoga teacher and wish I could see more often. Everyone from Trinity Camping. Jo. My wonderful January Yoga Motivation Group (who have been there for much longer than the month of January and for much more than just yoga motivation). The Coven – what can I say? Let's enchant the world. The 'girls' in the village for much-needed nights of too much booze and just the right amount of chatter. Jen Hiscock (hereafter, Jen H), and all the incredible and awe-inspiring ladies of Women in Supramolecular Chemistry (WISC). My cheerleader, work-buddy, and adopted baby brother Elliott. Bee for being a sounding board for revisions and generally being great. Mudimo for helping me find time to return to my body. The NADSN STEMM Action Group for action, activism, and community. Emma, who has been my best friend since I was 10, and who is now my co-conspirator at work. You have made my life so much better, thank you. All the incredible and inspiring people I work with day-to-day as students, co-researchers, and interns. I need to thank all the funders and supporters who have made this work possible; the Society for Research into Higher Education (Newer Researchers Prize), UKRI (Future Leaders Fellowship Grant Number: MR/T020415/1), Royal Society (Grant Number: APX\R1\201170), Royal Society of Chemistry (Inclusion and Diversity Fund), Scot Chem, Biochemical Society (Diversity in Science grant), ChemPlusChem, Crystal Growth & Design, Strem Chemicals, University College London, Università degli Studi di Cagliari, Christian-Albrechts-Universität zu Kiel, and the University of Kent. And finally, so many of my colleagues at the University of Kent – let's keep making Kent and the world a better place! To all of these people, and to everyone who is not named but has been there – thank you.

Foreword

Aimee Grant
Cardiff, UK

I was delighted to be asked to write this foreword for Jennifer Leigh's book. I have consistently been fascinated by the range and breadth of experience and literature that she weaves into her research, and this book is no exception! These days, it is very common for funders and other bodies to suggest that research should be *interdisciplinary*, however, how this should be achieved is much less clear. Furthermore, at a time when there is a push for these methods, the dearth of research methods literature to guide the way is a striking absence, surely diluting the potential impacts of interdisciplinary collaboration. As such, this book fills a much-needed gap in the literature.

Based upon her decades of experience as a scientist, therapist, and educator, Leigh's research is consistently at the cutting edge of *interdisciplinary* research, for example, involving hard science – in this case chemistry – with consideration of *embodied* practices. It is this cutting-edge exploration, described in a highly accessible way, that researchers can find within *Borders of Qualitative Research.* In doing so, Leigh identifies ways in which the subjectivities and embodied realities of scientists impact on their practice, challenging the dominance of positivist world views and opening up a range of ontological perspectives. In doing so, the potential for harm to (under-supported) researchers is front and centre, raising important questions about the support provided to novice researchers, which are relevant to new and seasoned researcher alike.

Although these types of philosophical debates and considerations of how to change the academy for the better are challenging, Leigh takes readers on a gentle journey, sharing her own experiences to illustrate key points. First, she considers subjective research practices, including the use of qualitative methods, including those which rely on creative methods and embodied practices. Later she establishes current disciplinary boundaries, from art, science and ethics, before finally showing interdisciplinarity through a series of case studies. I am sure that by the end of reading this book any reader will be considering their practice through a different lens, which can help to identify ways in which creativity and embodiment can *add* to hard science research, while simultaneously reducing the potential for harm.

This book is highly relevant to current research trends, and the case studies will be of interest and have relevance to an exceptionally wide audience. I have no doubt that reading this book will open up new ontological opportunities for readers, and that this book will continue to have relevance for decades to come.

Aimee Grant is a Senior Lecturer and Wellcome Trust Career Development Fellow at Swansea University, and author of *Doing Your Research Project with Documents: A step-by-step guide to take you from start to finish* (2022, Policy Press) and *Doing EXCELLENT Social Research with Documents: Practical examples and guidance for qualitative researchers* (2019, Routledge).

PART I

Introduction to qualitative, creative, and embodied research

Introduction to Part I

I am an interdisciplinary researcher. My passion is utilising embodied and creative qualitative research to capture transient evocative moments and authentic stories of people's lives (Leigh and Brown 2021a). I am particularly interested in exploring and sharing the subjective experiences of those who are marginalised, and highlighting these testimonials in order to effect change. The life I lived beyond academia as a scientist, therapist, teacher, and artist taught me lessons about intention and impact imperative for all qualitative researchers; particularly those using creative and embodied methods. It showed me how art, education, therapy, and qualitative research share borders and lie adjacent to science. A naive or unwary researcher, artist, or educator can easily get lost, or even harm themselves and their participants if they find themselves in unfamiliar therapeutic territory. Researchers, artists, therapists, and educators are trained to navigate in different lands.

I am a researcher. However, before I became a researcher I was a scientist,[1] and I accepted that there was an objective and absolute truth, and purity in the scientific method. Before I became a researcher, I was a therapist. I worked therapeutically with a humanistic and person-centred ethos using movement, words, and creative outputs such as drawing or mark-making in the service of others to help them process difficult experiences. My work facilitated others to learn from and take what they needed from their own

[1] Throughout this book I use 'science' and 'scientists' to denote those engaged in the natural and physical sciences such as biology, chemistry, and physics, as well as those located within STEMM (Science, Technology, Engineering, Mathematics, and Medicine) disciplines. This is in line with Thomas Kuhn's (1962) definition of 'hard' and 'soft' disciplines. Although this definition is obviously far from ideal, it can be a useful tool (Matthew and Pritchard 2010), particularly when it comes to delineating what is expected from and of those engaged with the 'hard' or more traditional sciences and those working within more human-orientated subjects such as the social sciences or psychology. There are very real differences between science and social science, for example in the ways in which students are taught, the constructions of knowledge, and how academic identity is developed. Despite attempts for social science to emulate the natural and physical sciences:

> The natural science approach simply does not work in the social sciences. … We should promote social sciences that are strong where natural science is weak – that is, in reflexive analysis and deliberation about values and interests aimed at praxis, which are essential to social and economic development in society. We should promote value rationality over epistemic rationality, in order to arrive at social science that matters. (Flyvbjerg 2006: 38)

lives and their relationships with the world and others around them, and to let go of what they no longer needed. Before I became a researcher, I was a teacher. I trained to teach children aged 11–19 in science, and worked with children aged four and older with and without special educational needs across the curriculum in the UK. Before I became a researcher, I was an artist, using movement and fibre to capture ephemeral moments of creativity in a spinning web for others to notice and play with.

So why am I writing this book? What am I saying that is unique, or, more importantly, do I feel needs to be said yet has not been shared so far within existing literature?

Scientific researchers are trained to fervently and unquestioningly trust in the scientific method and the myth of objectivity. For research like mine to be effective and give voice to others there must be an acceptance of the subjective other and their experience. If the moments under investigation are sensitive, personal, or traumatic, as is often the case with those who are marginalised due to any reason, for this process to not be exploitative or damaging to either party there has to be trust and a relationship between the researcher and the participant.

Therapists are trained to build rapport, and to establish relationships and trust with others, while safeguarding themselves and their client from harm as they talk about the most painful aspects of their lives. Researchers are not, though the conversations that they have with participants may elicit stories and reminiscences of pain or trauma, particularly when using embodied or creative methods.

Teachers and educators are trained to facilitate others to learn from experiences, to observe, to manage group dynamics, and to support and guide their students' development. Researchers are not, though they may find themselves running focus groups, conducting an ethnography, interventions, or working with children or vulnerable adults to gather research data.

Artists use their work to evoke emotion in or a reaction from their audiences. Researchers are trained to produce outputs that meet externally imposed criteria of excellence and academicity.

It is rare to be a qualitative researcher who has training and experience across therapy, education, art, and science. It is only through working in and across them all that I have been able to see what is missing from current research mores and texts and trainings, and the potential for harm to both researchers and participants. This potential for harm is magnified with the use of the embodied and creative methods that I treasure, because of their capacity to build rapport and relationships, and take people beyond the conscious, surface layers of their experiences and expose their hidden, unconscious, richer truths.

This book is not a consideration of the different theoretical perspectives that underlie embodiment within academic disciplines; that can be found in my book *Conversations on Embodiment* (Leigh 2019a). This is not a methods or instructional book on how to 'do' Embodied Inquiry, develop embodied conscious self-awareness, reflexivity, or positionality; that can be found in my book *Embodied Inquiry: Research methods* (Leigh and Brown 2021a). This is neither the call-to-arms and theorisation for activist research that addresses marginalisation that can be found in my book *Ableism in Academia* (Brown and Leigh 2020). It is also not a demonstration of how creative and embodied research can highlight lived experiences of marginalisation through words, images, and creative writing to collectively share true stories that are not real; as this can be found in my book *Women in Supramolecular Chemistry* (Leigh et al 2022c). My vision for *this* book, the reason why I believe it needed to be written, is so that researchers can understand more about how the work they do borders onto therapy, education, or art, and how therapists, artists, and educators can understand how their work borders onto research and fits alongside science.

This book is a demonstration of how I have reflected on my ontological perspective and its shaping of my research. Ontology is the study of existence and its nature, and, interwoven with beliefs, assumptions, and societal and cultural values, is a concept that can be hard to understand and get to grips with as a researcher. I would love it if this book helped other researchers to take the time and space they need to reflect on their own ontological positioning and how it relates to their research design, questions, goals, and plans.

The lessons I share highlight the importance of identifying and reflecting on intention. They foreground the importance of being self-aware and present to embodied experiences, on our own as well as in relation to and with others. Being present to all the possible implications of research will help ensure that we and/or our work do not unwittingly stray over a border. If we understand where these borders are we can avoid or at least minimise the accidental or unintentional harm that can unwittingly be done to ourselves and others.

The structure of this book

This book is divided into three parts. Part I introduces qualitative research with an emphasis on embodied and creative approaches, and sets out three lessons I believe are vital. These are:

- reflection (which I learned most from my training and practice in education);
- awareness (which I learned most from my training and practice in somatics and embodiment); and
- relationship (which I learned most from my training and practice in therapy).

Part II is shorter, and sets out the lessons that can be learned from art, science and ethics. In this section of the book I discuss the similarities between artistic research (research on art), Practice-as-Research (research into and formed by artistic practice where the result is art), and arts-based methods (creative methods such as painting, collage, drama and the like used for research in any discipline), where they are fundamentally different, and what researchers can learn from them. I discuss problems with the scientific method and ideal, and how scientific knowledge and understanding can be used to enable us to become better qualitative researchers.

Part III is comprised of four case studies, which practically illustrate how qualitative research borders onto therapy, art, education, science, and ethics. Finally, there is a short chapter that aims to draw the threads of the book together, and 'tidy up' or 'weave in' any loose ends.

Qualitative, creative, and embodied research

Qualitative research is about finding meaning (Braun and Clarke 2013); it is engaged with finding out about people's experiences so we can learn and make new knowledge. Qualitative research values subjectivity and reflexivity (Evans-Winters 2019). As qualitative researchers, we do not have to aspire to a 'scientific ideal' of a disassociated and objective brain divorced from the messiness and reality of the lived world, although some social science researchers do hold fast to the idea that they are scientists seeking an objective, provable truth (Flyvbjerg 2006). Instead, qualitative researchers, particularly those of us using embodied and creative methods, *use* the messiness and realities of the lived world. We can intentionally draw on our messy, real, bodies and incorporate them into what, how, and why we research. Embodied, sensory, participatory, and creative approaches all allow researchers to gain richer data, to be more explicitly reflexive, and to work with vulnerable participants and those less able to use their voices. I explore the borders of embodied and creative qualitative research where the hinterlands merge with art, therapy, education, and science. These borders are not clear, in fact they are fluid, porous, and can both be affected by and themselves influence decisions around factors including ethics, burn-out, honesty (of researcher and participant), supervision, and vulnerability. They can be imagined as a psychogeographical map showing distinct lands with overlapping boundaries and shared landmarks (see Figure 1). A map is a representation of a different space or reality; one that shows the relationship between different points or elements. In mathematical terms, mapping is the product of transforming points from one space onto the same or different space. For example, the 'real' world of roads and landmarks is transformed onto a piece of paper or an image. Mapping and conceptualising the ideas around art, therapy, education, science, and qualitative research, how

Figure 1: Psychogeographical map illustrating the borders between research, therapy, art, education, and science

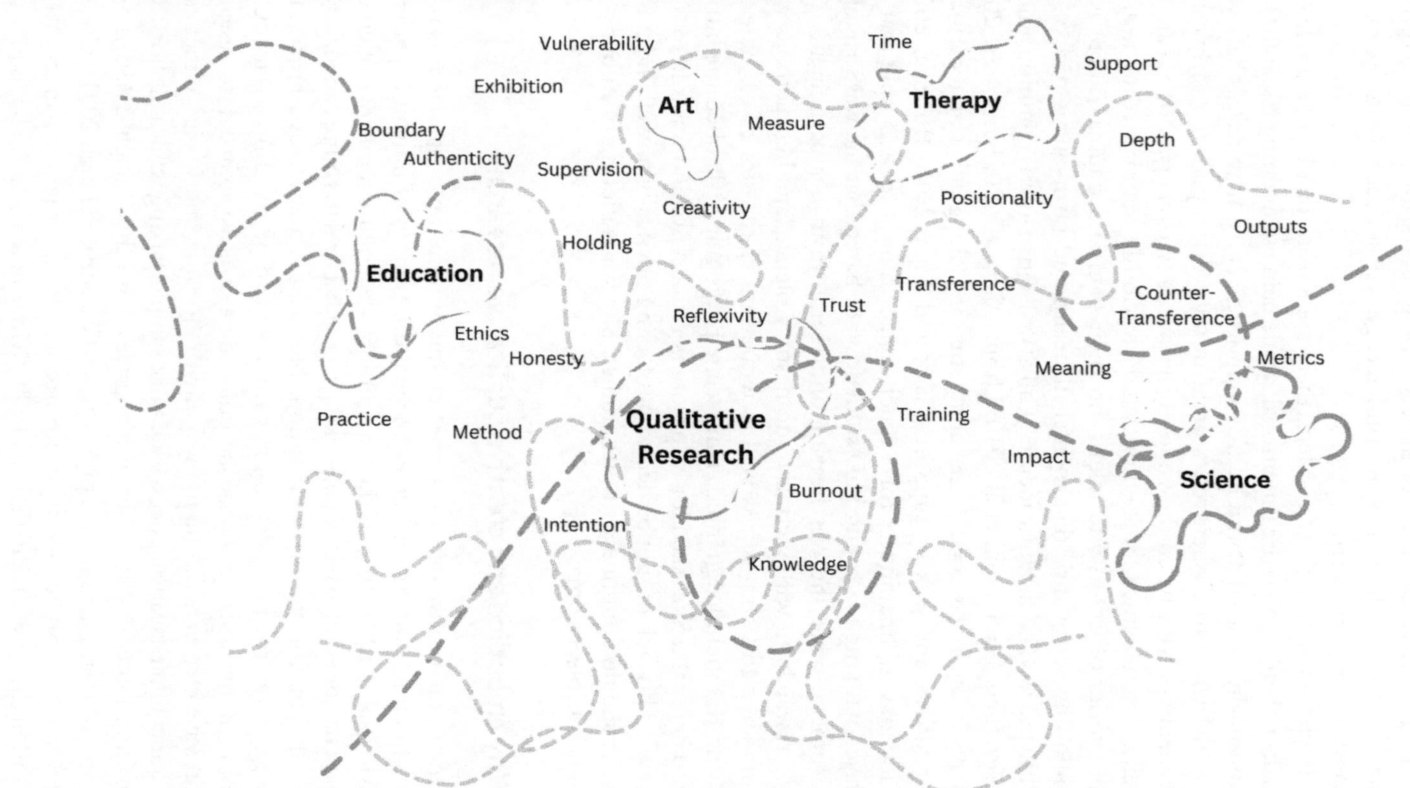

they connect and how they relate to each other (the *psycho* element of psychogeographical) brings both artistic expression (see Lessons from art in Part II) and a visual means of understanding and relating, by transforming them onto the different space and recognised concepts of geographical borders and boundaries.

Beyond mapping these borders, there are lessons that can be learned to make us better and more intentional, while being safer doing research. I am continually amazed at the lack of support given to new researchers who are 'thrown' into qualitative research. In my work supporting early career academics I have heard the same stories over and over again of researchers being overwhelmed, burned out, and vicariously traumatised by hearing the stories of others and taking on their pain and trauma. There is an unhealthy acceptance that mental ill health and burn-out is part of the PhD process and life in academia (Gill 2016). Burn-out is common among researchers (Archibong et al 2010; Urbina-Garcia 2020; Rolle et al 2021; Ayres 2022), and is eased by managing stressors, taking time out, rebalancing workloads, and seeking support (Clark and Sousa 2018; Boynton 2020). Vicarious trauma lingers for a much longer time. One example that has stayed with me is a young PhD student who shared that she was struggling to process what she was hearing and seeing from her participants. She was researching with victims of domestic violence, and her methods were embodied and creative. As well as witnessing victim stories of abuse and harm, this included graphic crime scene photographs that became burned into her brain. She asked for help from her supervisor and was told to 'suck it up'. This lack of support led to her feeling physically unwell and unsure if she should continue with her studies. She was suffering from burn-out *and* vicarious trauma.

Why embodied and creative qualitative research?

One of the motivations for a research question in the social sciences is the intention to understand 'the essences and meanings of human experience' (Moustakas 1994: 105). Others might include a desire to uncover elements of behaviour and experience, seeking to predict or determine causal factors, or illumination through description. Not least is research as a process that engages the total self, sustaining passionate and personal involvement. All these motivations can be satisfied through a creative approach to research. Creative elements can be used to elicit reflections and stories, either as an adjunct to the creative process itself (for example, talking while collaboratively making something together or alongside each other (Leigh 2019a)), or in response to artefacts such as photographs (Watson and Leigh 2021). Creative research can also be used to create artefacts, films, or performances that are 'stuff in their own right' (Latour 1999). Movement itself can be used as part of the research process, a research tool, and in dissemination, and I will explore this more in Lesson 2, Lessons from art, and Case Study 3.

Creative research encompasses a wide range of research methods, approaches, and techniques that go beyond conventional qualitative methods such as surveys, questionnaires, focus groups, or interviews (Kara 2015). I find creative data more exciting and authentic than conventional qualitative data (Wilson 2008). Creative research is most commonly associated with arts-based and participatory research methods (Lyon 2016). This can include the co-creation of artefacts (Leavy 2015), and also incorporates fiction as research (Leavy 2016), video as method (Harris 2016), and movement or somatics (Bacon 2010). Creative research is often used to break down power dynamics between researcher and researchee as it can involve the co-creation or generation of knowledge (Mannay et al 2017). As such, creative research fits well within paradigms with a critical or activist agenda (Shildrick 1997; Johns et al 2022). Venus Evans-Winters (2019) discussed how qualitative research needs to have outcomes, be action-orientated, and provide a counter-narrative to racist and patriarchal portrayals of marginalised people to be transformative. As activist research becomes more common, researchers can be struck by conflicting desires to 'help' participants, further their cause, and have concrete outcomes as a result of their research. Creative research has also been credited with allowing participants to be more honest, express more emotions, share not only what is easily expressed in words but go deeper and be more reflective (Brown and Leigh 2018a). The creative aspect of research can happen at any stage from design, data gathering, to analysis or dissemination (Leigh and Brown 2021a). Creative approaches 'breathe life into research participants' personal histories and commentary in ways that emotionally connect the reader to the research subject at hand' (Evans-Winters 2019: 1). More than that, in her book *Black Feminism in Qualitative Inquiry*, Evans-Winters described the approach as 'soul work' (2019: 7). This kind of comment about qualitative research serves to emphasise the border it shares with psychotherapy.

My approach to creative research is from an embodied perspective. This is not unique; Laura Ellingson (2017), Derek McCormack (2013), Sarah Pink (2009), and Evans-Winters (2019) all wrote about their approach to qualitative research which either explicitly or implicitly included an embodied perspective. An embodied perspective is aligned with multimodal processes and communication (Jewitt et al 2016), and can encompass more than 'just' body language and alternative ways of communicating. Creative methods within a phenomenological or qualitative research project allow a researcher to access deeper, richer, and more emotional stories. An embodied approach enhances the likelihood that the researcher will recognise the resonances of these stories in their own body. Creative methods tap into deeper and more unconscious layers of experience, and by using these approaches the researcher is much more likely to touch on stories and experiences that a more conventional technique would not reveal. In other words, creative research allows researchers to take a 'short cut' to creating emotional intimacy between them and their participants. Emotional intimacy is a necessary part of an effective therapeutic relationship, highlighting its border onto therapy.

An illustration of how creative research can create emotional intimacy is a technique that asks people to use an object as a metaphorical representation (Lakoff and Johnson 2003). If I am part of a group of people who do not know each other and are asked to introduce themselves for the first time, it is likely everyone would say their names and their jobs – in other words what they *do*. Potentially, if the group is facilitated or in a research context the group might share why they are present, what they research, what they are hoping to get out of the meeting, or how they are feeling about it. Those last answers are likely to be in direct response to requests from the facilitator. Now, imagine that before meeting a new group you are asked to bring an object or picture that represents your response to a specific question. Examples of questions in research projects and workshops I have facilitated have been 'Who are you as a teacher?', 'Who are you as a researcher?', 'Who are you as a dancer?', or 'Who are you as a scientist?'. The introduction then becomes a showing or sharing of each person's object or image, and the telling of the story of how and why it represents that aspect of their identity. I am sure you can imagine the quality and depth of information and narrative is tangibly different from when people 'just' introduce themselves, as they share who they *are* rather than what they *do*. This creates an emotional connection and intimacy far beyond that achieved in a conventional introduction. My role in this is as a facilitator and also a boundary holder – ensuring everyone gets to speak and share, holding the time frame for the session, and ensuring the activity serves its purpose (for example, as a learning event, part of a workshop, data gathering for a research project, or the first meeting of a new collaborative autoethnography group).

The boundary of a specific question is important. Although the questions are deliberately open-ended and hard to answer, they are still specific, directed, and contained. A group will likely share more personal and emotional aspects of their stories than they would in a conventional introduction, and by creating a container or boundary with a specific question it is easier to allow people to keep private those parts of their stories that are more painful or less relevant. When I use this technique I always go first, because it sets the tone and allows others to see the richness of a story and what is expected. Although I obviously think about the object or image I will share in response to the question, I generally do not plan what I will say too much. I have surprised myself by how, even when I use the same object to answer the same or similar question in a different setting, my story changes as my relationship to that aspect of myself changes. If I am sharing an object that relates to my identity as a researcher, I can choose not to talk about when I lived in poverty as a single parent, or aspects of my identity such as my religion or my journey with chronic illness or disability. I *can* choose to share that information – but I do not have to. However, if I am asked to share an object in response to a broader 'Who are you?' prompt, I would do myself a disservice if I did not mention those facets of my story. It can be interesting to ask people to represent different aspects of their identity in the same space. I remember leading a session for a group of educational developers and asking them to bring objects to answer both 'Who are you as a teacher?', and 'Who are you as a researcher?'. The differences in how they saw themselves and their authority in those arenas, which were both features of their day-to-day academic job, was enlightening for everyone. The questions can also be forward looking; I asked one group 'Who do you want to be as a scientist?' which revealed very different answers to 'Who are you as a scientist?'. The answers and objects shared for the first question were aspirational and wide rather than drawn down into the everyday reality of life and work which can be very different from what people dream of being. As well as exploring questions around identity, these kinds of techniques can be particularly valuable when researching into experiences that are hard to put into words, such as traumatic, emotional, or embodied experiences (Leigh and Brown 2021a), as well as for reaching groups who may find it hard to express themselves and allow their stories to be captured (Leigh 2017; Leigh 2020a).

A reflective and autoethnographic approach

Autoethnography, specifically evocative autoethnography as developed by Caroline Elis and Art Bochner (Bochner and Ellis 2016), is a form of academic and creative writing and another example of creative research practice that centres stories. Autoethnography is the study of self in relation to society, and is used to shed light on experiences and evoke emotions and responses in the audience. It is also a useful tool for researchers to reflect on and understand their ontological perspective, and how they might draw the threads of their research together. I would strongly encourage every researcher to take the time and space to reflect on their journey.

My background and route to creative and embodied qualitative research was not mapped out and linear (Leigh 2020b, 2021), and nor was the process of writing this book. Concepts and ideas that I encountered chronologically as I have woven my way through life (Leigh 2020b) became a tangled and matted ball of yarn that was hard to follow or make sense of. I often explain my holistic approach to research by describing myself as a 'star child born of hippies' with parents who were self-employed naturopaths and osteopaths. I was brought up vegetarian, practising yoga with my mother who qualified as a counselling psychologist when I was a teenager. As I read and reflected on my relationship to therapeutic practice and how it touches on so many aspects of the way I conduct qualitative research, I realised I needed to dwell a little more on the impact that this had, and why my approach is so important to what I do and who I am. It is enlightening to reflect on who we are, how we came to be, and how this can shape us. I say 'can' because the act of reflecting allows us to act reflexively – we can choose how we act and respond and the paths that we take rather than allowing our unconscious prior shaping to guide us.

My mother studied for an Open University distance learning degree in psychology when my brother and I were young children. It took her many years as she fitted courses and modules in around working, home-educating, and looking after us. I remember her testing out theories she had read about in child development by asking us to do tasks (like forward rolls or roly polies) to make a link between theories and practice of social, physical, and intellectual development (Piaget 1928, 1976; Vygotsky 1987). I remember a few weeks where she had a Siamese fighting fish in a tank and taught him to swim through hoops for a reward as a demonstration of positive behaviour training and conditioning (Skinner 1948; Pavlov 2010). She maintained an interest in psychology and education, and qualified as a counsellor while I was growing up. I was a teenager when she decided to go to graduate school on the first cohort of a master's degree in counselling that was recognised by the British Psychological Society for chartered status in counselling psychology. Years later in 2009, the Health and Care Professions Council awarded statutory registration for this course at doctoral level as the first stage of what became the establishment of counselling psychologists alongside clinical psychologists. Her master's degree was taught over an evening and a day each week. On her study night, she would travel to London and not be home until 11 or 12 pm before going to study again the next day. The days she was out the rest of us either had to fend for ourselves or, more often, eat a casserole that she would prepare in the morning before leaving. I loved those casseroles, with crispy potatoes and a yeasty marmitey flavour, though I remember my brother and father being less keen.

I have vivid memories of my mother being in what I would now recognise as a normal stage of graduate study – where your mind feels blown by information, and you just want to share and talk about it. I was a willing sponge, eager to learn whatever I could. My older daughters had parallel experiences when I returned to study, learning to pronounce 'phenomenology' in a sing song tone, and even now my youngest wants to know what I am writing, what I am researching, and why it is important. As a teenager I wanted to meet the course mates my mother spoke so much about – I would hear some of their voices when they called the house phone to talk to her (including one who had the most incredible chocolatey smooth

Irish-American accent). She took me to a couple of social events, and I met them and her tutor – who physically embodied a caricature of what you might imagine a stereotypical psychology professor to look like – he was short, dark-haired, with bright eyes, a neat beard, a quick way of talking, and a pipe clamped in his hand, mouth, or both. I cannot accurately remember what he wore that night any more than I remember my own clothes that day, but in my imagination he was enveloped in tweed, with elbow patches in the appropriate spots. My mother's interest and resonance was with humanistic and person-centred theories and practices of psychotherapy, and it is no surprise that these were what she spoke about most keenly, and I found myself immersed with her. Carl Rogers' unconditional positive regard for and acceptance of the client (Rogers 1967) became a fundamental and non-negotiable tenet of therapeutic interaction for me. Actually, Rogers' work became fundamental tenets and ideals for all interactions that resonated with not only my therapeutic trainings, but the way that I approached education, research, and tried to interact with my family and colleagues. Why would you not want to recognise the beauty and humanness in everyone and work to support them?[2] Of course, I am not claiming that I live up to these ideals all the time, particularly when tired, feeling hangry, or under stress. I do think it is fair to claim that I aspire to though.

Academically I was an all-rounder, although focused on science in my later school years. Toward the end of my education I became very ill, missing much of my final year, but I completed my A-Levels and was desperate to get 'back to normal' and study at university. I turned down a place at the University of Oxford to read chemistry at the University of Birmingham and threw myself into student life, wanting to make up for what felt like lost time. With hindsight, I was overwhelmed with the transition from being an invalid as well as coming from an all-girls grammar school to a university course with less than 10% women. I found myself in an environment where for the first time in my life (thank you misogyny (Ahmed 2017)) fluttering my eyelashes, wearing a short skirt, or *crying* could let me get away with pretty much anything. Prior to this my teachers had a short shrift with feminine wiles. Women in chemistry and science were at that time very much in the minority (Colwell and Bertsch McGrayne 2020). Unfortunately, despite longstanding concerted programmes and efforts to address gender balance and the lack of diversity in science, it is still not a welcoming place (Rosser 1988, 2004, 2012, 2017; Royal Society of Chemistry 2018; Royal Society 2021). The need for equity, diversity, and inclusion in science and academia is one of my current research areas (Caltagirone et al 2021b; Egambaram et al 2022; Leigh et al 2022b, 2022c, 2024a), and although most of the time

[2] This is, of course, a rhetorical question, and one I recommend returning to often.

I identify as a social scientist rather than a chemist, my two older daughters have both chosen to study science. One is in the final stages of a chemistry PhD, and the other studying computer science. She chose to talk about gender inequality in her subject for an assessed presentation – the apple does not fall far from the tree!

I do not think it would shock anyone who knew me at that age to say that I went a bit wild and off the rails in my second year at university. I ended up failing a course and falling pregnant aged 19, taking a year out to have a baby (the one now completing her PhD). When I returned to finish my degree, it was with a renewed sense of seriousness about my education as well as an attitude that meant I preferred to ask a question and potentially look stupid rather than sit and not know – a strategy that was particularly useful when learning quantum mechanics. I worked weekdays and term times while the nursery was open. I finished my final year top in physical chemistry, with a mitigated overall degree grade that acknowledged this and downplayed my second-year results. I had applied for a place on a PGCE (teacher training course) in secondary science, but before I could take it up I was offered a fully funded PhD in computational chemistry by my undergraduate dissertation supervisor. I took up the PhD, though shortly after beginning my supervisor left to join industry. This led to a spiral of events that resulted in my being expelled from the university while pregnant with my second child (the computer scientist). These experiences definitely influenced the ways in which I approach my work with marginalised groups in science and chemistry.

During my first pregnancy I started antenatal yoga, and as a PhD student I found Iyengar yoga (Iyengar 1966) classes at the university. I began a three-year yoga teacher training course and started running my own classes as a yoga teacher. Here, the learning from my mother about working in service to others really came to the forefront. Teaching yoga meant that I also needed to practise too, and to become aware of where I felt things and how they worked. When I was planning a class, I needed to be clear on what I wanted my students to get out of it, so that I could work to adjust things for them appropriately. Yoga was less about *achieving* the external form of a pose, and more about the *internal* process and work. The first step of this was to develop awareness, a step that is also necessary for the reflexivity demanded in education, therapy, and research. After leaving my doctorate I undertook four years of a training in somatic movement therapy. This training from Linda Hartley included developmental movement and play (Hartley 1989), somatic psychology (Hartley 2004), Authentic Movement (Adler 2002), and the development of therapeutic presence and self in relation to others (Hartley 2005). Hartley's background was in Body Mind Centering©, Dance Movement Therapy, and Jungian and Gestalt psychologies. Her humanistic approach resonated with my mother's, though I do not recall

Hartley directly referring to Rogers or person-centred approaches. I do recall conversations with my mother as I discussed my training though – on looking at the syllabus and content she compared it directly to one she was by then teaching, saying that it was body-based rather than talking therapy. That is not to say we did not talk in somatic movement therapy, more that talk originated from and was grounded in the body, and that the body was used to embody, experience, and process emotions and feelings that were either less accessible to the conscious 'talking' mind, or that were hard to express. The joy of somatics was that it didn't have to be therapeutic. It could be used artistically, as an educational tool for people of all ages, to treat a specific bodily injury, or just enjoyed for the pure pleasure and fun of it. For several years I worked providing bespoke classes for SureStart centres and local Primary Care Trusts. At the same time, I worked in schools and private therapeutic practice. The SureStart classes focused on infants and young children with their care-giver, using baby massage and baby yoga along with developmental play. I offered a safer space where women could either engage with or have space from their babies and children. There was a creche set up in a corner and I was perfectly happy to hold a baby while a mother exercised or rested. The sessions were more structured than a 'mommy and baby' group, and allowed people to chat and interact or not, depending on what was more comfortable for them. In support of the then government's focus on healthy eating, we also provided a nutritious snack lunch. The SureStart centres were set up in areas of social deprivation, aiming to engage those who were 'hard to reach' or marginalised. The classes proved incredibly popular with locals, and were an easy way for the centres to meet targets around community involvement.

It was during this time that I started developing my artistic practice – initially in movement. I collaborated with institutions including the Birmingham Royal Ballet, and worked privately with musicians and dancers. I also began exploring textile and fibre art after learning to knit as something to keep my hands busy when I stopped smoking. I started with the usual squares and scarfs and quickly moved on to more challenging pieces such as 'Mary the Alien' which I made out of cashmere for my then three-year-old's birthday. Mary was made out of cashmere and stuffed with weighted fibres. Inside her tummy I hid a bag filled with heavy glass beads and semi-precious crystals (I was born of hippies after all). Mary was used as a most beloved pillow, and underwent several surgeries to mend her as her flesh wore thin and tore. She has now retired to a safe shelf where she oversees goings on, and sports a Babygro purloined from my youngest to protect her from further damage. I started working with knitted felt to create three-dimensional pieces using short-rows to give torsion and topographical shape (see Figure 2). I enjoyed making pieces that were unusual or technically challenging, such as devil horns or fairy wings. My designs were published in several leading knitting

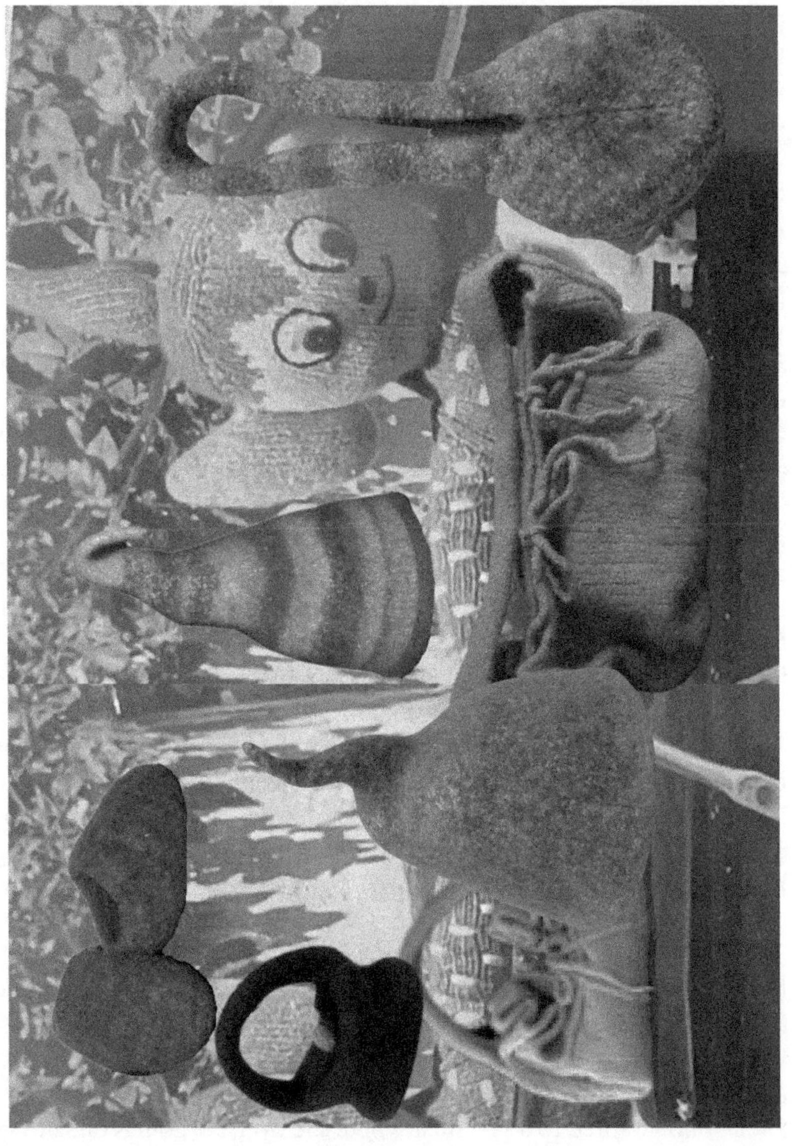

Figure 2: Some examples of knitted designs, and Mary the Alien when she was new

journals and magazines, and I was even offered a book deal. I turned it down because I thought the terms were unfavourable – I was yet to come across academic publishing! I tended to design for a specific person, and after I had made an item I gave it away. The copies of the journals have disappeared among several moves and so I have no images of many of my pieces. Some of my designs are still available on the website Ravelry.com under my married name Jennifer Hilton.

I left Birmingham to move back to Kent and be nearer my parents when my children were ten and five. My then business partner and I had applied to the Arts Council for funding to support a project working with children with special needs and their families. The feedback was that they wanted us to partner with a university to provide evaluation. At that point in my life, I decided I did not want someone else to get a PhD from my work. I applied to several doctoral programmes, and eventually accepted a place at Roehampton University, with Professor Richard Bailey as my supervisor. This second PhD explored how children perceived, embodied, and reflected on their sense of embodiment through movement (Leigh 2012). I worked with children aged four to eleven within a school, using creative methods to encourage reflection (Leigh 2020a), and expression and self-regulation of emotions (Leigh 2017). A few months later I also began a PGCE (teacher training) in Secondary Science on an iTeach distant learning programme run by Canterbury Christ Church University and Hibernia College. This second course was to pay the bills, because at that time student teachers in shortage subjects were given a training bursary and I had two young children and a mortgage. During this period my husband of ten years left. My youngest was so distressed she barely spoke for a year. I was single, and solely financially responsible for my family and home. I finished my teacher training course, then, despite being offered a full-time position teaching science at a school for autistic children, took the decision to take at least a year out to care for my own children and continue my PhD part-time, which had had to be put on hold. The following year I started a Research Associateship (a postdoctoral research position), despite not quite having submitted my thesis. This post-doc was in psychology, looking at the impact of quality of care on individuals with profound and multiple disabilities (Beadle-Brown et al 2016; Bradshaw et al 2018). I continued onto a second post-doc associated with the research project *Imagining Autism*.

When I started my (second) PhD which is referred to throughout the book and in Case Study 1, I became aware of the tensions between working therapeutically, educationally, or as a researcher, when I had to negotiate an ethics application. This was denied twice because I wrote that the participants were more important than the research. Reflection and reflexivity, both mine and my participants' and the ways this was enhanced through creative methods, became an important theme of my thesis, and one that transferred into my work in higher education (Leigh and Bailey 2013; Leigh 2016). I remember my supervisor telling me that I had reflected on my reflections, and had gone a bit 'deeper' than was expected or was normal. I was hired for the first post-doc because my ethical and therapeutic perspective prioritised the participants over research, which was in line with the Active Support mentality of the principle investigators (Mansell and Beadle-Brown 2012). The second post-doc, *Imagining Autism*, was around the use of improvised drama with children with autism (Trimingham and Shaughnessy 2016; Beadle-Brown et al 2018). I headed up the research team, and a separate team of drama academics and practitioners delivered the drama content (Shaughnessy 2017). While the actual work with autistic children was very similar in feel to my own movement work, the drama academics and practitioners had not had the therapeutic background that I had. In conversations with those involved in a small follow-up study two years after the project (Leigh and Brown 2021b), we spoke about what counted as research, and the boundaries between art, therapy, and education. I draw from this experience and these interviews in Lessons from art, and Case Study 2.

Towards the end of that post-doc, I began a fixed-term part-time lectureship in Academic Practice and Higher Education, working with new lecturers and PhD students as they began their academic careers, and learned the skills needed to teach within higher education and develop an academic career (Fanghanel 2012). This role, which was varied to a full-time, open-ended position within ten months, was the fourth discipline change in my career – from chemistry to education to psychology to higher education. Higher education as a field is relatively new (Jones 2012), and the majority of researchers and educational developers come from a different home discipline. Initially I struggled to find my place and credibility (Leigh 2019d), as I tried to fit into what felt like an incredibly cognitive and critical environment (Leigh 2019b). I reached out to other academics who incorporated embodiment into their teaching, practice, or research (Leigh 2019a) to learn more. I use a case study of work with academics who shared their embodied practice with me in Case Study 3.

In 2014 I had my third child, and at delivery suffered a haemorrhage that led to chronic illness and disability (Leigh 2021). This, together with a late diagnosis of ADHD (Attention Deficit and Hyperactivity Disorder) and Autism led to an interest in ableism in academia and neurodiversity (Brown and Leigh 2018b, 2020; Grant et al 2022). I am Co-Chair for the University's Staff Disability Network, Co-Lead for the International STEMM (Science, Technology, Mathematics, and Medicine) Action Group of the National Association for Disabled Staff Networks, the disability representative for the Athena Forum – 'the expert voice from within and for the science community [for] discussion and dissemination of examples of good practice in addressing the under-representation of women in academic STEMM' (kamila_k_benova 2015) – and was asked to sit on the Wellcome Trust's Inclusive Research Design Practice Expert Advisory Group. These roles are active ways I support and lead changes around policy and practice to support disabled and other marginalised staff in higher education, and I manage them alongside doing my best to support my older daughters as they make their way into the world, and my youngest as she explores who she is and what she wants to be (aged 8 she is currently expressing a great interest in musical theatre having gained the part of Matilda in a local production of Tim Minchin's musical).

Why have I started this book with a detailed encounter of who I am and where I came from? In research, art, education, therapy, and even in science, it is impossible and undesirable to disassociate who you are and your context from what you do. I am choosing to reveal more of my background and my journey in the hope that you will understand why I am writing this book and the ways in which these worlds have intersected for me. Where we sit and how we position ourselves and the things that influence us are pertinent and relevant for people working with creative approaches, with participant groups who are vulnerable, or who are looking to increase engagement with different audiences.

I am a qualitative researcher who has traversed, trained, and worked in education, therapy, art, and science. There are lessons for qualitative researchers from these lands: on reflection and reflexivity, awareness, and relationships with and to others.

Lesson 1

Reflection

It is vitally important that a qualitative researcher is self-aware, reflective, and reflexive; particularly one using creative and embodied methods (Leigh and Brown 2021a). Reflection and reflexivity can be used interchangeably, and though they are linked, they are not the same (Leigh and Bailey 2013). Being reflective is the process of looking and examining what is there, how we reacted, or what has happened – the literal act of looking into a mirror – ideally performed without judgement, enhancement, or filters. Reflection is a necessary element of being reflexive, and being consciously self-aware enhances the ability to be reflective. Being reflexive can be understood as the process of reflecting on those reflections, taking into account the context, positionality, and using that insight to act rather than react, and *choose* what happens next.

I am not a lone voice calling for reflection and reflexivity in researchers. Ian Stronach and colleagues described how reflexivity, and different models of reflexivity are intrinsic to creative methodology in educational, scientific, and artistic research (Stronach et al 2007). Mike Poltorak saw embodied reflexivity as crucial in visual anthropology research and education (Poltorak 2019). Susan Hall stated it is essential in action research (Hall 1996a). Sarah Pink (2007, 2009) and Venus Evans-Winters (2019) saw it as essential to ethnographic research, and Aimee Grant (2018) for documentary analysis. Virginia Braun and Victoria Clarke developed a widely adopted approach to qualitative analysis 'Reflexive Thematic Analysis' which demands reflexivity to ensure quality[1] (Braun et al 2012, 2019; Braun and Clarke 2013, 2016, 2019, 2021a, 2021b; Clarke and Braun 2019). Amanda Moffat and colleagues believed that reflexivity is key for a researcher's self-care (Moffat et al 2016). It might seem obvious to say that reflexivity is essential throughout a qualitative research process from design, to data generation, and analysis (Leigh and Brown 2021a). However, Ben Newton and colleagues found that far too often reflexivity is still lacking in qualitative research (Newton et al 2011). The ways in which researchers are supposed to develop reflexivity

[1] Interestingly, despite developing influential work that had already been cited over 200,000 times by February 2023, Victoria Clarke had not yet been made a full professor; in her words 'because the criteria are inherently ableist & I have lived with chronic illness for 15 years & I don't have the energy' (Clarke 2021). So much for meritocracy.

are 'hardly discussed' (Pink 2009: 50). This may be because reflection and reflexivity are seen as hard to teach (Leigh and Bailey 2013), and researchers are lacking the skills they need to reflect effectively.

Research training

The increased popularity and recognition of qualitative research has led to a significant intensification of research skills training. Training sessions and literature focus on how to do research. They might include specific methods or analytic techniques (Phillips 1971; Cresswell and Miller 2000; Cresswell 2003), general skills such as how to conduct research interviews to facilitate a connection with participants (Oakley 1981; Brinkmann and Kvale 2014), or research with specific participant groups such as young children (see, for example, Greig and Taylor 1999; Punch 2002; Irwin and Johnson 2006; Einarsdottir 2007; Greene 2014). Training and resources for researchers wanting to utilise creative or arts-based approaches have increased drastically (see, for example, Gauntlett and Holzwarth 2006; Thomson 2008; Buckingham 2009; Lapum et al 2011; Kara 2015). Creative methods and approaches benefit researchers in that they can capture rich data that 'haunts' the audience (Wilson 2018), and often fit within a research axiology that moves away from privileging Euro-Western ideas of rigour and knowledge (Kara 2018; Wilson 2008). They are particularly useful for questions that are hard to answer, and work with groups whose voices are marginalised. They can elicit emotional stories and evocative experiences that go beyond the surface-level responses participants and researchers might expect to be shared (Brown and Leigh 2018a). While this benefits research, it brings questions around whether conventional research training, ethics, and approaches are appropriate (Leigh and Brown 2021a). I return to the idea of ethics and axiology in Lessons from ethics. The kind of training a qualitative researcher will receive (or more often seek out for themselves), is nowhere near as in-depth or comprehensive as the training for either an educator or a therapist. There is at best only a very minimum, if any, required training before a researcher is 'let loose' for the first time, or before a more established researcher wants to try a new approach. It is rare indeed to have training or guidance around the emotional load of conducting qualitative research, as experienced by the poor PhD student I mentioned earlier.

Reflexivity and positionality are talked about a lot in qualitative research methods, from ethnography to interviews and everything in between. These ideas and concepts are just as important for researchers who do not use qualitative research methods – that is, scientists (Latour 1999; Kara 2022). As an interdisciplinary scholar and someone who has trained across disciplines, I have personal experience of the differences in how subjects such as these are taught and the different skills and knowledge that are valued. Although some social scientists might assert that they too are scientists (Flyvbjerg 2006), there are fundamental differences when it comes to the expectations of a student or researcher and the shape of the knowledge that they learn or contribute to, whether they are an undergraduate, graduate, or independent researcher. Reflection and reflexivity are not taught within science. In 2019, I started working with he International WISC (Women in Supramolecular Chemistry) network ... As their Vice Chair (Research), I used qualitative and creative research methods to support their aims to build a sense of community and kinship and the progression and retention of women and other marginalised groups in the field. My primary method of achieving this was by teaching reflective and reflexive techniques. As a chemistry 'insider', and because all social science research methods were alien to them, I was able to introduce creative approaches to data gathering and analysis, including collaborative autoethnography and a programme of reflective meetings for graduate research students that incorporated elements of therapeutic group work (Leigh et al 2024b).

Positionality in research terms is often reduced to gender, class, or practice background. However, it is not always clear how much this goes beyond a one-time paragraph in a thesis that tries to give a semblance of objectivity to what is, at heart, a subjective process. It is possible to 'bracket' or set aside feelings or cultural assumptions. This technique is used in both research (May 1989; Merleau-Ponty 2002) and therapy (Finlay 2022) with slightly different meanings and connotations. However, if a fundamental tenet of interaction with others is non-judgemental acceptance and unconditional positive regard, we need to first accept that it starts with ourselves. Who we are is not reducible to easily defined social constructs. In order to accept ourselves non-judgementally and hold ourselves in unconditional positive regard, we first have to *know who we are*. In therapeutic contexts, a therapist has to be acutely aware of who they are, where they are, and what they bring with them on any given day or hour. In movement-based therapy, the living, breathing body is also important as the practitioner needs to be aware of how they are moving and holding themselves in space in response to their client. Part of the therapeutic process to create this awareness is training and supervision (see Lesson 3) where a therapist has a safer space to talk about clients, unpicking how they are reacting to them, where they might feel stuck, how best to progress or move forward, or if they need to let go. In order to deal with the inherent stresses of listening to people's stories and avoid burn-out, a therapeutic training would include a conceptual framework and a prolonged process to become cognisant of edges and limitations and learn about self-awareness. In other words, therapists are trained to become aware of and pay attention to their own positionality and how it impacts on their work with others. This may be achieved through personal analysis, however they are also required to undertake supervision throughout the time they are working as a therapist: 'there is no doubt whatever that he needs prolonged personal supervision and monitored introspection of his own responses' (Cox 1988: 92). These processes are put in place to safeguard both therapist and client. A therapist is taught to support their practice by reflecting on their own and, with support, to develop self-awareness and 'an equally deep connection with their own embodied life' (Totton 2003: 79). I will return to therapeutic training and its intent to safeguard both therapist and client in Lesson 3. The level of self-awareness I briefly mention here would be useful if taught as part of researcher training on reflection and positionality. An effective reflective practice would enable researchers to become more aware of their intent and intuition. This would support them to be more fully present when using the creative methods that evoke emotional intimacy, and ensure that a research encounter does not move into a therapeutic space unless they are equipped to hold the boundary of it for themselves and others.

Reflective practice

The rhetoric about and around reflective practice is slippery, and can be compared with David Best's (1978) discussion of the slipperiness of philosophy of movement. There are many definitions of reflection (see, for example, Dewey 1933; Schön 1987; Calderhead 1989; Tremmel 1993; Hatton and Smith 1995; Cordingley 1999; Jay and Johnson 2002; Moon 2007; Smears 2009; Hickson 2011; Miles 2011; Leigh and Bailey 2013). Likewise, there are many reasons given for the *purpose* of reflection (Shakespeare et al 1993; Osterman and Kottkamp 1993; Brookfield 1995; Ixer 1999; Ferraro 2000; Woronchak and Comeau 2016), and many examples of the experience of reflecting (Pereira 1999; Cole 2000; Clegg et al 2002; Ross 2014; Kennelly and McCormack 2015; Petsilas et al 2019a, 2019b). This does not help an individual wishing to learn about reflection. Indeed, reflection and reflexivity are often used interchangeably, when they are not the same thing. To reflect means to mirror, while reflexivity can be thought of as a way of accounting for our humanness (Dean 2017). Reflection is necessary for reflexivity (Leigh and Bailey 2013), but teaching reflection is not simple, and there is no one way that has been agreed to tackle it (Hatton and Smith 1995) or teach it (Bourner 2003; Smith 2011; Clarkeburn and Kettula 2012). Reflection is something we do *about* something. Like critical thinking, it cannot be taught in isolation and without context. Reflection cannot be de-contextualised. The very things that appear 'unconnected' may be those that eventually give the greatest insights. Donald Schön used the term 'artistry' to describe the process of reflection (Schön 1987). Artistry implies that it is not technical rationality that is important for reflexivity, but the intuitive insights gained through awareness and attention to feelings and emotions. Technical and rational thoughts can only confirm what is already known (Tremmel 1993). The reflexive mind has to be:

> Flexible and pliable. It is a mind that can attend to what is happening in the moment and respond directly ... it is, moreover, the mind that has the capacity to reach into the center of confusing situations, to see itself, and to shift the base of its operations or pull up stakes altogether to follow the flow of the action. (Tremmel 1993: 436)

How reflective practice is perceived depends on personal beliefs as well as the context of the reflection. However, just thinking about something is not enough to be reflexive:

> The process of reflection allows a sense of order to be brought to the descriptions of the experiences, and for them to be brought into conscious awareness. Just as it is not enough simply to have an experience and then think about it, 'it would be wrong to assume that simple exposure to a professional experience will bring about learning' (Miles 2011: 110). Contemplating on an experience or event is not necessarily purposeful and will not lead to new ways of thinking or behaving in practice. Reflective practice has to involve observational and analytical skills being turned towards the self, into a 'self-evaluation and the analysis of one's own actions ... to identify and critique [one's] own actions and behaviours' (Miles 2011: 114). ... By engaging with the body to achieve a greater embodied awareness, we can develop an effective, useful practice that does not degenerate into rumination, uncertainty, questions and a diminishing of self. (Leigh and Bailey 2013: 170)

In other words, reflection and reflexivity are most meaningful when they are embodied. Luckily, developing an embodied self-awareness allows context and data on which an individual can reflect, and there is a long history of evidence demonstrating that embodied self-awareness can be taught (Feldenkrais 1981; Hanna 1988; Hartley 1989; Bainbridge-Cohen 1993; Fogel 2009). Self-embodied awareness can start as simply the highlighting of 'appropriate body parts and how they feel ... [so that the] ... neuro-developmental process of self-awareness and self discovery [can] take root' (Fogel 2009: 208). Developing embodied self-awareness demands more than using and moving a body, as this can lead instead to self-consciousness. Self-conscious thoughts can occur that are thinking of the self without relation to any awareness of bodily state. These type of thoughts typically involve 'generalised judgements and evaluations of the self ("I'm too fat", "I'm not worthy of love") that are disconnected with the lived condition of the body' (Fogel 2009: 137) and are more akin to self-rumination than self-reflection.

Rumination is described by Alan Fogel as one form of suppressing underlying feelings and emotions that creates a highly distressing yet absorbing series of negative thoughts. He quoted Susan Nolen-Hoeksema and colleagues, defining rumination as 'the tendency to repetitively focus on symptoms of distress and possible causes and consequences of those symptoms without engaging in active problem solving' (Nolen-Hoeksema et al 2007: 198). This absorption into negative thoughts at first serves to guard against negative feelings, but in the long term affects the immune, cardiovascular, and neuroendocrine systems of the body in a way that maintains illnesses. Self-rumination can be defined as 'self-focus motivated by perceived threats, losses, or injuries to the self. This neurotic form of self-consciousness is characterised by recurrent, past-orientated, negative thinking about the self' (Lischetzke and Eid 2003: 362). It is associated with neuroticism, depression, anxiety, hostility, and vulnerability. Rumination is a process that neither enables a person to adopt another's perspective nor elicit empathic concern. In addition, the prevalence of depressed thoughts and negative self-evaluation become linked in a self-sustaining cycle (Fogel 2009). Rumination and absorption with the past, fantasies, or anxieties about the future 'pull one away from what is taking place in the present' (Brown and Ryan 2003: 823). Interestingly, despite self-awareness often being associated with mindfulness (Langer 2000; Salmon 2020), Kirk Brown and Richard Ryan believed that reflexive thought bore little or no relation to it. They believed mindfulness concerned 'the quality of consciousness itself' (Brown and Ryan 2003: 823) and was a purely intellectual activity not associated with the body at all. This view would be expected by Gert Biesta who thought much theory was 'rooted in the paradigm of the philosophy of consciousness' (Biesta 1994: 302).

One way to combat a negative ruminative thought spiral is to focus on the underlying feelings. Individuals reporting high clarity about their own feelings are more likely to rebound from negative moods and are less likely to engage in self-rumination (Lischetzke and Eid 2003). Fogel used clinical studies to support his claim that paying attention to embodied self-awareness assisted in changing thought patterns from ruminative negative ones to more positive and self-consistent patterns, and led to elevation of mood. Training individuals to engage in self-reflection rather than self-rumination can increase their ability to empathise, and reduce personal distress, feelings of guilt, shame, or worthlessness (Joireman et al 2002). Self-reflection, in contrast to rumination, is associated with an openness to experience, and is positively related to adaptive and facilitative forms of empathy. Attention to embodied feelings rather than thoughts decreases rumination, and non-ruminative self-awareness is linked to higher self-esteem and empathic concern for others. Elizabeth Smears considered how embodied reflection could be important for professional development:

> The more we reclaim body awareness, that is our capacity to observe and our willingness to feel, the more ways we can communicate. The development of skills to access embodied knowing is a critical resource for reflective practice and inter-professional communication. It can be argued that professionals, who develop an embodied awareness of self, have a further and useful resource to draw upon when communicating with others. (Smears 2009: 107)

By engaging with the body to achieve a greater embodied awareness, it is possible to develop an effective, useful practice that does not degenerate into rumination, uncertainty, questions, and a diminishing of self. Education about embodiment and how to increase and use levels of self-awareness can be used to develop empathy, reflective practice, and reflexivity. They are connected (Joireman et al 2002).

But what might embodied reflection and reflexivity entail? In order to reflect, an individual has to be self-aware. This begins with observational and analytical skills being turned toward the self, into a 'self-evaluation and the analysis of one's own actions … to identify and critique their own actions and behaviours' (Miles 2011: 114). Embodied self-awareness includes being aware of what is going on in the physical and physiological self, and how that relates to emotions, feelings, thoughts. For example, if you hurt, what kind of hurt is it (bone, tissue, muscle?); or a more general awareness of you, the world around you, and others. By making the link between embodied self-awareness and reflection, this self-awareness has a purpose and is not just self-absorption. Reflexivity is the step beyond reflection, taking self-aware reflective thoughts and using them to bring about change. Smears (2009) stated that reflexivity is a way to regain control over our personal world, which can bring self-confidence. Reflexivity might be an individual taking time to process their experiences of marginalisation in the workplace; reflecting on where they are and realising that they are not responsible for the actions of others. Within an educational context, reflexivity might be a teacher becoming self-aware of, and reflecting on, how they feel when they have to teach, and then implementing a routine that is more supportive and has a positive effect on their practice. Reflexivity is an iterative process that demands self-awareness and reflection to gain insight. Reflexivity reveals choices, and possibilities to take action and effect change. In research it might be a researcher reflecting on the data they are generating or the subject matter, and noticing that they have had an insight into what they are exploring and why, resulting in a connection of ideas and how they could be implemented.

Reflection in education

I undertook my doctoral research while I was training to be a teacher. This led to tension between the kinds of reflections required from me. In contrast to the somewhat *ad hoc* training for researchers, educators in schools usually have the equivalent of a year of postgraduate training before they are qualified. This can still leave a lot to be desired when it comes to self-awareness and reflection, despite reflective practice being fundamental to the art of teaching (Schön 1987). As a trainee teacher I was not exposed to the many discourses around reflective practice I discovered as a trainee researcher (Calderhead 1989; Osterman and Kottkamp 1993; Cordingley 1999). I received little guidance and less modelling of reflective practice and instead was presented with a framework to 'achieve' reflection; I needed to write reflections to pass assignments. This is not unusual. Many teaching trainees are simply told to reflect. Tom Russell (2006) developed an explicit strategy to teach relective practice to new professional teachers, concluding that it was a necessary step to ensure that they were able to experience the full benefit and understand how it differed from 'normal' reflection. Some teacher training programmes separate out the reflexive process from the professional practice of reflection by providing private learning journal spaces for students that are not assessed, but that are followed up by dialogue (Whewell 2005). Reflection and reflexivity should not be a search for solutions. Neither reflection nor reflexivity is a linear process, despite that often being how they are presented; with lists of questions, tasks, journals, or elements to be completed and achieved. Although frameworks may be useful, they do not necessarily encourage a process that is intuitive and emerges from the self; instead, they promote a practice that is rule-bound (Brookfield 1995).

Mixed messages about the purpose and processes of reflection mean that students are likely to end up ruminating on their experiences rather than reflecting. Despite the detrimental mental and physical effects of rumination, it is stated as a desired aspect of reflection by some educators. For example Joelle Jay and Kerry Johnson (2002) believed that reflection should entail recognition, examination, and rumination. Not surprisingly then, in a list of descriptive questions they designed to elicit reflection from student teachers, only one out of eight had any relation to the embodied or self-aware processes of the trainee (Jay and Johnson 2002). Unfortunately, this is not an isolated case. In an explanation of the weakness of student teachers' reflections, James Calderhead implied it was because they did not ruminate: 'they are reluctant to be self-critical and dwell upon their weaknesses' (Calderhead 1989: 46). This emphasis on rumination and dwelling on the negative can turn a potentially useful process into a negative experience (Joireman et al 2002). Reflection should be taught as a skill rather than a subject which can be passed or failed, as assessed reflection does not facilitate effective reflection (Leigh

2016). Assessed reflection is more likely to result in superficial reflection (Calderhead 1989) than a lifelong practice (Tremmel 1993). Graham Ixer asked a stark question of whether reflection should be assessed at all within social work programmes, as the assessor's conceptions of reflection may be poorly formed, not match those of the students, and are likely to compound the imbalance of power between them, with particular oppression of vulnerable learners who do not fit their ideas of what reflective learning may be (Ixer 1999). Ixer did not recognise reflection as 'a competence … a measurable skill readily available to standard assessment criteria' (Ixer 1999: 514). If this is the case with reflection in social work, then how can it be assessed and measured as a competence elsewhere? If reflections form part of an assessment for a taught course, then this implies that the reflections are less about thoughts and feelings, and more an opportunity to demonstrate a competence at reflecting or, more accurately, being seen to reflect.

I had first-hand experience of this when completing my teacher training course. The academic teacher training I undertook had a real impact on my understanding of what it was to be an educator in contrast to being a therapist or a researcher and how these boundaries could be kept distinct or blur. My teaching practices were not all comfortable places for me. I had ongoing issues with the course director who had agreed part-time placements in two schools to fit around my doctoral field work, then asked me to find a third and switch to full-time within a week of my husband walking out and abandoning me and our two children. I felt powerless, and at a loss. I wrote in my private reflexive journal at the time: 'reflecting on how the words [from the children] in this session and the last "power", "nervous", "anxious" reflect on the situation I find myself in whilst on teaching practice' (Reflexive Journal), wondering 'how [my course] is "influencing" research – again big difference between teaching, working, researching' (Reflexive Journal). These were not feelings I shared in my assessed teaching practice reflective journal. I had initially chosen the teacher training programme because it explicitly emphasised developing reflective teachers, however that seemed evident only in the inclusion of this mandated and assessed journal. My approach to that assignment – in that it was an integral part of my training in which I had to prove my ability, my competence, and evidence my journey as a trainee – was one recommended by Bruce Macfarlane and Lesley Gourlay (2009). They likened a reflective assignment to a reality television show. Although this may have been slightly tongue-in-cheek, it fit with my experience. The assessment of reflection 'in a way that reinforces behavioural conformism' (Macfarlane and Gourlay 2009: 457) did not encourage critical engagement. Instead, reflective writing became 'little short of a confidence trick, or perhaps more worryingly, an exercise in self-justification and conformism with the psychologised curriculum of learning and teaching' (Macfarlane and Gourlay 2009: 457). However, concerns about assessment of reflection do not feature in many discussions on reflective practice (Calderhead 1989; Cordingley 1999; Cole 2000; Ferraro 2000; Jay and Johnson 2002).

As an academic developer and teacher in the university sector, I built reflection into all the modules that I taught, and developed a specific course to look critically at models, theories and practices, reflective practice, and reflexivity within teaching, practice, and research in higher education. This module provided space for university teachers and researchers to process what they understood about reflection, look critically at how it was used, develop more of a sense of their own embodied self-awareness, and experiment with artistic means to provoke reflection. It incorporated a wide range of literature and scholarship on reflection. Thankfully, teacher education is more likely to include creative means to facilitate effective reflection than it was when I completed my training (Sidebottom and Ball 2018).

Before including a reflective assessment for others, I believe an educator should experience what it feels like to be seen or witnessed while reflecting, then reflect further on how this compares to assessing or judging reflective assignments from others (Leigh 2016). If people are expected to reflect on and in their practice, whatever their role, then their training needs to encompass this. In contrast to directly assessed reflections, a required but non-assessed journal can be incredibly valuable as a means of promoting the development of self-awareness, and facilitating effective reflection and reflexivity. What is key, in any model of reflection, is that the participants are self-aware and engage with their embodied 'knowing' as well as with the literature and theoretical knowledge, as in this way they can progress from reflective practice to a holistic reflexivity (Bleakley 1999).

Reflexivity

My work and research, on one level, is all about what it means to reflect as an embodied being, and using reflexive and embodied self-awareness to provide material on which to reflect. This work, and the reflective and reflexive processes associated with it, are the same whether I identify as a researcher, artist, therapist, or educator. An educator might reflect on how they feel when they have to teach, and reflexively implement a routine that is more supportive for themselves and their students and has a positive effect on their practice. As an educator, now most often with university colleagues and students rather than in schools with children, I am able to model what a reflective practice is to my students, teaching them 'the art of "paying attention" as a way of nurturing reflective practice' (Tremmel 1993: 435). A therapist has to reflect and be reflexive in order to stay present with their client and serve their needs as best they can. As an artist I found reflection and reflexivity were implied and expected, but not taught explicitly. Conservatoire training is changing to address this lack (Gaunt 2016; Woronchak and Comeau 2016; Petsilas et al 2019b).

Reflection and reflexivity are often described as requirements for researchers (Shakespeare et al 1993; Pereira 1999; Stronach et al 2007). A researcher has to reflect and be reflexive during the processes of their research from design, where they must maintain an awareness of how their positionality impacts on the questions they ask and the ways they go about answering them, through the generation of data, to analysis, and dissemination. A lack of reflexivity can lead to the same 'feelings of staleness, rigidity and defensiveness' (Hawkins and Shohet 1989: 5) experienced by therapists working without adequate supervision, that in turn lead towards illness, burn-out, or a stale artistic practice (Joireman et al 2002; Nolen-Hoeksema et al 2007).

Reflexivity on movement might be a process of watching, imitating, experimenting, and reflecting to make it possible to not just copy but inhabit the experience and integrate knowledge into action and understanding. Through movement work it is possible to show or to write about a moment of experience. Bodies allow people to experience more of the world around them, and are the expression of what they feel on every level. There is a history of connecting movement and awareness of movement with research and philosophy of experience. Linda Bain (1987: 45) credited the philosopher Kitaro Nishida (1870–1945) with the idea that bodily movement is the route by which every process of expression is possible. Indeed, movement is described by Maxine Sheets-Johnstone as 'the change itself, the dynamic happening, and needs to be phenomenologically analysed and properly understood as such' (Sheets-Johnstone 2010a: 121). In a description of Edmund Husserl's approach to phenomenology, Eric Zuesse wrote that his analysis 'has a fascinating resemblance to the psychology of Hindu and Buddhist yoga' (Zuesse 1985: 56), and stated that according to Maurice Merleau-Ponty 'the body and its movements … are the foundations for all reflective thought' (Zuesse 1985: 64). The work of phenomenologist and philosopher Martin Heidegger is also thought to have been influenced by East Asian texts and ideas (May 1989). Reflection is linked to phenomenology because it is a means of giving language to an experience or phenomenon. This allows the processing of experiences and events: 'because they are embodied, affective phenomena are always somewhat ineffable: they have a quite literally unspeakable aspect that renders them elusive to, and always slightly disjunctive with, language' (Cromby 2011: 83). It is useful because this enables an individual to process their experience, or sort out the feelings, emotions, and thoughts around what has been encountered. Without reflection this is challenging, as 'embodied, affective phenomena are always somewhat ineffable: they have a quite literally unspeakable aspect that renders them elusive to, and always slightly disjunctive with, language' (Cromby 2011: 83).

I understand embodiment to be both a state of being mind-body and an ongoing process of cultivating and developing self-awareness (Leigh 2012). This understanding and assumption of embodiment is part of somatics (Hanna 1988), which was explicitly connected with phenomenology by Bain (1995). Similar conceptions of embodiment are found in work in diverse fields, including sport pedagogy (Cote and Hay 2002), physical education (Bailey et al 2009), Dance Movement Therapy (Chodrow 2009), dance (Green 1999), human geography (Longhurst 1997; Alexis-Martin 2019), psychology (Fogel 2009), education (Tremmel 1993), special needs education (Powell et al 2006), philosophy (Sheets-Johnstone 2009), psychotherapy (Hartley 2004), sociology (Back 2007), anthropology (Ruby 1980; Csordas 2002), media studies (Bowman 2019), and health studies (Junker et al 2004).

My reflexive practice is built on embodied self-awareness. This has been cultivated through positive movement practices including somatics, bodywork training, yoga, and Authentic Movement (Adler 2002). Similarly, Smears attributed her ability to perceive a situation through, and reflect with, the subjective and sentient body, to a range of somatic practices and techniques, including Alexander Technique, Feldenkrais, and the work of Hartley. It can be challenging to take the time needed to be reflexive. Like many habits, it takes time to develop, and it is easier to instruct others that they should practise than it is to do it oneself. Having a reflexive practice means taking the necessary time to reflect on and analyse actions, being aware of oneself and others, and using these insights to improve. As an autoethnographer, I 'ground' feelings, reflections, and emotions in my body. I do this reflectively and reflexively through the embodied self-awareness I developed through my practice of movement, together with a practice of non-judgemental acceptance (Leigh 2019d; Leigh and Brown 2021a). Moment-to-moment I am conscious of my breathing rate, heart rate, feelings, emotions, and associated images and thoughts. I am aware of the pain and discomfort in my somewhat broken body and how my ease or lack of ease in movement ebb and flow. I am also aware of my stream of consciousness and how my gaze and focus are directed around a room. I am open to the physical signs I see from those around me, while not projecting my own interpretations onto them. This awareness from my embodied self feeds into my research and practice at every stage from design, to data gathering, analysis, and dissemination. For example, it allows me to access and recall detailed information that is recorded in field notes when conducting ethnographic or observational research, providing content I can reflect on at a later time as part of my reflexive practice.

The idea of reflecting in an embodied way links somatics to the worlds of education, therapy, art, and of course research. If an individual has not had the opportunity to develop self-awareness then they are limited in the amount and quality of information to reflect on and then be reflexive with. An effective reflexive practice requires reflection moment-to-moment, self-awareness, awareness of others, and a sense of instant knowing that arises from the body and the world around the body rather than an organised, critical, and analytical process. As I shall demonstrate in Lesson 2, embodied self-awareness and non-judgemental acceptance of the body make it possible to develop an understanding of the body as it relates to the world. I explore non-judgemental acceptance within humanistic and person-centred therapeutic approaches and the ethos of 'being in service to' (Rogers 1967) and how it fundamentally differs to other approaches, for example Psychodynamic or Psychoanalytic psychotherapy, in Lesson 3. Somatic awareness allows people to experience and know a situation or context experientially, accessing sensory information, perceptions, and judgements, and developing empathy, and non-judgemental acceptance of the body contrasts to developing a view of it as a gendered and socially constructed thing.

Lesson 2

Awareness

In order to be the best qualitative researcher possible, it is essential to reflect. The previous lesson demonstrated that this is most effective when it results from embodied self-awareness. This long lesson begins with exploring the discourses of embodiment, bodies, and moving bodies, before investigating somatics as a tool for developing awareness, and how it can be used both therapeutically and educationally as well as for research. I end with an example of using somatics to teach young children to become more aware. But to start, what do I even mean when I use the term 'embodiment'?

Embodiment

The idea of embodiment is contested (Sheets-Johnstone 2015). 'Embodiment' can describe the way our bodies represent ourselves at an individual or cultural level. This would be the definition used by many sociologists, such as Chris Shilling (2005, 2008, 2012) or Nick Crossley (2006). My use of embodiment rests on 'fundamentally different assumptions' from those of many sociologists (Totton 2009: 189). For example, Crossley's work on Reflexive Embodiment includes 'practices of body modification, maintenance and … body-image' (Crossley 2006: 1). His understanding of 'bodywork' is work that is done on the body to change its appearance or function. Although he includes feelings and emotions we have about our bodies in his discussions of the social and constructed meanings attached to diverse bodywork or practices such as tattooing, eating, and exercise; his view of embodiment does not necessarily mean a self-awareness and consciousness being brought to the feelings and sensations within the body. Or Laura Ellingson, who rather than seeing her body and mind to be connected, saw her body as 'troublesome' (Ellingson 2017: 5) demanding her 'continual attention and accommodation, making it impossible to ignore the ways in which embodiment necessarily affects (and is affected by) [her] research processes' (Ellingson 2017: 5). Crossley and other sociologists might say that everything we do is embodied because we are embodied beings – living, breathing, meat sacks moving about the world. They would not necessarily agree with my definition that embodiment equates to conscious self-awareness of the body. Maxine Sheets-Johnstone, a dancer and philosopher, would say that my use of the word is wrong and what I mean by embodiment is instead 'kinaesthetic awareness'. However, I feel I include more in my usage of the term than just the proprioceptive awareness of the body implied by kinaesthetic awareness, as I incorporate the physical experience of movement through space together with the thoughts, images, feelings, perceptions, and sensations that arise within and through it. Thomas Hanna would say that I should use the term 'somatics' instead of embodiment. If I am honest, I do not completely disagree with him, but I continue to use the word embodiment in academic spheres as it means something (if not quite the same thing) to more people than somatics. I tend to use somatics to describe a form of 'bodywork' as a means to embodiment, as I will show later in this chapter. Embodiment is an experience rooted in the physical as much as the theoretical or spiritual worlds. However embodiment is understood or defined, it can be agreed that it concerns the body, which itself is an idea subject to many discourses.

Body discourse

Plato defined the body as an 'endless source of trouble' (Russell 1946: 151) and Socrates is credited with describing it as 'a hindrance in the acquisition of knowledge' (Russell 1946: 150). The idea of a 'decorporealised' or 'disembodied' existence in Western society can, in part, be attributed to the hold of the Cartesian paradigm which separates the mind from the body, with the body often relegated to a secondary or oppositional role from a Platonic 'purified soul' (Leder 1990). This duality of mind and matter or body and soul is associated with discourses of power, imbalance, and patriarchy where the body is ascribed lesser valued attributes correlated with emotion/nature/female and the mind the more valued and valuable attributes of intellect/culture/male (Gatens 1988). This, which is still the dominant paradigm of the body, is promoted through dogmatism or indoctrination (Bailey 2010) much as dominant paradigms are transferred to the young in other fields such as science education (Bailey 2006). In Lesson 3, I will explore how this discourse impacted the development and practice of psychotherapy.

The Cartesian duality and power relation of mind over body can be linked to the patriarchal structures of Western society: 'Women have consistently been associated with the bodily sphere. They have been linked with nature, sexuality, and the passions, whereas men have been identified with the rational mind. This equation implicitly legitimizes structures of domination' (Leder 1990: 154). This comparison with hierarchies of gender oppression can be applied to oppressions of class, race, nature, religion, disability, and the like. In each case, one (subjugated) aspect is identified with the emotional body; the other (the oppressor) with the rational mind. The Cartesian view of seeing an inferior, external 'Other' that is mindless and in need of control justifies subjugation. Phenomenology can be used as a tool to logically refute or criticise a dualist approach. However, if it is made without experiential knowledge and understanding it can become yet another discourse that panders to the intellectual, and ignores not only the body, but the reality of an embodied self.

Perceptions of bodies can change depending on context (Brown et al 2009) or habitus (Bourdieu 1990). Margaret Duncan (2007) explored six somewhat objective views of 'bodies' that inform perceptions; the imagined body, the consumer body, the transgressive body, the disciplined body, the practised body, and the discursive body. The imagined body is described as the body image an individual holds of themself, or 'how our own bodies look to others' (Duncan 2007: 56). This is seen by a 'panoptic gaze, a kind of self-surveillance, in which a woman or girl regards her body through the eyes of others. … Are her clothes too tight? Do they make her thighs look big?' (Duncan 2007: 57). This inner gaze encourages surveying, 'with degrees of distress, their own bodies for signs of abnormality against an unrealistic image' (Markula and Pringle 2006: 43). The consumer body refers to the body as an object to be altered through consumption of exercise, diet, or surgery to meet a desired 'ideal' outcome. The transgressive and disciplined body are two sides of the same coin. The transgressive 'deviates from the social norm and defies social expectations' (Duncan 2007: 60). It might include 'the pierced and tattooed body, the disabled body, the hypermuscular body' (Duncan 2007: 60). The disciplined body is disciplined through exercise and dieting, has been medicalised, or is the object and target of power (Markula and Pringle 2006). Duncan links the disciplined body to the moral imperative for 'good' bodies and adherence to 'good' behaviours. These definitions and identification with 'good' and 'bad' bodies raise questions about where a body would fit if it intersects these two domains; for example, the disabled athlete who adheres to a strict training regime or diet, or the tattooed dancer who does the same. This has been explored within physical education research (Dyck and Archetti 2003), and this kind of intersection can be seen in certain types of dance. For example, the assumption is that ballet dancers' bodies would automatically fall into the disciplined category by adhering to the exercise and diet regime necessary to appear and move in the accepted way for a ballet dancer. Yet many ballet practices can be injurious, and the individual dancer could easily, if not inevitably, fall outside of the social norm due to the extended hours of practice and rehearsals necessary to succeed, which goes beyond innate talent (Bailey and Toms 2010). Further, achieving the ballet body can become an obsession for dancers, thereby crossing into the transgressive body domain (Pickard 2007). The practiced body is identified with a skilled athlete, one who rehearses movement sequences again and again. Duncan highlights the importance of social practices within this, giving an example of becoming adept at the Korean martial art Tae Kwon Do where a critical part is learning correct social codes of discipline, strength, and self-confidence within a group as much as the moves. For many Tae Kwon Do afficionados, 'mastery of the body is second to the social benefits of the martial arts' (Duncan 2007: 62). This could be interpreted as movement being used as a social practice to control and transform the individual and to bend them to the will of authority. Tae Kwon Do is particularly hierarchical, as are many martial arts (Delamont 2006). Other sports, for example gymnastics and football, have hierarchical elements in their talent development systems (Bailey and Toms 2010). Last, the discursive body is the body evoked in language. Once again, the language used by Duncan objectifies the body using examples of medicalisation and obesity. The importance of language cannot be underestimated, as it is a vital element in our understanding and experience of our bodies: 'Our understandings of these things are embedded in our words, not separate from them. In a real sense language is constitutive; there is no reality that stands apart from it, nor is language merely a reflection of the actual thing. … For this reason words have power' (Duncan 2007: 62–63).

Another discourse found in sport and education body theory is the negotiation of male identity. Body theory has been described as being disembodied and masculinist (Sparkes and Smith 2002). In a discussion of masculinity, gender, and the construction of men's sporting identities, Ian Wellard sought to 'provide evidence of the way in which early experience of sport contributed to the formation of individual sporting identities' (Wellard 2006: 111). Gendered masculine bodies attract most cultural capital when they exhibit prowess in sport and bodily strength. If a body does not conform to cultural ideas, it can become 'a major source of humiliation' (Wellard 2006: 112). Wellard explored the attitudes of male physical education degree students taking part in a dance group when their previous experience of sport was more traditional (2006). Initially they viewed dance to be outside of their definitions of sport and 'girly', however they were aware of its value for both boys and girls in the context of physical education, even if it was seen as 'an enticement for those non-sporting types to take part in sport' (Wellard 2006: 6). The body plays a 'central role in determining who the participants should be' (Wellard 2006: 109) in sport, and this relates to social normative codes and requirements.

There are many discourses on the body, not least by philosophers including Edmund Husserl (Carman 1999), Maurice Merleau-Ponty (2002), Jean-Paul Sartre (1969), Gabriel Marcel (2011), Leo Straus (1935/1963), and Hans Jonas (2001). Michel Foucault regarded discipline of the body as one of the means by which the 'mad' (or those who were seen to be deviants from the norm) could be brought back to an 'affirmation of social standards' (Dreyfus and Rabinow 1982: 9), and 'a crucial site of conflict between various forms of power and resistance to power, like a contested territory' (Totton 2009: 191). And yet, bodies can be seen as irrelevant to the research process (Denzin 1997). The idea of the absent body has been raised by Jacques Derrida (1987), Robert Sokolowski (2000), Merleau-Ponty (2002), and Drew Leder (1990). Leder believed the body only became visible when in a state of distress or disabled (Leigh 2021). He stated, 'I dwell in a world of ideas, paying little heed to my physical sensations or posture' (Leder 1990: 1). The idea of the disappearing body would resonate with Ellingson's experience of her disabled body, which only became present to her when it was not working as it should (Ellingson 2017). While it is true that bodies that are disabled or in pain demand more attention and consideration, it is possible to be aware of a body without experiencing pain or discomfort (Leigh 2021). However, Leder stated explicitly that human experience was incarnated, or 'embodied'. This illustrates a tension between the thoughts, theories, and philosophies of the body and embodiment that arise from experiential understandings of movement and the conscious self-awareness of the moving body, and those that arise from people who think, write, or talk about embodiment while mainly sitting rather than moving with awareness.

Jean Hardy (1996) described a model of the Higher Self, a context of personality, comprised of the physical, feeling, and mental body. Chunlei Lu, Johanna Tito, and Jeanne Kentel (2009: 354) argued a subjective view of the body required a qualitative, hermeneutic methodology, describing the 'lived body as a text to be interpreted'. They explained that 'hermeneutics' includes body image, how one comports oneself, and how one relates to the world and to others. Also included is the body's function to problematise or alter identity, to serve as a political statement, and how it can be used to transgress stereotypes and change power relations (Oliver and Lalik 2001; Evans et al 2004; Crossley 2006; Pickard 2007). Within these discourses, embodiment is often taken to mean just the outward expression of the self to the world (Young 1980; Buote et al 2011; Shilling 2012). Embodiment is understood as an expression of belonging or identity represented by clothes, decorations such as tattoos, or 'disciplining' a body so that it inhabits a particular space and shape, such as the different disciplined bodies of a competitive weight lifter, sumo wrestler, or long-distance runner.

This type of sociological discussion is an alternative to a more spiritual or transpersonal view of embodiment, as the body's 'unspeakable' aspect, or ineffability 'has long been remarked upon by philosophers … consequently it is something to be managed rather than resolved' (Cromby 2011: 83). For example, Derrida stated 'spirit is not the thing, spirit is not the body' (Derrida 1987: 15). Derrida shared Martin Heidegger's view, that certain terms such as 'spirit' should be avoided. This avoidance of spirit is in almost direct opposition to the incorporation of mind/body/spirit that is central to somatic principles and Transpersonal Therapy (Rowan 1993). In fact, the body, along with the outside and the inanimate is described as being 'the opposite of spirit' (Derrida 1987: 25). Becoming more embodied or self-aware about the body, how it moves, and how it is part of our conscious and unconscious expression and communications to the world, may be a route to regaining an embodied connection to the ineffable. Without non-judgemental acceptance, self-awareness can become self-consciousness, with a critical inner gaze that seeks to judge and control a body into conformity (Markula and Pringle 2006; Duncan 2007). Perceiving and understanding the body-mind as a whole and unified thing rather than a dualist split body and mind is a different ontological standpoint. A key aspect to embodied self-awareness is that the inner experience of moving is key, rather than external performance which might be assumed given the previous focus on sporting and athletic bodies. The focus here is phenomenological, that is, on the individual, personal, and internal experience of movement. However, phenomenological understanding of self-movement remains 'incomplete' (Sheets-Johnstone 2010b: 113). While this is particularly true for the 'actual experience of one's own movement' (Sheets-Johnstone 2010b: 113) this may be because the phenomenon of self-movement is under-examined.

Moving bodies

Bodies move all the time. At the micro level, each cell inside our bodies moves and respires continuously until it dies, expanding and contracting as it takes in all that it needs and releases all that no longer serves through its membranes. This movement and other movements of cells are incorporated into an internal bodily cell motility and form part of its internal rhythm. On the meso level, our bodies' systems move as they function: the digestive system with its waves of contractions extracting what we need from the food we eat; our cardiovascular system pumping oxygenated and deoxygenated blood serving all those individual cells; our cerebrospinal fluid washing around our brains; our lymph, excretory, and nervous systems – they are all in movement. On a macro and at the physical level, we all move as we breathe, as we blink, as we shift our weight and adjust our posture. Movement is not the privilege of the elite, athletes, or only accessible to a few. Movement is inclusive to all bodies in every state because everyone moves. We *all* move *all the time*, though we are not always alert to, or aware of, those movements, particularly at the level of the micro and meso. Becoming aware of and reflecting on experiences of movement has consequences for the way in which we think and construct meaning, as well as how we are seen by others and see ourselves. When I worked as a yoga teacher, I found that becoming more aware of my body made me more aware of the tiny aches and pains and uncomfortableness associated with exercise, or sitting or holding my body in a way that had been habitual but was not balanced or even. I felt when my muscles had worked and were tired. My students told me they began to notice how they felt when they slumped for example, and they were able to make choices about using their bodies differently as a result. Pain is not always a bad thing if it can be utilised to stimulate change. Vanda Scaravelli and Mary Stewart, two yoga and movement teachers, are attributed with saying 'it is not so much the performance of the exercises that matters, but rather the way of doing them' (Phillips 2001: 45). This awareness of internal motility, and soft, fluid approach to movement speaks to the idea that movement is a means of learning how to pay attention to the embodied self. However, movement and the awareness of movement does not guarantee the absence of pain or injury.

As human animals, people have all been nurtured by an original capacity to think in movement, a capacity that can become submerged or hidden by the practice of thinking in words. Even as a foetus in utero an infant has a sense of gravity, a sense of their joints, and a tactile kinaesthetic sense of their own body as an articulable, essentially dynamic form (Brook n.d.). While thinking in movement can be opaque to language, 'language is profoundly embodied as an element of thought' (Cromby 2011: 86); spatio-temporal-energic concepts come from experiences of movement. A common kinetic theme can be said to weave between improvisational dance and human development. It is the non-separation of thinking and doing, and the non-separation of sensing and moving. A body that is dynamically attuned and knows the world and makes its way within it kinetically, is thoughtfully attuned to the quality of its own movement and the movement of the things that surround it (Sheets-Johnstone 2009).

Philosophy often separates thinking and language from feeling. Yet thoughts and movement are linked (Manning 2016). Phenomenological research into the body and movement is hampered in that 'qualitative investigations of embodied, affective phenomena encounter a further difficulty because most qualitative analysis presumes a linguistic epistemology' (Cromby 2011: 83); that is, in order to understand an experience we need to express it and consciously put it into language. Movement and the expression of movement can be through non-verbal means as well as spoken or written language. An individual's experience is referenced through movement *and* language (Thorburn 2008). Language remains important as a means to bring the unconscious into consciousness. Fuller and freer expression allows more opportunity to make sense of the world, share perceptions of it, and become more intelligible to others. In fact, bringing bodily experience into language can be an important part of a healing process (Chaiklin 2009). From a developmental perspective, a child's view of the world and of the language used to describe it is formed in relation to how the world and the objects within it move in relation to themselves (Bloom 1993). This ties in with how both Hermann von Helmholtz and Husserl described how humans learn. It can be said that movement is a foundational character of the world, and an infant's (or adult's) knowledge of the surrounding world is derived from their physical knowledge of it. According to Sheets-Johnstone (2010a), language is 'post-kinetic', that is, language acquisition occurs after movement rather than the more customary opinion that movement is pre-verbal. Language cannot easily be separated from movement of the body: 'The signs of language are never separate from the signs of the body: what we speak and what we hear is always influenced by what we feel and vice-versa. Meaningful signs arise directly through and within the body, as well as through and in language' (Cromby 2011: 84).

It is commonly assumed, because of the dominance of Cartesian duality, that thinking is tied to language, that it takes place only via language, and that only thinking and language are tied in an exclusive way to rationality. If thinking is separated from its expression, it can only ever be transcribed or transliterated into movement. Pushing one step further is the possibility that movement constitutes thoughts themselves: 'movement and non-verbal communication ... essentially involve emotion and embodied cognition' (Fischman 2009: 43). Movement then becomes the *presence* of thought (Merleau-Ponty 2002). However, it must be noted that neither thinking or feeling in movement nor a descriptive account of thinking in movement is challenging a linkage between thinking and language, thinking and rationality, or even thinking and symbolic systems of thought. Thinking in movement solely challenges the view that there are *no other* forms of thinking: that language *is* thought. A subject's experience is referenced through movement and language. Assumptions that it does more than this are often accompanied by assumptions rooted in a Cartesian separation of mind and body (Leder 1990): 'thought and language are qualities of the body itself and separating them off from the body acts to reinstate the body-mind split' (Totton 2003: 133). Judith Butler wrote that people use the information from their senses before even forming thoughts (Butler 2015). The arguments made by Ludwig Wittgenstein (1963) and Merleau-Ponty (2002) with respect to thoughts existing separately to their expression in language, apply also to their corporeal expression in movement. There are not necessarily meanings going through a mind in addition to expression of thought through language. Yet it is still language. Similarly, movement may or may not have conscious meaning ascribed to it by the mover. This implies that *thinking in movement* is not always subject to an outside or critical eye. In improvisational dance, for example, there is no external choreographer. As in other forms of thinking in movement, it is not subject to a judgemental outside presence, and this 'thought in action' can be seen as the work of a mindful body. This does not make it less worthy of being researched or analysed, though careful attention needs to be paid to ensure that analysis of movement is not used as a form of critical judgement, and instead is undertaken to increase understanding and knowledge.

When it comes to emotions, Sheets-Johnston cites Charles Darwin's observations of animal movements and reactions to emotional stimuli (such as alarm) to testify to the 'intimate connection between movement and emotion' (Sheets-Johnstone 2010a: 4). The body is connected to the mind with movement acting as the dynamic between them: 'when we are speaking of the body, we are not only describing the functional aspect of movement, but how our psyche and emotions are affected by our thinking and how movement itself effects change within them' (Chaiklin 2009: 5). For example, language is associated with both movement and emotion: 'words, phrases and metaphors ... attempt to portray the somatic components of emotion' (Cromby 2011: 89). Emotions, and our experience and expression of them, are areas well suited to phenomenological explorations, as 'to be in an emotion state is to be in a particular phenomenological state, because emotion states are personal-level attitudes that themselves are essentially something it is like to be in or to have' (Lambie and Marcel 2002: 220).

By integrating expression through movement and language, it may be possible to facilitate young people's developing self-awareness as well as their motor skills (Bresler 2004). Movement can be therapeutic because it gives access to expression. Movement can also be a quick way or a short cut to access process-orientated psychology (Mindell 1995). Movement is the form in which it is possible to express and validate a sense of self. It is the bridge between how people affect and sense the world around them. Movement can bring awareness, attention, and expression to thoughts that have previously been invisible or unconscious. The experiences of moving and enjoying and experiencing bodies in activities such as somatic movement as a child or adult may increase both future participation in other forms of exercise and physical activity, and reflexive self-awareness of the body and the thoughts, feelings, and emotions that arise from it.

How an individual perceives their body, and perceives what a body looks like and how it moves, can colour how they feel about themselves. If people are allowed to gain pleasurable experiences and memories of the physical expression of their body, then this will inform how they view their ability to move and increase their confidence in doing so. If, instead, they are subjected to activities and experiences they do not enjoy or that they are unable to conform to, perhaps in physical education classes which is the most common introduction to movement education within schools, then it is likely that enjoyment of and participation in any form of movement will decrease (Wellard 2006).

There is an ongoing debate about the position, value, purpose, and definition of physical education and movement within education. Physical education may be seen as useful for health and fitness (Barrow 2008), or vital to integrate students' lived-body experiences and acquisition of subject knowledge (Thorburn 2008). Different types of movement education have different outcomes. For example, a feeling of achievement has been identified as a motivation factor for participation in sport, referenced by perceived competence, effort, task mastery, improvement; or comparison with others, norm-referenced perceptions of competence, or winning (Pickard and Bailey 2009). The goal-orientated motivation that is a necessary outcome for young dancers and athletes can be compared with the non-competitive, process-orientated nature of positive movement practices. Positive practices, including yoga, martial arts, some forms of dance or meditation and the like, are seen as optional by Leder, only being sought out by those actively seeking them despite their capacity to increase self-awareness. For example, the use of Eastern Movement Disciplines (EMDs) can be used to develop mindfulness (Lu et al 2009). Mindfulness is holistic in the sense that is assumes an embodiment of the soul or spirit in the physical corporal body (Hanna 1988). These movement practices embody a 'philosophy of mindfulness which they teach through physical movement' (Hanna 1988: 356) addressing the three core issues of philosophy, health, and education. It is fairly contentious to lump together so many disparate forms and practices into one category of 'EMDs', including 'Yoga, and Qi Gong … Eastern martial arts and Eastern meditations' (Hanna 1988: 356). Even within one form of movement discipline there may be many schools, views, and allegiances. Added to this, not all positive movement practices that might be encountered are particularly positive, for example when one element of a holistic practice such as yoga or a martial art is lifted out, sold, and marketed independently of its wider philosophical context (for example, 'disco yoga', 'stretch and tone' or 'boxercise'). In addition, competing for customers in a consumerist environment means that such practices are often promoted with exaggerated claims, devaluing the work of others engaged in the same basic task of 'regaining a measure of fleshy sanity' (Johnson 1995: xiv). Leder gives the opinion that although there are Western equivalents to positive movement forms like yoga and martial arts that increase relaxation, coordination, ecstasy, and concentration, in general philosophical and religious traditions take a negative view toward the body and do not place an emphasis on cultivating it. This becomes a self-fulfilling cycle: if positive body affirming and awareness practices are not habitually part of life, then awareness of the body is remembered mostly when it is injured, in pain, tired, lustful, diseased, or dying (Leigh 2021). By not experiencing the body positively, it becomes more likely that it is subjected to abuse and neglect that leads to more illness, injury, and physical decline, thus perpetuating the cycle (Leder 1990; Fogel 2009). This is not to say that all illness, injury, and physical decline is caused by abuse and neglect of the body.

In contrast to Duncan's 'bodies' of knowledge, using the body to increase a sense of embodied self-awareness through movement practices is an aim of somatics, whether these are forms of bodywork, movement practices, artistic, educational, or therapeutic techniques (Fogel 2009). The history of somatics is fragmentary (Johnson 1995). Such divisions have contributed to the underground nature of this work as each school or form has a tendency to use different language to describe what they do. These differences may lead people to believe that their own practice is different from others', rather than viewing it as an alternative means of reconnecting with their body or increasing a sense of embodiment. The value of the somatic approaches discussed in the next section of this chapter is that they challenge 'the dominant models of exercise, manipulation, and self-awareness that alienate people from their bodies' (Johnson 1995: xv). For example, while discussing the idea of teaching self-control through somatics and dance education, Sue Stinson (2004) reflected on the edge of empowering children to make choices and manipulating them subtly to choose only within carefully presented options. In this scenario, while children are free to express their emotions, there can be a denial of any but the happiest emotions. An emotion such as anger can be expressed physically through movement, and perceived negatively. Not all feelings and movements are seen as 'nice', although only those might be expected or even preferred within an educational or therapeutic context (Ecclestone and Hayes 2009). Manipulating children and controlling their emotional range or awareness of what are 'good' or acceptable emotions is hardly equipping them with education that will allow them to lead a flourishing life with the full range of options and expressions open to them (Brighouse 2005). An important element of the Humanistic or Person-Centred approaches explored in Lesson 3 is that all feelings are allowed, and there is no expectation or limitation placed on what should be felt (Kirschenbaum and Henderson 1990). Somatics and embodiment have at their core an emphasis on individual expression and freedom of choice (Johnson 1995; Fogel 2009; Leigh 2019a). This comes about in part through self-reflection and a focus on self-transformation. For example, the expression of emotions through movement is a natural part of the therapeutic element of somatics (Leigh 2017).

Somatics

I am aware that I have been using the term 'somatics', and it would be helpful to take a moment to define it, as it can come across as somewhat jargonistic. Somatics or somatic movement, whether it is educational or therapeutic, includes a diverse range of practices and methods. In this section I will name and explain some of these to demonstrate their range and diversity, and in order to show how even when these practices arose organically in the West, they have been adopted, adapted, and renamed in order to create artificial boundaries to capitalise on and monetise them.

Three principles set somatic movement practices apart from other dance, sport, or exercise forms (Leigh 2012: 13):

> The first principle sets out the 'What?' of somatic movement. The starting point is that the body and mind are connected and through movement we can increase our body's intelligence and our mind's embodiment.
>
> The second principle answers 'Why?'. Somatic movement is an on-going process, an exploration of self that is undertaken as a life-time commitment or path for many practitioners. It is possible to bring awareness to every movement and moment of our body. The belief that it will enable us to develop towards a higher sense of self is a reason for taking somatic movement off the mat, or out of the room and into every aspect of life.
>
> The 'How?' of somatic movement is through conscious awareness, or the intention behind the practice. Not all somatic forms will look the same, nor will they necessarily feel the same. However, each practice, therapy or technique will either have explicitly defined these principles or implicitly adhere to them.

Thomas Hanna is credited with first using the phrase 'somatic' in the 1970s. He defined it as having 'evolved to mean the living body in its wholeness' (Hanna 1988: 6), and used it to mean the living body, from the Greek root σωμα. In contrast to classical philosophy, somatic implies an underlying philosophical belief that the mind is embodied. Somatics involve 'the use of sensory-motor learning to gain greater voluntary control of one's physiological process' (Hanna 1990: unpaged), and focus on an ethos of acceptance (Kirschenbaum and Henderson 1990). Any activity, from observing the breath or paying attention to the motility of the cells in our body, can be seen as somatics or somatic movement. Somatics includes the processes by which the absent or invisible body described by Merleau-Ponty (2002) and Leder (1990) is made to become more present or visible. There is a vast range of movement and bodywork practices that would fall under this definition (Juhan 1987; Johnson 1995). While not all somatic movement forms are explicit about their philosophy, they share an implicit or explicit belief that it is desirable to balance the mind and body through exploring the 'relationship between body and mind in movement' (Hartley 2004: 4), exploring a balance where 'mind doesn't dominate body, it becomes body – body and mind are one' (Pert 1999: 82–83).

The term 'somatic bodywork' equates to the skillful touch utilised in hands-on work and manipulation techniques designed to facilitate awareness of the body (Juhan 1987). Most somatic bodywork practices involve 'hands-on' work or touch. The use of touch, and the significance of human touch on the skin has long been recognised as important both to our psyche and within language (Montagu 1971). Touch is 'intrinsic to communication' and '"chief" amongst the language of our senses' (Westland 2011: 21). If a moment is significant, we call it 'touching'; if a person is irritable, we call them 'touchy'. We touch or feel others through our skin, and this is reflected through language. 'Feelings' refer to emotions, and someone who is 'unfeeling' could be referred to as 'callous', which originates from the Latin *callum* meaning hard skin. Being thin- or thick-skinned, again implies a judgement on emotional capacity, and to be 'tactful' is to have a sense of what is right when dealing with other people. In somatic movement education and therapy, there is often an importance placed on the expression, in language, of experience (Fogel 2009). A practitioner uses touch to facilitate a change in the body state of the client, paying attention to breath and bringing their awareness to areas of tension or holding. Although the approach does not intentionally probe the origins of any blocks to relaxation, 'the client may become aware of the emotional content of the barrier and thereby gain access to a new way of behaving' (Mayland 1991: 36).

Yoga

Yoga is probably one of the best-known somatic movement or bodywork practices. It has been known as a philosophy and form for over 3,000 years. For example, in India one of the earliest yoga writings is a practical 'how to' manual called the Hatha Yoga Pradipika (Vishnu-devanander 1997) and is thought to date from the 15th century BCE, compiled by Svatmarama. This guide for the aspiring yogi begins from the premise that we are all working towards 'raja yoga', or self-actualisation, and does not separate the physical from the spiritual or transformational. Yoga was ordered, coordinated, and systemised by Patanjali in the Yoga Sutras (Iyengar 1993). According to Patanjali, the goal of *samadhi*, or enlightenment, is the purpose behind all yoga. Yoga is often translated as meaning union, yoking, or communion, and is 'a poise of the soul which enables one to look at life in all its aspects evenly' (Gandhi 1929: ix). Although yoga has been associated with religion, including Hinduism and Buddhism, it is not in itself a religion. In fact, yoga can be described as either an 'Art' or a 'Science' (Iyengar 1966). Yoga can even be considered as something akin to a Western form of psychotherapy, or 'a critique of culture' (Watts 1957: 7) as it has at its heart the aim of personal liberation, a concept described as individuation or self-actualisation. The perception of yoga as a religion has led to its banishment from some church halls. The purely physical aspect of yoga, hatha yoga and its asanas (postures), has been emphasised in Western society sometimes to the exclusion of all else, turning yoga practice into an exercise form. Even as such it has been 'generally accepted as being highly positive' (Carbonneau et al 2010: 452).

However, yoga is much more than just physical movements for the body. The underlying philosophy of yoga can be present regardless of how one may initially encounter it, as changing the physical body can impact the mind and emotions regardless of whether that is the intention at the start or not. The practice of being still is one aspect that separates it from physical education and other physical activities (Phillips 2001), although many martial arts, such as budo, also incorporate stillness or meditation in their practice (Stevens 2001). Stillness, or the 'moving into stillness in order to experience the truth of who you are' (Schiffmann 1996: 4) is an alternative way of expressing the focus of a yoga movement or asana practice. By allowing a meditative awareness to focus in on the body in a non-judgemental and accepting way, it is possible to release negative perceptions that are held by both the mind and the body. There is stillness even in movement – a practitioner who endorses a very strong, powerful, and dynamic practice describes 'a healing sense of relief followed by a profoundly soothing inner peace, an even "at-easeness" – a stillness' (Schiffmann 1996: 6).

Many aspects of hatha yoga focus on the inner experience and awareness of the body in space, increasing the direct experience of the body (Prichard 2007). The focus on internal sensations and experiences, rather than external, competitive, or performance aspects, can help reduce self-objectification and the importance given to physical appearance. Controlling the mind and developing mental discipline facilitates a state of independence, liberty, or freedom from the world around. This does not mean death or unconsciousness, but an ability to live and not be ruled by circumstances: 'both mind and body … all things of the body and senses, and all states of the activities of the mind are merely phenomena, playthings' (Wood 1959: 20). Yoga focuses on 'the development and maintenance of the natural balance between the mind, the body, and the soul' (Wood 1959: 456), as the body and mind are understood as inseparable aspects of the same human existence (Dychtwald 1977). The core belief of yoga and many other somatic movement practices and bodywork forms is that a body/mind split or duality is not a desired state of being. Instead, somatics cultivate and develop conscious awareness in the individual, which can lead to a greater health and wellbeing, creativity, choices, and responsibility (Hartley 2004). New forms of somatics seemed to flourish during the late 19th and early 20th centuries. They offered 'some kind of translation into the Western vocabulary' (Bainbridge-Cohen 1993: 11) of concepts long found in yoga and other movement and bodywork forms traditionally associated with the East and across Africa.

Western somatics

Many somatic movement forms and bodywork practices have developed alongside each other, with some better known than others. They all share the underlying principles of an assumption of a mind–body connection and that embodiment is an exploration of self through conscious embodied awareness. This time period was one of revolution within many spheres, as Rudolf von Laban, Emile Jacques Dalcroze, Frederick Alexander, and Sigmund Freud were all contemporaries. Similar embodied work also developed within other spheres including music, performance, and theatre (see, for example, Grotowski 1975; Allain 2009; Trimingham 2010; Maloney 2018; Weir 2018).

Rudolf von Laban (1870–1958) developed a training that came from his study of martial arts designed for 'exploring your own capacities in the movement' (Rubenfeld 1977: 11), along with Labanotation which was a way of recording movement for dancers and choreographers. Irmgard Bartenieff (1900–81) brought Laban's work to the USA, and developed work that would later become Dance Movement Therapy (Chodrow 2009; Wengrower 2009; Wengrower and Chaiklin 2020), using movement to address 'mental problems as well as the physical' (Rubenfeld 1977: 11). Dance Movement Therapy is now a psychotherapeutic technique particularly useful for those suffering after trauma, and is regulated by national professional bodies.

Frederick Alexander (1869–1955) took a more structural approach to the body one-to-one. Alexander Technique involved learning to inhibit automatic reactions, move with grace and ease, and being fully present to remove habitual patterns and inhibitions. Alexander worked for 20 years with educator and philosopher John Dewey: 'Pragmatism and Progressive Education bear the marks of his work' (Johnson 1995: 85). Alexander's niece, student, and Master teacher, Marjory Barlow (1915–2006), described the aim of teaching 'people to know how to work on themselves' (Schirle 1987: 24). Alexander Technique encourages letting go of old habits to bring new patterns of movement into every aspect of daily life: 'the smoker can abstain from smoking without interrupting the necessary activities of his daily life' (Alexander 1932: 86). It is commonly found on the curriculum within music and drama conservatoires.

Jacques Dalcroze (1865–1950) developed a system of music education for children to experience music with their whole body. One of his students, Gerda Alexander (1908–94), developed her own less imitative system of 'living movement which freed the personality' (Bersin 1983: 5). She began to use the work in therapy, looking to bring 'the person into greater awareness and contact with himself … awareness of mind, sensation of the outer form of the body, in contact with the surroundings, awareness of breathing, circulation, tissues, inner space with organs and bone' (Bersin 1983: 8). Like Alexander Technique, Eutony is associated with music and drama training as well as free schools such as Summerhill (Vaughan 2006).

Elsa Gindler (1885–1961) developed Gymnastik, a Westernised form of meditation which she described as 'not the learning of certain movements, but rather the achievement of concentration' (Gindler 1986: 35). Her emphases were on bringing full consciousness and intelligence to actions, and self-care: 'each of us must try to gain understanding … of our own constitution in order to learn how to take care of ourselves' (Gindler 1995: 39). Although most of her writings were destroyed by Nazis at the end of the Second World War, her students, including Carola Spreads (1900–99) and Charlotte Selver (1901–2003), disseminated her work across Europe and the USA. Selver immigrated to the USA in 1938. Selver spoke of the dangers of becoming so involved in the study of self that connections with the world and reality were lost. She taught people to 'wake up … trust their own sensations' (Schick 1987: unpaged). Spreads applied Gindler's work to breathing, naming it Physical Re-education. She recognised 'this type of work had to do with much more than the mere physiological' (Hanna 1981: unpaged), and that embodied self-awareness as much as movement was fundamental for mental and physical wellbeing: 'all too often sports training is so mechanical that it does not develop any sensing of the body at all' (Spreads 1986: 13). Unlike obstetrician Frédérik Leboyer (1918–2017) who also wrote of the importance of breath (1974), Spreads did not believe that the way people breathed was set irreversibly at birth. She taught that awareness and attention could increase the quality of breath at any stage of life or health, 'as if your breathing had waited for the chance to be freed!' (Spreads 1986: 15).

Ilse Middendorf (1910–2009) developed an approach combining breath work, psychology, and movement. It included stretching, pressure points, vowel-space breathing, cave breathing, and movements out of breathing. Her method was a response to the inherently male ways of breathing taught in yoga (Beringer 1988). She believed if 'a person finds his way based on the experience of his breathing, he finds his own power and creativity' (Beringer 1988: unpaged). Her aim was to increase sensory awareness of breathing at all times, as she believed that breath was the key to corporality – the embodied self – which needed to be experienced rather than understood (Middendorf 1990).

Moshe Feldenkrais (1904–84) developed another structural hands-on approach. He pioneered group sessions of 'Awareness through Movement' and one-to-one 'Functional Integration'. His sessions were innovative, creative, and improvised: 'he would do what was necessary in order to discover how to do a movement more efficiently … he would explore his body for hours at a time in order to discover the process and its connections' (Hanna 1985: 8). A student of his, Mia Segal, trained in Judo in Japan and realised 'their philosophy is the same as Moshe's; that is, in the way both consider the whole body as a unit' (Hanna 1985: 18). It was the 'how' of the approach, not the 'what' that was important to Feldenkrais. Although Feldenkrais sessions may appear from the outside to look like physical therapy or dance, as with yoga it is the inner awareness and experience of the participant that is the work: 'to understand how my techniques work

… I have deliberately avoided answering the whys' (Feldenkrais 1981: 1). Feldenkrais worked with people who came to him in pain, either physical or mental. He felt it was the learning of his clients that contributed to their healing: 'the accent is on the learning process rather than the teaching technique' (Feldenkrais 1981: 10). He saw that after sessions they breathed easier, their eyes were brighter, and they felt lighter and taller. Feldenkrais denied he had 'healing hands', and rather than healing them said he danced with them: 'I bring about a state in which they learn to do something without my teaching them, any more than the woman taught the dancer' (Feldenkrais 1981: 11). Unsurprisingly, Feldenkrais is still associated with contemporary dance training.

Marion Rosen (1914–2012) developed the Rosen Method from physical therapy and clinical practice as 'a pathway to self-awareness and self-acceptance' (Mayland 1991: 18). Rosen was trained by Lucy and Gustav Heyer, who combined massage, breath work, relaxation, and psychoanalysis. Lucy (1891–1991) was Elsa Gindler's student, and Gustav (1890–1967) studied and worked with psychiatrist Carl Jung (1875–1961). The Heyers' mixed approach claimed to reduce treatment times for patients undergoing psychoanalysis. Rosen moved to the USA after spending some time in the UK working as a physical therapist.

Ida Rolf (1896–1979) developed Rolfing from what she knew about yoga, osteopathy, and homeopathy (Feitis 1978). Rolfing is a form of deep tissue manipulation that uses touch to bring about healing effects. Rolfing differs from osteopathy because soft tissues are manipulated to realign the bones of the body rather than direct manipulation of the bones. The body is seen as a whole, and if one aspect is out of balance it will affect the rest. Rolf's practice of yoga led her to believe 'that work with the body will improve not only the physical but the emotional and spiritual life of the individual as well' (Feitis 1978: 6), and that 'a balanced body will give rise to a better human being' (Feitis 1978: 6). Rolf did not appreciate others taking elements of her method and incorporating them into their own work, and in order to put a stop to others stealing her ideas, she developed a sequence of treatment that could be applied equally to all bodies. Judith Aston trained in Rolfing following severe spinal injuries, then adapted into a softer, less painful form known as Aston Patterning®. Aston Patterning® combines gentle manipulation of soft tissue and the redesign of the environment to support balance and promote flexibility. Aston was fascinated by movement as a child and trained in dance. Her view was that 'if you begin where people are already successful, you can help them transition into the new material, step by step' (Aston 1995: 209). The registering of approaches and names as practitioners sought to find secure business models for their work and protect its integrity is endemic within somatics, and has contributed to its fragmentation and lack of wider recognition (Johnson 1995).

Bonnie Bainbridge-Cohen developed Body Mind Centering® (BMC®) in the USA in the 1970s, using 'ideas of effortlessness, and the lengthening rather than the stretching of muscles, taking inspiration from modern dancer Erik Hawkins, who used Japanese aesthetics, Greek civilization and Zen Buddhism' (Leigh and Brown 2021a: 16). She developed an approach that 'involves a study of the relationship between body and mind in movement, through a detailed and subtle exploration of human anatomy, physiology, infant development, movement and perception' (Hartley 2004: 4). Bainbridge-Cohen said her work reorganised the brain through a combination of movement and touch. She included experiential anatomy into her classes – that is the lived and experienced exploration of the body, its organs, and systems (Olsen 1998). Although this type of exploratory movement and bodywork was considered different and new, Bainbridge-Cohen said:

> [F]or yoga to have developed, somebody somewhere must have had the awareness that one could initiate from all of the various organs. And in the martial arts, people speak of points or centers, and I think it must be internal, organic energy they're talking about. I don't feel what we're doing is new. (Bainbridge-Cohen 1993: 11)

Linda Hartley, a student of Bainbridge-Cohen, used the principles of BMC®, transpersonal psychotherapy, process-orientated psychology, and Dance Movement Therapy to develop her own framework of Integrative Bodywork and Movement Therapy (Hartley 1989, 2004). In Integrative Bodywork and Movement Therapy, the psychological process of the client is emphasised alongside an experiential exploration of anatomy and movement patterns. The client is asked to be aware of the psychological and emotional processes that may be touched on, whether they are addressed specifically or not. Hartley related the development of her work to that of Wilhem Reich and Jung (Hartley 2004). They both emphasised the need to treat a whole person. Reich saw character as a whole-body attitude, which led to muscular body armouring, and focused his work on healing the body/mind split. Hartley used Authentic Movement (Whitehouse 1995; Adler 2002, 2022) to develop her students' sense of therapeutic presence so 'the therapist's perceptions can be offered to a client, but owned for what they are – her own interpretations, judgements and projections' (Hartley 2004: 30). Authentic Movement was created by Mary Starks Whitehouse (1911–79) as a ritualised form of movement or dance therapy: 'At its simplest, Authentic Movement involves moving from felt internal impulses, and nurturing the feelings and emotions that are released. According to Dance Movement Therapists, Authentic Movement offers a powerful form within which the depths of the inner psyche can speak directly through the body' (Leigh and Brown 2021a: 17). Authentic Movement utilises

Jung's Transpersonal Psychotherapeutic principles (Jung 1957) to allow the unconscious knowledge of the body to permeate consciousness. The form includes a held boundary, and dedicated roles of witness and mover to create a dialogue and facilitate process work. Whitehouse focused on the direct experience of a mover (Whitehouse 1995), and the form was developed by Janet Adler to include the witness (Adler 2002, 2022). In the book *Embodied Inquiry: Research methods*, I explained:

> Authentic Movement can be practised in its ground form, with one mover and a witness. It is the role of the witness to create the witness circle, a safe, held space in which the mover moves with eyes closed, following internal impulses. The shutting of the eyes enables the mover to give her full attention to what she senses internally and imagines. The form and expression of the inner story is allowed to unfold, until, usually after a mutually agreed time, the witness signals the end of the movement session by the ringing of a bell or other signal. Both the mover and the witness attend to their own experiences whilst the mover moves; however, it is the role of the witness to contain the experience by marking the time boundary. The experiences are anchored into the consciousness by recalling it to the witness, or recording it through artwork or writing. The witness then offers her personal responses to the mover, helping to bring unconscious material into consciousness, and integrating the unconscious with the conscious. According to the Jungian process of active imagination, the final stage of integration occurs without great effort and resistance, and from there it is possible to make changes in everyday life (Adler 2002). If we liken this process to that of researcher and researched, we can see that the researcher (witness) holds the boundary and safeguards the researched (mover), and it is the process of articulating the experience that allows it to be processed. (Leigh and Brown 2021a: 18)

Somatics work to consciously align the body and mind; identifying, articulating, differentiating, and then integrating the smallest internal cellular movements to the external expression of movement and mind, to promote more efficient functioning (Bainbridge-Cohen 1993). This efficiency, together with an awareness of the relationships inside the embodied self and acting from that awareness, creates a state of knowing, of intuition, or inner wisdom (Hartley 1989). This inner knowing, connection, trust, and relationship with the self is an essential part of the reflexivity necessary in embodied and creative research. It allows both the researcher and the researchee to be authentic.

Research has begun to show empirically what the somatics practitioner, meditator, and intuitive mover all reported through experience; that the mind, emotions, and bodily processes are not separate, and each influences the other through subtle and complicated interactions. For example, the body stores and receives neuro-peptides in many more locations than just the brain (Pert 1999), which was postulated by Bainbridge-Cohen in her initial explorations of the body in the 1970s (Bainbridge-Cohen 1993): 'mind doesn't dominate body, it becomes body – body and mind are one' (Pert 1999: unpaged). The traditional Western view of a body/mind split is not based in physiological fact, and this has begun to influence philosophical views, as in post-humanistic writing (Barad 2007). In the book *Embodied Inquiry: Research methods* (Leigh and Brown 2021a), I gave an overview of how embodiment and embodiment techniques have been used as a research approach and used Authentic Movement and the role of the witness to illustrate the ways in which embodied self-awareness could be utilised throughout a research process (see Case Study 3 for more details). I went into detail about the form and what it entailed and looked like. I also spoke about ethnography and autoethnography, and how they could be used as embodied research approaches, particularly when focused on the sensory (Pink 2009). Ethnographic research has its own problems and critics (Hammersly 2006). Autoethnography relies on the subjective self as a research tool (Coffey 1999) and, as a result, has been critiqued as being self-indulgent, a form of navel-gazing, and lacking in rigour (Ellis 2009). As I sit here, with the light darkening outside due to the rain falling, my legs crossed underneath me, my computer resting on my lap, and my back heated by a warming pad, I am conscious of not wanting to replicate earlier work. This summary of somatic approaches gives an idea of the variety of forms and connections between practices from working with the breath; the structure of the body; giving sessions that are improvised and never repeated or a series of set manipulations; or using movement for music, drama, and dance education or therapy. Most forms can be used educationally, therapeutically, or for self-development and self-knowledge.

Somatic education or somatic therapy?

Somatics can be used as a means to educate or provide therapy. Although from the outside there may seem to be a similarity between them, there is a difference of intention between the two: 'The idea of the practitioner's thought and will shaping the process has similarities to Edmund Husserl's approach to phenomenology where "through intentionality we will our entire world into being and give it shape" (Zuesse 1985: 53)' (Leigh and Brown 2021a: 15). Somatics education is 'the educational field which examines the structure and function of the body as processes of lived experience, perception and consciousness' (Linden 1994: 1–2). For example, in yoga students learn to develop self-acceptance, physical and mental strength, clarify the mind, and enhance a mind–body connection (Farhi 2000). Somatics has been used to teach dance, reflection, or as an adjunct to training (Petsilas et al 2019a, 2019b), and can open possibilities to refine body perceptions, improve technique, aid the development of expression, and prevent injuries. Some somatics education crosses the border into therapeutic practice by claiming therapeutic intent or affect (Leigh and Brown 2021a). However, even when this is not the case, care has to be taken to ensure this is introduced in a way that is aware of the potential therapeutic (or transformative) aspects of increasing embodied self-awareness (Fogel 2009). There is a differentiation between educational material that may have therapeutic content (of which the practitioner needs to be aware), and a therapeutic intention from the outset. Therapeutic somatics can be used to increase a client's embodied self-awareness and address the issues or reasons that lie beneath its loss (Hartley 2004; Fogel 2009). It might incorporate the emotional content present in movement and the words in which we speak of and process movement, in addition to developmental movement patterns or the physiology of the body. Educational somatics, in contrast, would not seek to explicitly explore why an individual wished to increase their embodied sense of self-awareness, although a practitioner might choose to follow up any insights gained through sessions in personal therapy (Hartley 1989).

In order to choose between working educationally or therapeutically, a practitioner would need to have undergone a therapeutic training. Educational training alone does not equip a person to work therapeutically, and, as seen in Lesson 1, may well not even equip them with the skills needed to be reflective. In my own somatics training, the differentiation between therapist and educator occurred only at the point of accreditation and not in the training itself. The recognition of disparity in educational and therapeutic training or skills was not present in Kathryn Ecclestone and Dennis Hayes' (2009) discussion of therapeutic education, where they suggested that 'almost everyone in education now has some counselling or therapeutic aspect to their work' (Ecclestone and Hayes 2009: 128). They spoke of 'therapist/teachers', and implied that therapeutic elements in teacher training were detrimental to education. They did not seem to understand that therapeutic training is vastly different from teacher training. Their definition of therapeutic education had more to do with a perception of change in the purpose of education rather than an exploration of the therapeutic and educational aspects of teaching. The line between therapist and educator in somatics can be thin, and, as a consequence, there has been debate among somatic movement practitioners about what constitutes therapy or education – in part driven by legislation in Europe and the USA regarding the qualifications, insurances, and status of practitioners. For example, the UK Association for Humanistic Psychology Practitioners had a category of 'Bodywork Therapist' defined as 'someone trained in one or more of the schools of body therapy, such as bioenergetics, polarity therapy, postural integration, rebirthing etc., which tend to take the client into deep emotional or unconscious material quite quickly' (UKAHPP 2009). This would include many forms of somatic practices if their trainings met the requirements for hours and content. Due to the wide variety of somatic forms, the fact that they can be associated with 'New Age' or 'Alternative' health practices, and a lack of objective evidence to show effect, they have not always been widely accepted as bona fide therapies. Used educationally, somatics are not necessarily subject to the same regulations. The somatics I trained and have experience in are yoga (Iyengar 1966), Integrative Bodywork and Movement Therapy, and Authentic Movement, which are all used educationally and therapeutically to help people develop their embodied self-awareness, whatever their age.

Teaching awareness

Even young children can be taught to become more self-aware and to use that self-awareness to reflect (Leigh 2017). There is a strong case for including the embodied mind and body in education (Varela et al 1993; Freedman and Stoddard Holmes 2003; O'Loughlin 2006). The idea that movement embodies meaning, and the relationship between the body, movement, the mind, and understanding, implies that movement has the capacity to enhance understanding, substantiating its importance (Barrow 2008). An embodied approach to physical education could address the need for increasing activity in children's lives (Bailey 2019). Movement activities that develop a mind–body connection, such as free play, somatics, and dance are vital 'not only as a means to an educational end, but as an end in itself' (Adele Kentel and Dobson 2007: 145). The children in my doctoral study (see Case Study 1 for more details) demonstrated they were able to use movement to begin a journey to develop their embodied self-awareness. I used somatic education, including developmental play, experiential anatomy, and yoga, with children aged four to 11 over a period of two years. I gave them time to journal and draw in each session, and, at the end of the study showed them the collection of their work and talked to them about how it felt. The children were able to reflect on their experiences, even those who had been only four years old when they first started working with me. They were able to reflect on their emotions, experiences, and even the processes of reflecting itself (Leigh 2020a). However, not all found it easy to have an awareness of their body to start with:

Me: And what did it feel like when you drew pictures of you doing stuff?

EM: A bit nervous because I didn't know what I looked like because I didn't have a mirror to look in.
Me: Do you need a mirror to see what you look like?
EM: Yes.
Me: Why do you need a mirror to see what you look like?
EM: Because my eyes can't go on my hands so I can see. (EM Age 6)

This idea of not being able to 'see' the body is the absent body as described by Leder: 'the body's own tendency toward self-concealment' (Leder 1990: 69). Leder implies that the visceral organic nature and senses of the body fade into the background when compared to a more 'engaging' verbal consciousness. He gave an example of the awareness of his legs disappearing as he sat and read a book, as his mind becomes engaged with the information. For him, and maybe for many people, the body can tend to fade into the background. Increasing levels of embodied self-awareness and proprioception (that is, the sense of the body in space when still and when it is in movement) make it possible to have the body as part of a continued consciousness, and to build a sense of 'knowing' about what you are feeling, experiencing, and where you are in space. In the practice of Authentic Movement this sense of knowing is practised through 'tracking' awareness of movement and sensations:

> I sit writing and thinking, and I am aware of my left-leg folded up underneath my right sitting bone, the toes of my left-foot extended and pressing against the arch and top of my right-foot. My weight is balancing mainly through my left-hip and I balance my computer on the outer-side of my right-leg. I am aware that this unevenness in posture will mean that soon I will stretch and shift my body to find another shape in which to work. For me, engagement in one activity does not necessarily equate to the disappearance of my body nor a sense of disembodiment. I focus on this task of writing whilst I remain present to my body and the environment in which I find myself, which includes the sounds of my children playing a make-believe game. (Reflective Writing)

Leder postulated that as an individual learns a new physical activity, 'the problematic nature of these novel gestures tends to provoke explicit body awareness' (Leder 1990: 31). This fits well with the idea that embodied self-awareness can be taught and achieved when the body is experienced in new ways. With these young children, one such new way of experiencing their bodies was learning to be still. The youngest children, aged only four to five, shared their thoughts on the idea of being still:

'Is blinking still?' (J Age 4)

'You're still if you are dead.' (F Age 4)

'But your heart is always beating.' (A Age 5)

These children described how even when our physical body is held in stillness our bodies are actually in constant motion – as we breathe, our lungs, ribs, diaphragms, and trunks all move, our hearts beat, our blood and lymph circulates, and at the microscopic level each of our cells is engaged in the cycle of expansion and contraction through respiration. Being physically still on the outside was a challenge for some children. JA reflected on this:

Me: Was that easy, staying still for one minute?
JA: No.
Me: No? Why not? Do you spend much time being still? No? Did it get easier being still or harder?
JA: Harder.
Me: Harder? We did some of that every week, didn't we? Did you like being still?
JA: Yes.
Me: Yes? So even though it was hard, you liked it? Why? You're not sure? No? (JA Age 6)

Another slightly older boy, spoke about being still when reflecting on and looking through his work:

Me: And this was finding places to be still.
J: I remember that as well actually.
Me: Yeah? What do you remember about it?
J: We had to stay still and stuff and then we had to try and stay still for a long time and then we would stop and then do some more yoga I think.
Me: And was it easy to be still, or was it hard to be still?
J: It's quite hard really.
Me: Is it something you do a lot, being still?
J: No.
Me: Is it something you would like to do more of?
J: Yeah. (J Age 7)

Although J remembered being still for 'a long time', the class was never asked to be still for more than a couple of minutes. Other children reflected on how they felt when they were being still:

> 'I feel happy and relaxed because I enjoyed it, not nervous. I felt happy.' (A Age 10)

> 'Very quiet – hard because I'm used to some noise, felt like I was going to be asleep. Got easier over the weeks – nice to relax. Everyone's normally shouting in class.' (W Age 11)

Stillness was different for the children, and not something they encountered in everyday school life. It could be uncomfortable and was not always easy, and yet they wanted to do more of it. Being still was not the only new way the children were encouraged to develop their self-awareness. Some found it easier to become aware of their bodies when they moved or stretched:

Me: And you've written: 'When I stretched, I felt in my back and my legs, when you stretch you don't hurt other people, we stretch so we don't pull our bones out when we do stuff.' And this is all about feelings and stretching, 'when somebody is mentally stretched they can be angry or sad or really excited. When somebody is …' …What does it say?

C: Is physically.

Me: 'Physically stretched, they look like they go red in the face. I feel more stretched in my legs and my arms.'

C: I put the red in the face bit as a joke. (C Age 11)

Another girl, A, said "I learnt that don't, like, push your body too much because it can hurt you. And like you've always got to stretch before you do like the … like when you do the handstands and all that, because if you don't stretch you can really hurt yourself." The idea of taking care of her body so that she could use it in the ways she wanted to (in this case to balance or to do handstands) was something that she related to. For C, the awareness of what her body was feeling and how she could choose her movements to take care of herself and not cause herself pain is contrary to Leder's perception that 'a trained yogi can learn to ignore pain entirely and suppress reflexive motor responses. But the powerful distractions, training or strength of will necessary to resist pain's call bear testimony to its original strength' (Leder 1990: 73). I disagree with the view that embodied self-awareness developed through yoga or other forms of somatics would train someone to ignore, suppress, and resist the body's responses to pain or any other body sensation. On the contrary, yoga is a means to accept the body as it is in any given moment (Yee and Zolotow 2002). Yoga is practised; it is not something in which you train (Pattabhi Jois 1999). This might be a small distinction, but I believe it is important as it likens yoga and yogis more to artists or musicians than athletes. Similarly, you 'play' Tai Chi Chuan, likening that ancient art to music. The children's perceptions of their still and moving bodies were grounded by and in their physical experiences. Through moving, writing, sharing, and modelling, they were able to reflect on the sensations of their bodies and begin to conceptualise their meaning, increasing their sense of embodied self-awareness. They were encouraged to accept and experience themselves without judgement. Increasing their embodied self-awareness and developing their proprioception allowed them to begin to learn and identify sensations as feelings, and be open to the emotions and images that could be evoked by movement, which in turn allowed them to learn how to reflect.

If we want to conduct qualitative research and use our fleshy, meaty, bodies to do so; awash as they are with sensations, hormones, blood, and bile; then, just like these children, we first have to learn to notice them. This lesson has explored how awareness can be developed, what embodiment means and how it is understood and interpreted, and how it, or at least embodied awareness, can be taught through movement. Movement and self-awareness of movement can contribute to understanding the phenomenology of self. Teaching an individual to increase their sense of embodiment or embodied self-awareness through somatics is a way to support the development of an effective reflective practice, which in turn leads to reflexivity. I have been writing about embodiment and somatics for over 10 years. My own practice has waned and waxed in that time. When I was a PhD student I was practising Ashtanga Yoga (Pattabhi Jois 1999) up to six days a week, and running four times a week (Mipham 2013). Physically I was fit and healthy. Now, due to chronic illness and disability, I find myself doing my best to remember to extend the back of my neck, and acknowledge and try to process the way that my eyes struggle to focus due to sheer exhaustion. This might have impacted on my work and mean that I valued the embodied or the somatic less. My embodied body at times feels less safe, less known, and more of an enemy than it used to. I mourn the loss of my fit and flexible self. And yet, while I may not take the luxury (is self-care a luxury?) of listening and honouring all of the messages I receive from my body, the importance of being aware of them is still fundamental to understanding myself, the world, and people within the world.

In order to focus on the sensory and embodied experience of the body, it is necessary to 'have a clear idea of what sensory and embodied experience involve[s]' (Pink 2009: 24). Sarah Pink spoke of the meeting points between research (specifically sensory ethnographic research), scholarship, art, and intervention. There are inherent tensions between the critical, cognitive, and competitive nature of academia and the more accepting and non-judgemental philosophy associated with many somatic or embodied practices. It is important that every researcher takes care to maintain the relationship between the need to make an academic contribution to scholarship and discussion, performing a service or intervention, and maintaining a professional duty of care towards their participants. There can be thin, porous borders between therapy and education. I have used somatics and embodiment to illustrate this, however the same is true for many creative arts-based approaches, and I discuss this more in Lesson 3. The same arts-based methods can be used as part of an artistic practice, to work educationally, therapeutically, or to gather or generate data as part of research or Practice-as-Research. If a qualitative researcher is inexperienced in or new to the method they are employing, and misunderstands this or is ignorant of the theoretical underpinning of that approach, it can lead to harm to both researcher and participants. Using an embodied or creative research approach blurs borders due to the intensity and characteristics of the relationships between educator/researcher/therapist and learner/participant/client. The intention of the educator/researcher/therapist, and their ability and experience to develop a secure relational field and hold a safer space, are crucial. The next lesson explores the characteristics of a therapeutic relationship, and how these can be utilised by a qualitative researcher.

Lesson 3

Relationship

The vast majority of qualitative research involves others; as participants, co-creators, or audience. Leaving aside audiences for now, when a qualitative researcher is working with participants or co-creators and wants to elicit data or engage, they have to form a relationship with them. The same is true for educators when they educate others, and for artists who work with or for community groups. However, it is *therapists* who receive training on how to form, build, and contain relationships with a specific intent. This lesson draws on psychotherapy to understand the constituents of a therapeutic encounter or relationship, so researchers, educators, and artists might better understand the encounters they have and the relationships they form with their participants, students, or co-creators.

The purpose of psychotherapy

Psychotherapeutic approaches are intended to allow others (clients) to share and explore their stories with trained therapists so that they can process their experiences and heal. As such, psychotherapists undergo specific training to support their work and development as a therapist. While these trainings vary in length and content depending on the specific nature of the psychotherapeutic approach, they would all cover similar general principles in order to adhere to the guidelines and codes set by the professional bodies in their country (examples of these are the Standards of Conduct, Performance and Ethics set out by the UK Health and Care Professions Council; Codes of Ethics and Conduct from the British Psychological Society; Ethical Principles of Psychologists and Code of Conduct from the American Psychological Association; the Association of Family Therapy Code of Ethics and Practice; and similar codes set by various bodies including the UK Council for Psychotherapy and the British Association for Counselling and Psychotherapy). These codes all include practical ways of engaging and building a relationship with a client, establishing trust, boundaries, and creating an environment in which the client is happy to share personal and often emotional stories and the therapist is working to strict professional ethics to safeguard their own safety and that of their client. The purpose of therapeutic training is to build and facilitate the natural skills of the therapist (Budd et al 2020). The general objectives for any training programme would support the trainee to develop and acquire therapeutic skills and determine the type of therapy and range of client problem and personalities they are able to work with effectively. The particular theoretical approach they choose might direct the shape and content of their training, and the level they want to practise at may determine its length and depth. Some training programmes will focus on one approach from the beginning, while others give an overview of different practices and allow the trainee to align themselves where they best fit.

Psychotherapeutic approaches

There are many different theoretical forms of psychotherapy, and, as alluded to, they do not all have the same view or purpose of practice. For a comprehensive overview of psychotherapeutic practices and their history, I recommend the *Psychotherapy in Britain* book series edited by Windy Dryden. Incidentally Dryden went to school with my father and was my mother's master's tutor. When I was a young teen he told me he had attained his PhD in just 18 months and said no one needed to take three years or more. His attitude obviously made an impact as I completed my own PhD part-time in four years (equating to around two years of full-time study). In my defence for taking longer than 18 months I was a single parent at the time. My own bias is towards psychotherapeutic techniques and frames that centre the client and their needs; such as humanistic approaches, Carl Rogers' Person-Centred approach (Rogers 1967; Kirschenbaum and Henderson 1990), and those that implicitly or explicitly involve the body. The resonance of this perspective with my trainings in yoga and somatics, together with all of the teenage conversations I had with my mother as she studied for her master's in counselling and the way I approach teaching led me to erroneously believe that *all* psychotherapists would put the needs of their client first and practise in service to them. However, this is not always the case.

The development of many psychotherapeutic approaches has been dominated by Western, white, men. In 1982, a book bringing together 'some of the most outstanding and best known contemporary psychiatrists' (Shepherd 1982: x) who had been chosen specifically to include variation in age, nationality, background, and theoretical standpoint included just 12 men – 11 of whom were from Europe or the USA. In Britain, psychotherapy has Victorian roots, and this period is seen as a focus for historians of psychiatric practice (Scull 1977; Donnelly 1983). Psychiatry, or 'moral therapy', was originally seen as a way to re-socialise 'deviants' (Pilgrim 1990). In Victorian times deviance was seen as illness. Biological models of aetiology and treatment predominated over psychological or social models within medicine; and medical terminology is still utilised within psychotherapy in the present day. The First World War dramatically changed the status of psychotherapy. Victorian moral therapy had at its core an idea of biodeterminism, that is that mental disorder or ill health was due to inherited degeneracy or weakness. The war, and treatment of soldiers from all classes and backgrounds with what would almost certainly now be characterised as Post Traumatic Stress Disorder (PTSD) helped legitimise the role of talking therapies within medicine. It seemed incomprehensible and unpatriotic to believe that all these men were degenerate. Psychotherapeutic ideas about shell shock flourished, and asylums began to fall out of fashion. Political decisions such as the running down of hospital-based mental health services in favour of community-based options in the 1960s brought about a contentious shift. The siting of mental health services away from other medical specialities had implications for its legitimacy and role. Biological and clinical psychology did not always sit easily alongside psychotherapy with its emphasis on talking; bringing psychiatrists, psychologists, and psychotherapists into dispute (Pilgrim 1990).

Different theoretical frameworks require different modes of doing and ways of being with a client (Finlay 2022). While many therapeutic approaches value the bond formed between therapist and client, the idea of equality or mutuality between them is one most closely aligned with Person-Centred Therapy, Jungian therapy, Gestalt Therapy, Transactional Analysis, Cognitive Therapy, and Adlerian Therapy (Dryden 1990). In other approaches, such as Existential Therapy, although the client and therapist are seen to be equal as human beings, there is more of a tutor/pupil relationship between the two. Similarly, in Personal Construct Therapy, the role might be likened to the PhD student/supervisor relationship. In Cognitive and Behavioural Therapy, the relationship could also be described as tutor/pupil due to the emphasis placed upon the therapist's technical expertise. In terms of interpersonal closeness, in Freudian Psychodynamic Therapy the therapist is seen to be a participant observer to the process as they adopt a neutral and anonymous stance. Kleinian therapists are also anonymous, though less neutral and more confrontational. Jungian therapists might use their idea of 'self' but in a restrained way. While they would be a participant observer, they would be more likely to intervene than Freudian or Kleinian therapists.

Historically, psychotherapy operates very much on a Cartesian duality and privilege of mind (or words) over body (and experience). The emphasis is on the words spoken by and to the client and the meanings attributed to those words rather than the experience of the body (Clark and Clark 1977). This bias towards the cognitive has been described as 'curious' (Finlay 2022: 88). Linda Finlay goes on:

> [S]o much of counselling/psychotherapy seems to be focused on a verbal ('talking therapy') level, while the body in all its complexity is relegated to a secondary, separate status. I believe it is an

> ethical-professional obligation to find a way to bring the body (whether of client or therapist) holistically into our work. Engaging bodily, we help the client to own more of their fuller being-in-the-world. … Our bodies are the home of our being and every experience, emotion, thought, interaction. Even when we're dissociated from our bodies – or disembodied (in the case of online work) we are still embodying those states; bodily disconnection (or absence of a bodily presence) itself carries important meaning. The body holds untapped wisdom. We just need to find ways to release it. (Finlay 2022: 88)

Since the early 20th century, alternative forms of therapeutic approaches have been innovated including Primal Integration Therapy, Feminist Therapy, Psychodrama, Transpersonal Psychotherapy, and Neuro-Linguistic Programming (Dryden and Rowan 1988). As a therapeutic framing, Transpersonal Therapy takes the body as the 'base' level. A five-level model is used – the body, emotions, intellect, soul, and spirit (Rowan 1993). Transpersonal Therapy resonates with my training in somatic movement therapy (Hartley 2004) and yoga (Iyengar 1966; Buddhananda 1978). Transpersonal Therapy places an emphasis on self-awareness and knowing, and an awareness of the different levels of consciousness that can be equated to the mind/body/spirit connection discussed in yoga (Buddhananda 1978) or the interplay between the body and the mind (Fogel 2009). Spirituality is often more associated with philosophy and religion (Wilber 2006) than therapy. However Transpersonal Therapy and approaches that draw on Jungian archetypes use spirituality to offer perspectives on psychic distress and illness (Hartley 2001) which align with much of my work around authenticity, ableism, and disability (Brown and Leigh 2020; Leigh 2021). This can be seen in contrast to the Psychoanalytic and Freudian emphasis on the individual being responsible for their own illness.

Person-Centred therapists place emphasis on being genuine and congruent with their clients (Mearns and Thorne 1998), and, coming from this perspective, like many others I struggle to see the detached stance of Freudian, Psychoanalytic, or Psychodynamic therapists to be therapeutic: 'Therapist neutrality, withholding, and inactivity were experienced as aversive, and participants expressed a desire for explicit evidence of clinician humanity' (Goldstein 2020). Initiating therapeutic encounters that establish a relationship based on empathy, genuineness, and respect is core to Humanistic therapies such as Person-Centred Therapy, Gestalt Therapy, Transactional Analysis, Cognitive and Behaviour Therapy, Adlerian Therapy, and other approaches such as Psychosynthesis, Transpersonal, and Existential Therapy. A Psychodynamic therapist is unlikely to suit someone who wants a therapist who will be interactive and have a real presence within the relationship. Regardless of the mode of therapy, it is more likely to be effective if the therapist and client are well matched, can form a bond, and have productive encounters. Whatever the theoretical approach, psychotherapy generally has the purpose of relieving clients' distress. Some, like Freudian and other Psychodynamic approaches, are open-ended, and do not emphasise goal-setting with clients. Many other approaches encourage either goal-setting as collaborative endeavours – and these can be wide life goals such as to be a better or wiser person – or more tangible and achievable tasks that can be measured. However, Gestalt therapists and Personal Construct therapists do not see themselves as 'change agents', and may actively display scepticism towards client goals, particularly with respect to the language and manner in which they are declared. Instead, they see their role as integrating the aspects of the client that want to change together with the aspects that want to stay the same. The process of individual psychotherapy can vary from a contract of a set number of sessions over a fixed time period (for example, in Behavioural or Cognitive Therapy) to several sessions a week for an open-ended amount of time (more common in Psychodynamic Therapy).

Therapeutic encounters

Therapeutic encounters are the means by which a client's habitual and taken-for-granted reality is deconstructed, opening the way for new possibilities. It can be defined as an encounter in which the goal is to change the internal experience of one person through the therapeutic relationship, and within the therapeutic frame (Gray 1994). The frame is the context and the boundaries of where and how the encounters occur and the relationship takes place, which can depend on the psychotherapeutic approach. Possibly the earliest recorded account of a therapeutic encounter was by Aristotle, though given that this was in the context of the play *Poetics* it could be seen as a *cathartic* rather than therapeutic encounter.

A client might come to therapy to ask fundamental questions about human experience such as: 'Who am I? What are other people like? What is my place in the social world?' (Bott and Howard 2012: 18). These basic existential questions are easily comparable to the research questions formulated and answered by qualitative researchers. Both therapists and researchers need to reflect on and find their own authentic answers in order to have meaningful encounters with others, and to place those encounters in a context that will help them to answer the demands of their profession. This does not mean that encounters need to be serious at all times. On the contrary, they should be able to bring to each encounter elements of creativity, humour, playfulness, and spontaneity (Bott and Howard 2012; Brown and Leigh 2018a). In order to be successful, an encounter needs to engage the other in a way that will make them feel that their story will be heard. For therapy this is not enough, the encounter needs to be substantially different from other relationships they might have. They also need the therapist to 'give the message that more of the same is not going to take place in the room. This is not a place where the client will be able to alienate, control or seduce the other in familiar ways in which they conduct their intimate relationships outside' (Bott and Howard 2012: 29). Finlay described three ways to encounter another: using the instrumental self, where the therapist would apply their skills and techniques; using the authentic self, characterised by more spontaneous person–person contacts allowing for self-disclosure and mutual co-creation of the relationship; and the transpersonal self, where the therapist would be attentive to the happenings between and beyond their own self and the client (Finlay 2022).

The setting of the boundaries of a relationship or encounter happens from the very start (Rowan 1993). A therapeutic relationship 'might be created in the interest of healing one person, but in which two people take an equally active and responsible role' (Bott and Howard 2012: 3). Therapeutic relationships can be fragile. The clarification of what the encounter and relationship will involve, and how a safe space will be created and maintained is key (Finlay 2022). In order to create a relationship in a space, a therapist would have to find a point of connection, be aware to what their client is saying and how they are reacting, and attend to their own wellbeing (Sleater and Scheiner 2022).

Encounters put people into relationship with each other. It is 'through relationship that we find out who we are, form views of others and take a place in the world' (Bott and Howard 2012: 92). In both therapeutic and research encounters there are two people involved in the relationship, and it is the role of the therapist or researcher to endeavour to remain aware of their own stories and experiences and how they feed into and bear on the relationship. The therapist or researcher takes the place of a guest in the client or participant's world. They gain a view of their internal or external world, and, as a guest, should endeavour to be respectful (Finlay 2022). A research encounter can easily begin to border onto a therapeutic encounter. This is made more likely when a researcher is using creative methods designed to elicit deeper or more emotionally loaded stories (Brown and Leigh 2018a; Leigh and Brown 2021a). A researcher needs to be aware and mindful that participants can be vulnerable. This is exemplified when thinking of the power balance. David Bott and Pamela Howard describe this in their book *The Therapeutic Encounter*:

> The therapeutic other, in his role of benign witness, is the one who holds the power to detoxify the shame of the client. Having the tenacity to stay close to the client's material, not to rescue or reframe, the therapist must overcome his urge to symbolically look away or move things on too fast. (Bott and Howard 2012: 49)

It is easy to imagine how a researcher has similar power within an encounter as they question or interrogate the other, or how they might unintentionally react with their words, tone, gestures, or expressions and unintentionally cause harm.

While some researchers may find the process of research cathartic or therapeutic, this does not make a research encounter therapeutic for either person. A researcher holding this position may be in dire need of understanding the concepts of therapeutic containment, boundary, or holding. Boundaries are held by a therapist through the use of contracts or agreements, defined structures in which to contain the work, a secure relational field, and through the bodies of the therapist and client. Similarly, researchers will generally contain the nature of an encounter by time, place, etc. There is a difference between one-off interviews or focus groups, and a longer term ethnographic project, for example. What is not always conscious in a research encounter is the holding (or not) of the boundary for the other person.

Researchers carry out studies in order to answer questions and generate knowledge. While research encounters can be healing or cathartic, the intention and purpose are not the same as the intention and purpose behind a therapeutic encounter. Catharsis, or the powerful expression of emotion, can have a place within therapy but it has to be approached with care, as it does not always equate with anything productive. Cathartic expression without boundaries or containment can be disastrous (Bott and Howard 2012). Boundaries and containment require awareness on the part of the therapist. In order to act as a container for another, it is vital to know where our cracks or thin parts or leaks might be. Lacking awareness, or not taking sufficient care to be reflexive, can lead to unhealthy encounters and abuse of power (Finlay 2022). However, developing awareness is just the start:

> Once we have developed our awareness, we confront the ethical challenge of monitoring and containing our wounded process. This is to avoid projecting it unhealthily onto others, sublimating it or dissociating from it (which results in dissociating from our client's pain as well as our own). Part of the challenge involves managing our own counter-transferences so that we don't become shredded by reminders of our own fragility or traumas. We need to find ways to avoid vicarious traumatisation. (Finlay 2022: 147)

Talking therapy is a process where the 'client's taken-for-granted linguistic reality is deconstructed, opening the way for new possibilities to be brought into language' (Bott and Howard 2012: 11). This process can be likened to research analysis, where text or data is deconstructed and new knowledge is generated. Creative research will almost always incorporate a creative and multimodal approach to data and knowledge (Jewitt et al 2016). In participatory research, where meanings are co-constructed with participants, there are analogies with therapy, as meanings and narratives can be co-constructed with clients as well (Bott and Howard 2012). Just as with psychotherapeutic approaches, researching experiences might impact both the ways in which we interact with our research participants and how we process the emotions that arise when we do. These encounters can be impactful. Although Bott and Howard write for therapists, their words are just as true for researchers: 'we spend whole stretches of time shut in a confined space within which painful stories are told and powerful stories expressed. This will inevitably trigger a response in us. We can find ourselves feeling inadequate, angry, and inclined to do the least helpful thing – retreat' (Bott and Howard 2012: 95). It becomes the role of the therapist to process their own feelings through adequate training and supervision, and I believe that researchers have much to learn from this process.

Psychotherapeutic training

There are a number of different routes to therapeutic patient-orientated work, with variations in emphasis, depth, and length, though all work of this nature requires adherence to strict ethical and professional guidelines relating to client or patient interactions as set out by the appropriate regulating bodies such as those named previously. To train as a psychotherapist takes between three and five years. Psychoanalytic training (regulated by the British Psychoanalytic Council in the UK) would take around seven years. There is very little practical difference between counselling and psychotherapy regardless of the therapeutic approach. It used to be that counselling was seen as less academic, required less training, and was used for short-term work with clients. Counselling training varied from a weekend course to diploma or degree after an initial introduction; while psychotherapy was generally a postgraduate training resulting in an academic qualification. Now both have short and long trainings and can be studied at a postgraduate level. There are two other options to qualify for therapeutic work of this kind: clinical or counselling psychology which requires an accredited undergraduate degree in psychology and a professional doctorate; and psychiatry, which necessitates a medical degree before postgraduate qualifications in psychotherapy.

Therapeutic trainings almost always incorporate an element or requirement of personal therapeutic work and ongoing therapeutic supervision in order for the would-be therapist to understand their own personal context and triggers, and their reasons and motivations for the work that they do. This can be seen in contrast to training for researchers which tends to focus on methods, theories, and analytic techniques despite often interacting with people on a one-to-one basis in interviews or the like. Mark Aveline listed the specific objectives of psychotherapeutic training in order of priority (Aveline 1990: 317):

1. To learn to listen to what is said and not said by patients and to develop with them shared languages of personal meaning.
2. To develop the capacity to keep in contact with patients in their pain and anger-filled explorations.
3. In interaction with patients, to learn to move between participation and observation. To get a sense of when and when not to intervene.
4. To gain a coherent conceptual frame with which to understand what happens and is intended to happen in therapy.
5. To study human development, the process of learning, and the functioning of naturally occurring personal relationships between friends, couples and in families and the artificial, constructed relationships in psychotherapy where strangers are brought together.
6. To understand and bring to bear both the therapeutic factors that types of therapy have in common … and those that are approach specific.
7. To gain confidence in the practice of the preferred type of therapy. To make full use of one's own emotional responses, theoretical constructs and techniques in resolving patients' problems.
8. To increase one's own level of self-awareness and to work towards the resolution of personal conflicts which may interfere with the process of therapy.
9. To come to know personal limitations and be able to obtain and use supervision.
10. To know the features of major psychiatric illnesses and the indications and contra-indications for psychotropic medication.
11. To make valid diagnostic assessments psychiatrically, psychologically, and dynamically.
12. To be sufficiently knowledgeable about other types of therapy so as to match optimally, by referring on, patient and approach (and therapist).
13. To consider ethical dilemmas and internalize high ethical standards.
14. To cultivate humility, compassion and modesty as well as a proper degree of self-confidence.
15. To be familiar with the chosen theoretical system and aware of its areas of greatest utility and its limitations. To appreciate the significance of cultural and social factors and to adjust therapy accordingly.
16. To evaluate critically what is enduring truth and what is mere habit or unsubstantiated dogma in the practice of psychotherapy through experience of clinical practice, being supervised, and studying the research literature.
17. At the level of career psychotherapist, to acquire that professional identity.

What is interesting in examining Aveline's list of objectives and priorities are where it resonates with and diverges from the objectives and priorities of a qualitative researcher. Initially I was struck by the language: the people Aveline's would-be therapists would work with are described as 'patients', a word that automatically pathologises them and places the therapist in the role of someone trained to 'diagnose', 'treat', or 'cure'. Person-Centred approaches use 'client' instead. Within research there are parallels between conventional models that research *on* participants, and more novel, participatory methods that research *with* participants. The first principle or objective Aveline sets out – the ability to listen to what is said and what is not said – is indubitably key to qualitative research when it involves any level of communication with a participant. However, research is not therapy, and the intention behind a research interview or interaction is the capture or creation of data rather than the 'healing' of a patient. The objectives of keeping someone in contact with their experience and emotion and knowing when or whether to intervene could be considered part of interviewing skills (Brinkmann and Kvale 2014). Likewise, knowledge and expertise on conceptual and theoretical frames could just as easily apply to the epistemological and ontological frames a researcher uses to position their work. Objectives 5–7 could be said to be specific to a therapist and not to a researcher. However, objectives 8 and 9, the need to increase one's own self-awareness, resolve personal conflicts, and know limitations, are again key for qualitative research. In research, self-awareness and the critical examination of this and its implications for practice are generally called reflexivity and positionality. However, where reflexivity or positionality is discussed in research training, it is often in the context of the research rather than with the intention for the researchers to work on themselves. This is something that was discussed in detail in Lessons 1 and 2, and will be considered again in the case studies. Suffice to say this objective should be high on the priority list for all researchers no matter their discipline. The ability to use supervision though, is something that is not the same in the research context. Research supervision is firmly in place for students to enable them to progress and complete their projects. Supervision for therapists is a different beast altogether, and something that is considered later in this chapter.

Objectives 10–12 are firmly rooted in therapeutic practice, but the final five (with some modification) are relevant for researchers. It is imperative that researchers are ethical, that they abide by high ethical and axiological standards, and above all that they do no harm (Finlay 2022). Ethics and the ethics of qualitative research is a topic that is considered in more detail in Lessons from ethics in Part II. I see humility, compassion, and self-confidence as part of self-awareness and the wider positionality and reflexivity that is demanded of high-quality researchers. Likewise, knowledge of theory, the wider context in which research sits, a critical approach to research and literature, and a sense of professionalism are valuable traits in a qualitative researcher as much as in a psychotherapist.

The lengthy trainings and ongoing supervision in place for psychotherapists are to manage the ongoing challenges they face while working with clients individually or in groups. These include issues around burn-out and knowing when to terminate work with a particular client, and the benefits and difficulties in working in different contexts over time-limited periods and over longer stretches of time (Hawkins and Shohet 1989; Leigh 1998). In addition to safeguarding participants, a large proportion of therapeutic training is also around safeguarding the therapist, making them aware of transference and countertransference, empathy or compassion fatigue, burn-out, and how to process and handle others' sensitive, emotional, and often heart-rending stories (Rogers 1967; Leigh 1998).

One concept that occurs in the literature around qualitative research and psychotherapy is that of bracketing. Bracketing comes from phenomenological philosophy (May 1989; Carman 1999; Merleau-Ponty 2002), and means the putting of one's assumptions or understandings into metaphorical brackets to be held aside for reflexive awareness. Bracketing may be useful to set aside our own knowledge or inclination to jump to conclusions or judgements, our own feelings, or cultural assumptions. It is part of the ethical practice of being a therapist to have 'sufficient robustness, emotional literacy and containment to avoid loading clients with distress accumulated from our own past experience' (Finlay 2022: 146). However, 'the process of bracketing is beset with misunderstanding' (Finlay 2022: 47). It is important for a therapist to 'avoid unduly leaking our emotions (or at least minimise their negative impact) so as not to drown out our clients. It is destructive, exploitative and unethical to use the client's therapy for their own support' (Finlay 2022: 46). This is just as vital for researchers, particularly those who err towards research as their own catharsis. Bracketing can be thought of as a non-judgemental focused awareness, which allows for empathy. Empathy can be shown in the ways in which we listen and are receptive, and is a co-created experience requiring mutual communication. It can be an indicator of a good therapeutic outcome, and as such it is no surprise that an empathic researcher might find their encounters bordering on, or moving into, an unexpected therapeutic space.

Countertransference is an interesting concept, and one that is not much discussed outside of a therapeutic context (and then not within every model of therapeutic work). Transference and countertransference are the unconscious processes where the client (transference) or the therapist (countertransference) projects feelings on to the other. The therapist may also experience countertransference in response to the client's transference. These feelings may be unresolved, and reflect conflict, trauma, or dependency that results from previous relationships such as parent and child dynamics.

Countertransference can be a useful tool to gain understanding and reflexive awareness of processes at play within therapy, and reveal feelings that are unspoken or hidden. The impact of another's feelings or emotions is not unique to therapy. It is common among helping and healing professions to have an emotional resonance or connection with another, or be impacted by their feelings (Cox 1988). Within a research context, the closest analogy to countertransference might be the researcher's reflexivity, where they use their own feelings and emotional responses to a situation (or data) to reveal hidden layers of meaning (Leigh and Brown 2021a). This is particularly important when the content or data is related to traumatic or very personal stories that evoke responses. In a therapeutic encounter the psychotherapist would be careful to ensure 'grounding' work was carried out before beginning to explore trauma in detail, and that the client was given tools to help them regulate their reactions to remembered trauma (Zaleski et al 2016). The same is not true in research. Researchers have much to learn here in terms of techniques to support and safeguard their participants so that participation is not harmful (and best case is potentially helpful), and so that they as researchers have the opportunity to process what they have heard, do not use research encounters as sources of catharsis for their own unresolved personal issues, and do not become burned out or suffer vicarious trauma. If insufficient attention is given to this then research encounters have much more possibility to become exploitative, with an abuse of power. Abuse of power can happen in therapeutic encounters as well, at which point the relationship would no longer be therapeutic. One of the key ways in which this is monitored within the therapeutic frame is through supervised practice.

Supervision

Therapeutic supervision is essential within therapeutic practice (Cox 1988) and is a mandatory part of practice required within the profession. Supervision is a site of learning, and separate from a psychotherapist's own personal counselling or therapy which is often required as a part of the training process. Supervision allows the therapist to process the emotional disturbances they feel in response to clients' negative attacks, and the emanations from countertransference they feel towards their clients (Mearns and Thorne 1998). Supervision gives structured time to reflect and learn from therapeutic encounters (Hawkins and Shohet 1989). A supervisor often negotiates the oversight of the therapists' client management together with an educational and supportive role towards them. It is incredibly challenging 'to witness and hold people's pain and trauma, day in, day out, and do so without becoming overwhelmed' (Finlay 2022: 143). Supervision provides a point of reference and check on the more hidden sides of helping. Supervision allows therapists to spot darker or dysfunctional motivations, such as a hidden need for power over others. Getting support from supervision is one of the skills that is taught and modelled on therapeutic training programmes. Being able to receive support is a different skill from that of helping others, and requires a pro-active supervisor and supervisee to be successful. Supervision can be less effective if undertaken by a line manager (though this is common within health care settings), or when it is rushed and not given sufficient weight and priority.

Within a therapeutic model of reflection and supervision it is not expected or demanded that a practitioner holds the space to do this alone. Both the supervisor and supervisee take responsibility for recognising fear and negativity, ensuring the quality of work, and building empathy. The supervisee is expected to begin to learn self-supervision where they appraise themselves, and by taking these thoughts into the clinical supervision setting they can take the opportunity to process them and form part of their ongoing self-development, self-care, self-awareness, and commitment. Therapeutic supervision is a non-judgemental process where the supervisor's role allows 'the emotional disturbance to be felt within the safer setting of the supervisory relationship, where it can be survived, reflected upon and learnt from' (Hawkins and Shohet 1989: 3).

Supervision can support a therapist to become aware of their self and values. The sociocultural and/or diversity lens through which people operate impacts on the ways they view and act on ethical issues or their choices to work (or not work) with certain groups of people: 'It is critically important for us to be reflexively self-aware of our being and doing and to examine our approach with an ethical-professional lens. Without such awareness, therapists run the risk of reproducing reductionist, habitual, routinised ways of working. Even worse … turning care into harm' (Finlay 2022: 18).

While Finlay speaks to therapists, her words are poignant and true for researchers, educators, and artists. Clinical or therapeutic supervision gives space and room for reflection on critical judgements and practice, and to learn self-regulation. Self-regulation, the process of learning from the past and feeding into future behaviour, is necessary for both therapists and researchers (Bott and Howard 2012). There can be dysfunctional motivators to work as a psychotherapist (Guy 1987). For example, an individual's own emotional distress, where they look for and find self-healing in the work. While familiarity with some level of emotional pain is essential, a therapist's own unresolved needs need to be at a level that does not impact on the client (Aveline 1990). Another dysfunctional motivator is vicarious coping, whereby the therapist engages in a somewhat voyeuristic element to the therapeutic relationship where they feel better in comparison to others. Working as a psychotherapist can be a way to compensate for a sense of loneliness and isolation, or it can fulfil a desire for power over others, or a need to provide succour to others. Working as a therapist can also be a way to express a rebellious nature, by getting clients to act out instead. In order to address these, it is necessary for a therapist to become self-aware and reflexive, supported through supervision.

A lack of supervision can lead to 'feelings of staleness, rigidity and defensiveness' (Hawkins and Shohet 1989: 5) that can, in turn, lead towards burn-out, a lack of empathy, or the maintaining of illness through rumination rather than reflection (Leigh and Bailey 2013). Staleness, rigidity, defensiveness, burn-out, loss of empathy, and illness can all affect researchers, educators, and artists who lack support. Many researchers describe being overwhelmed and vicariously traumatised by hearing the stories of others and taking on their pain and trauma without adequate support or training. The young PhD student who shared she was struggling to process her participants' experiences of domestic violence and was told to 'suck it up' by her supervisor was suffering from burn-out, vicarious trauma, or both, which led to her being physically and mentally unwell.

In contrast to therapeutic supervision, research supervision is focused on achieving success within a project; normally attainment of a specific degree or award. While it is a requirement for postgraduate research students, and often in place for undergraduate students completing research assignments, it is generally focused on academic concerns and outcomes rather than interactions with participants. It is unlikely that an academic supervisor would have undergone the specific and detailed training of a clinical supervisor in order to address work stress that might lead to burn-out, power dynamics, vicarious trauma, and issues caused by countertransference, which are all a focus of clinical or therapeutic supervision. The impact of these would likely be on the mental (or physical) health of the research student, and considered a pastoral concern. These are often thought about separately (Scaffidi and Berman 2011). Beyond research students, postdoctoral researchers may have a form of supervision from their Principal Investigators, however it is widely recognised that support for postdoctoral researchers is variable at best (Wellcome 2020). Whereas clinical supervision is ongoing, once a researcher has established their independence they would not be expected to continue supervision. They might seek out peers or a mentor to discuss work, though this is not mandatory nor even expected. A research project may have been designed with a steering group, however this is likely to be concerned with the overall success of a research project rather than safeguarding the researcher(s). One topic that deserves to be taken into supervision for researchers is their motivation. There can be many different motivations for undertaking research projects, and there is often an implicit or explicit personal reason or motivation. Although Finlay talks to psychotherapists and the trope of the 'wounded healer', her words are just as true for researchers: 'if wounds have not been processed sufficiently and mostly healed, there is a risk they will contaminate the field and impact negatively … wounds are unprocessed and leak out in damaging ways. The wounded can become someone who wounds' (Finlay 2022: 140). It is essential that a researcher becomes self-aware and reflexive about their own positionality and the ways in which this impacts and shapes the research they do, the relationships they form with their participants, and the ways they go about it.

Being in relationship

In both research and psychotherapy, people 'spend a great deal of their time together talking' (Salmon 2020: 1). Psychotherapists will develop rapport with clients and guide them through sharing their stories and experiences with the explicit intention to assist their processing of particular issues they want to deal with. Research might ask participants to share stories, but does not share the same intention of assisting their process and, as established, the majority of researchers are not trained to deliver therapeutic interventions.

Both therapeutic and research relationships require a sense of openness and presence (Finlay 2022). Being open and present can be likened to a state of unknowing, similar to that described within mindfulness (Langer 1989, 2000), and also found within Gestalt literature (Hycner and Jacobs 1995). The idea of presence within psychotherapy is particularly relevant in psychotherapy that looks beyond the spoken word (Weiss 2009).

Therapeutic trainings are designed to develop depth of practice as this, in turn, benefits the client (Sills 2000). The depth of reflexivity and awareness in my own practice allowed me to develop a quality that Alan Fogel defines as intersubjectivity. I learned this awareness and reflexivity through my somatic training and practice. Teaching reflection through a highly structured frame or an assessed process, as I was subject to in my teacher training, does not have the same result. Intersubjectivity allows a person to be more open to others' experiences, and requires them to remain self-aware while working with other people: 'the teacher or practitioner must herself embody a certain quality of openness and curiosity toward her own embodied self-awareness and to the discoveries made by her students' (Fogel 2009: 224). However, there may be times when intersubjectivity is not possible, or when it is possible but extracts a price: 'we have all been in situations where intersubjectivity is not possible' (Fogel 2009: 224). This is one reason that ethical codes for psychotherapists include regular, contracted supervision (BACP n.d.). Intersubjectivity allows one to tune in and be sensitive (Fogel 2009). In an educational context, it is within this intersubjective praxis that the educator and child form between them, both acting as competent partners within the relationship, that results in education (Biesta 1994). In psychotherapy, it is within this praxis that progress and insights are made for the benefit of the client. The idea of intersubjectivity may be less well used in qualitative research, but it can be seen that it is fundamental, and that a qualitative researcher should inhabit this same practice.

As well as intersubjectivity, in order to be effective for research or therapy relationships need to have trust, authenticity, and humanity. The initiator of the relationship (that is, the therapist or researcher) needs to create an open authentic relationship, and do this through giving of themselves without manipulating or controlling the other. This way the relationship is comforting rather than threatening. The extreme contrast of this would be the dehumanisation of others seen in the Holocaust where people were seen as less than human. In essence, this means allowing ourselves to be touched by the wonder and curiosity of the stories and experiences that are shared while holding our own assumptions, hopes, and expectations in check. This state forms part of the presence that allows us to hear and to listen. Finlay (2022) described the idea of presence as forming eight equal parts that feed into each other in a cycle (see Figure 3). Presence involves being grounded in our own embodied experience, so that we can 'receive' the other's experience (Geller and Greenberg 2002).

Establishing relationships that allow people to open up and share stories is important for both therapeutic and research encounters. However, while the border between the two can be thin, the intention behind research is different from the intention of therapy. Researchers carry out studies and encounter participants in order to answer questions and to generate knowledge, whereas therapists intend their encounters to change and affect their client.

Intention

One way of thinking about intent is by considering how the conscious mind works. Theories of mind and consciousness interested scientists as much as philosophers. As part of work on reflections, fantasies, and essays on the nature of the mind and consciousness, Douglas Hofstadter and Daniel Dennett wrote 'it is an attractive notion that the mysteries of quantum physics and the mysteries of consciousness are somehow one' (Hofstadter and Dennett 1981: 43). In their opinion, the mind can be modelled by non-quantum mechanical computations, and the 'observer' inherent to causal quantum mechanics is a concept not precisely defined. Rather than worrying about possible eigenstates and branching multiple universes, the effects fall back into the random of 'it either happens one way, or it does not' (much akin to the comment that all statistics are 50:50 – a statement designed to annoy mathematicians). The role of physics and where it lies in the Cartesian mind/body discourse and nature of consciousness is unclear. The ability of biologists and psychologists to uncover detailed physiology of the body and brain down to the molecular level and beyond has not realised the fear that 'psychology becomes a branch of physics, a result that

Figure 3: Finlay's cycle of presence

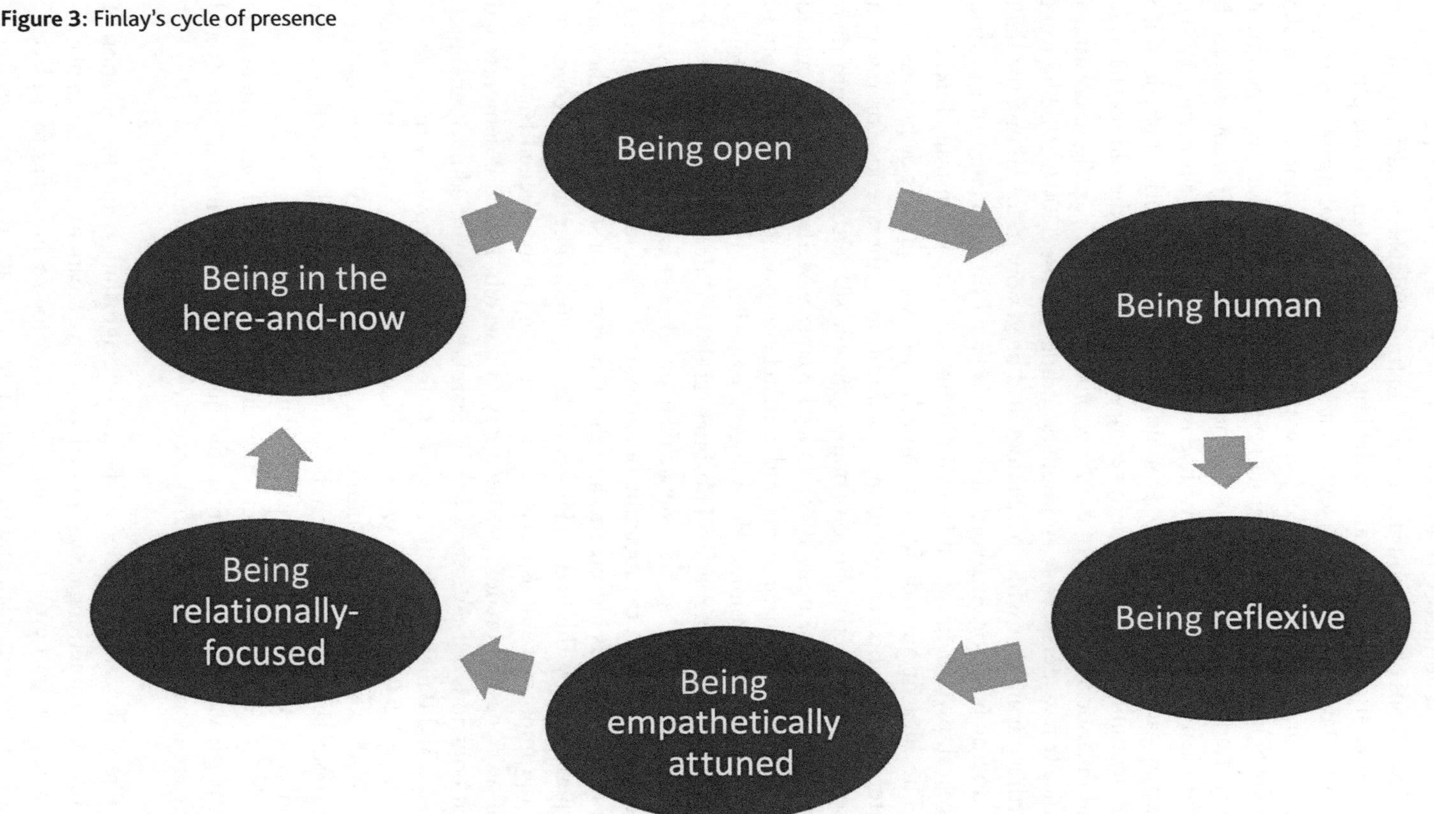

may cause some unease among both groups of professionals' (Morowitz 1981: 36). The theory of quantum mechanics and ideas that observation and conscious observation affect events in time and space linked new physics to consciousness and ideas about the importance of intent. Some physicists, such as Werner Heisenberg, even stated that the laws of nature no longer dealt with elementary particles but with the contents of minds. Others, like Erwin Schrödinger who is famous for the cat in the box thought experiment (Is it dead or not? Don't look or you might kill the cat!), moved towards mysticism and a sympathy with Eastern philosophies (Morowitz 1981). Hartley stated definitively 'the profound changes in the world of physics since the beginning of the twentieth century have uprooted the old mechanistic and dualistic world view of the Newtonian-Cartesian paradigm, creating a radically new perspective and understanding' (Hartley 2004: 19). She went further, saying that while psychology had been slow to 'catch up', the field of holistic body-orientated therapies was based on the view that spiritual, physical, psychological, and social dimensions were intrinsically linked.

The idea of an individual's thought and will shaping a process and determining whether something is educational, therapeutic, or research also evokes Husserl's phenomenology: people shape the world with their intention and will (Zuesse 1985). Indeed, Maurice Merleau-Ponty articulated a concept of lived space where, rather than being bound by reason/emotion, mind/body dichotomies, the subject's experience is referenced through movement and language (Thorburn 2008). Malcolm Thorburn went further and stated that 'the essence of an experience is its intentionality: the meaning of events, the meaning of embodied action including kinaesthetic awareness of one's movements and the importance of sensations as they are experienced by the body' (Thorburn 2008: 265). The acknowledgement of the importance of aspects such as intuition can be likened back to the self-awareness and reflexivity necessary in research. Lesson 2 demonstrated that conscious self-awareness can be learned and expanded into reflexivity (Leigh and Bailey 2013). Bodies are profoundly interwoven with a sense of self (Fogel 2009). Whether we are a researcher, educator, artist, or therapist, our body is a tool for communication and connection. We show through our body language how we can be trusted, and how we receive others. Our bodies are also tools that we can use and learn from.

This resonance of intention, embodied awareness, and phenomenology has particular implications for creative qualitative researchers. Creativity and play are incredibly valuable and necessary parts of therapy:

> Creativity can be defined as the use of original ideas and imagination to create something new. Applied to therapy, creativity comes into play when we go beyond the formality of protocols and rules to a place of imagination, play, and intuition. This is the artistry of therapy, the

> subtle process that dances in the mysterious 'between' of the therapy relationship. Being creative is about knowing your therapist self-as-an-artist and your therapy work as artistry. It's about the curiosity, passion, permissiveness, vitality, absurdity, joy, courage, and sheer heart and soul that can animate our work. (Finlay 2022: 107)

Finlay links creativity with therapy and art, and therapist as artist. Her words are just as true for researchers (Brown and Leigh 2018a). As Abraham Maslow said: 'When you are creative you are more self-accepting than average, less afraid of your own thoughts, and less afraid of being laughed at or disapproved of. You can let yourself be flooded by emotion and you waste less time and energy protecting yourself' (Maslow 1959: 88 cited in Mitchell 2016: 11). Engaging with creativity allows people to 'invoke imagery and metaphor' (Finlay 2022: 119). One might expect a research participant would know and be able to differentiate between experiences of being in a research interview or being in a therapeutic conversation. However, embodied and creative qualitative research intentionally creates research encounters that facilitate more emotional engagement from participants. It facilitates both participants and researchers to make connections between events that they had not been previously aware of, to be more emotional, embodied, and reveal hidden experiences. Unlike in conventional interviews, participants are less likely to be conscious of how much they choose to reveal, how much they share, and how much they enter into their own process.

Researchers often choose to study topics that they have a close personal connection to, or that they have personal experience of (Field-Springer 2020; Stronach et al 2007; Wellard 2010). It is important for researchers to reflect on who will benefit, and what motivations are behind their work. As researchers, and without the clear guidance of a professional body that mandates training, ethics, and guidance on supervision such as there is for psychotherapists, it is also vital to be aware of intentions towards the research participants. Using creative methods makes it easier to unwittingly move towards a therapeutic edge, particularly if the questions or research topic is more personal or sensitive. For this reason I believe that interviews, focus groups, or workshops that incorporate creative approaches are more likely to move towards the model of interactions between clients and psychotherapists. If choosing to use creative research methods takes researchers closer to the edges of therapeutic work, then they need to remain present and aware, and reflect on where they tread along those boundaries and how the porosity changes at different points during the process of research. With this knowledge and awareness, it becomes possible to choose to take paths appropriate to the project, experience of the researcher, time available, and participant group. In order to use embodied and creative research safely, a researcher's intention has to be clear. They should have awareness of their own motivations, and the need to establish a secure relational field or boundary for themselves and their participant to keep them both from unnecessary harm.

Relational field

I have been thinking on how the intent of the practitioner determines whether a creative practice event or activity is research, art, education, or therapy since my PhD study (for more details on this see Case Study 1). I had long conversations with drama practitioners and researchers as part of a project I conducted following up the interdisciplinary research study *Imagining Autism* (Leigh and Brown 2021b) where I explored this more (see also Case Study 2). I have to credit Melissa Trimingham with the idea that I should bring these thoughts into the form of a book. She told me quite correctly that there was too much to fit into one research paper. Trimingham was one of the pioneers of Practice-as-Research (Trimingham 2002). While discussing the boundaries between research, art, education, and therapy she told me that we have to divide them up into paradigm models "but as soon as you've got those boundaries of course you realise how unsatisfactory it is that there is a spillage from one to the other". She said we have to analyse and categorise things to try to understand the limits of these models.

As a researcher aware of the therapeutic potential of the material I am using, it is my role to be present with my full awareness and to hold space so that all can be heard, listen, and communicate to express themselves (Sills 2000). Trusting relationships and a contained relational field are essential to make people feel safe. Qualitative researchers and therapists want our participants and clients to feel safe so they can be honest, reflective, and share rich stories about their experiences. For example, when I worked with children I created that space through the ritual of making contact with those present, checking in with everyone, and more importantly allowing them time to check in with their own inner states. This established a 'field of listening' to make sure that everyone was seen and felt seen, and so they knew there would be room for everyone to show and share their feelings, thoughts, and experiences. In order to facilitate others' self-reflection, it is necessary to first feel seen and safe. The circle game was one way I did this, and it was a favourite with many children I worked with. The rules of the circle game were that everyone had to show *something*, either from the session, copying something someone else had done, or that they made up. This was to ensure that everyone was seen, recognised, and applauded. If a child did not know what to do or did not want to be in the circle on their own I would go in with them and we would do something together. Every child (or adult, as often accompanying adults enjoyed joining in) got a big round of applause from the group. Some children initially felt uncomfortable being the centre of attention in this way. Not all found being seen by others easy. In an interview after working with me for two years as part of my doctoral study, one girl told me how she felt about other people seeing what she had written or drawn:

C: That was pretty embarrassing to me, because you have to draw and then like show everyone.
Me: Okay, why was it embarrassing?
C: Because I don't really like … well, it's okay with me but I don't … showing people my work, it's not really my thing, you know, I don't want them knowing what …
Me: What you've done?
C: Yes.
Me: But you were all right with them watching you when you were moving, yes?
C: Yes. (C Age 8)

I was interested by C's response about sharing her drawings and writings, as this was not something we did in the sessions. We spoke a bit more to explore her experience:

Me: Do you remember we used to do the circle game, you have to get up and show, was that all right or was that embarrassing?
C: That was fun.
Me: Was it okay doing the writing and the drawing and the thinking about what it felt like to move? Was that bit all right? Was it just the sharing bit you didn't really enjoy?
C: Well, I kind of enjoyed the sharing bit because I like expressing my ideas but like just constantly sharing with others, we do show and tell with brain stuff and share them like that, we do that every week, so it's like people and sharing, but it's … I don't get like angry with it, it's a bit fun sharing my ideas.
Me: Okay. Is it kind of like an edge, like do you like it but you don't like it?
C: Well, it's 50:50
…
Me: What do you wish we'd done more of?
C: Probably more of the circle game. I liked that.
Me: Yes? Even though it's the sharing bit that you're kind of unsure about?
C: Sharing quite perks me up but too much sharing, then kind of perks me a bit down. (C Age 8)

Even though C expressed that being seen by others was something she struggled with, one of her favourite things was still a sharing activity. When I worked with children, I wanted each child to be able to gain confidence, and it was important to me that I built an atmosphere where there was trust, encouragement, and support. Key to this were the relationships I had built with the children and staff: 'relationship is the mirror in which you discover yourself. Without relationship you are not; to be is to be related; to be related is existence' (Krishnamurti 2002: 280). I encouraged recognising achievements at other times as well as during the circle game: 'K fab at balancing – smiling, whole class clapped when she balanced on one leg throughout the exercise' (Field Notes). I developed a contained relational field that allowed the children to feel seen, safe, and supported, which in turn allowed the potential for therapeutic work within my research.

My role is to ensure that everyone within the relational field I establish feels seen, and as safe and supported as possible. In my doctoral research the relational field encompassed all the children, myself, and any participating staff in each group. Similarly, when working with collaborative autoethnography or research groups, as in Case Study 4, the relational field has to expand to encompass all the members of the group. It is easier to establish a secure relational field working one-to-one, as I did with the academics exploring embodied identity in Case Study 3, than in groups.

Working with a group is different from working one-to-one. In a therapeutic one-to-one encounter the therapist can focus entirely on the needs of their client. In a group it is necessary to hold the 'energy', or focus, of the group together, and accommodate individuals as much as possible within that. Because of the compromises inherent in this, the therapist must be careful not to introduce material that may be too much to be held appropriately, and maintain a relationship with all present as much as possible. An example of where a secure relational field was not achieved with a group is with students on a dance degree given a 10-week course of bi-weekly classes in somatic education as part of an action research project (Fortin et al 2009). The classes included both theory and practice, and drew deeply on Feldenkrais' work (Feldenkrais 1981). However, the students described the sessions as destabilising. The authors reported these comments as revealing the 'ambivalence between, on the one hand, the desire to become aware of current situations in the dance milieu and, on the other hand, the discomfort this causes' (Fortin et al 2009: 54). However, given the importance of establishing a secure relational field, and the close borders between research, educational, and therapeutic work in somatics, I question the level of therapeutic holding present in the classes, and the rigour of conducting a short action research project rather than a longer study. In my experience, a duty of care should be present for students in such a class so that they are not left in a state that, in their words, left them not wanting to go to the next class 'out of fear that I would leave too shaken up by all sorts of self-questioning' (Fortin et al 2009: 54).

Another and more positive example of dance students and somatics can be found when B. Scot Nichols (2008) set out explicitly to research the interface between somatic education and somatic therapy. They designed three courses at different levels along that continuum and offered them to students who all had prior knowledge of somatics or movement. Each course offered experiential and theoretical components just as in Fortin, Viera and Tremblay's work. In contrast to the student evaluations from Fortin and colleagues, *all* Nichols' students fed back that they found the work to be transformative as well as informative, and the courses were observed and reported as being successful. It may be that students with less positive experiences declined to self-report, or were excluded from Nichols' final report. However, Nichols shared that they had progressively become more comfortable with their role as therapist and at designing and containing learning experiences that were able to move between education and therapy. They were able to establish and hold a secure relational field for the students they worked with. As a result, they saw deep growth in themselves and their students.

This chapter began to look at the importance of relationship, intention, the ways in which psychotherapy and research share boundaries with each other, where they touch on art and education, and where they diverge in terms of training and support. Part II focuses on the lessons to be learned from art, from science, and the ethical implications of embodied and creative qualitative research.

PART II

Disciplinary borders

Introduction to Part II

The first part of this book touched on ways in which qualitative research borders onto psychotherapy, education, and embodiment. In Part II, I will explore the lessons that can be learned from art, the challenging terrain that represents the no-man's land between science and qualitative research, and the practical and ethical implications of creative and embodied research.

Lessons from art

What does it mean to be an artist? An art researcher? Or a researcher who uses art? Is the definition of an artist someone who 'makes art', or is artistic expression an integral aspect of human identity open to everyone? If artists draw from their experiences to facilitate their own and others' creative processes, how and where is this process different from or the same as the ideas of reflection, awareness, and relationship I have discussed? How is it different from using creative research methods with participants? Just as using research methods that *can* have unintended therapeutic effect does not make a researcher a therapist working with therapeutic intent, using arts-based methods does not automatically make a researcher an artist.

Being an artist

There was a time, before I re-entered academia, that I described myself as an artist. In addition to the textile art I described in the introduction, my movement practice included creative work that served no extrinsic purpose other than to facilitate my clients to explore their body, the way it moved, and how it interacted with the environment around it. I acted as a consultant for bodies including Local Health Authorities, Primary Care Trusts, SureStart Centres, and Birmingham Royal Ballet, using my intuition and expertise to provide workshops and trainings (McMillan 2015). I used movement in many different ways to allow people to find out more about themselves and the ways in which they engaged with the world around them. My work spanned that of an educator, therapist, and participatory artist; using movement as the medium by which I engaged my audiences with the creative process and exploration of self and others rather than creating art for exhibition or performance. I was not a researcher.

When I began my doctoral studies and started my journey into research, my creative and artistic practice suffered. Coupled as it was with a turbulent and demanding time in my private and home life, I found that I did not have the capacity or space to feed an artistic practice beyond that funnelled into my creative research methods and writing. I was not completing a Practice-as-Research PhD, this was not an accepted form of doctorate in education. The majority of my work still integrates creative and playful approaches into phenomenological explorations (Brown and Leigh 2018a), and I often choose to use autoethnography, collaborative autoethnography, and co-creative participatory approaches, including video. As I have developed as a researcher, I have experimented with different creative methods including movement, drawing, mark-making, collage, film, and fiction. I see these securely as research methods. Although the outputs may be artistic, they are synthesised from, and in response to, research data. I have not described myself as an artist for many years, although as I write more autoethnographic fiction, direct more films, and use art to encourage expression, it is a descriptor I would like to reclaim and own again.

The formation of an artistic identity (or not) is often determined by social context, about what an artist is perceived to be, what they do, and the work that they 'should' produce. I am sure I am not the only person to have been in a modern art gallery or exhibition and thought something along the lines of "I could do that". As children, art is accessible to everyone. It forms a fundamental part of the educational and social experience for most children. This is evidenced by the prevalence of freely available pens, crayons, and colouring materials for children when they are having a meal in a restaurant, visiting a museum, attending a formal wedding, or waiting for an appointment in a hospital. Art is used for enrichment within schools, and is an activity that children are expected to enjoy. If I think about the activities I used as a teacher, things like drawing a picture, poster, or making a model were used to engage or reward children by allowing them an opportunity to be creative. Being creative is positive, and often the process of art-making is seen to be just as beneficial as the eventual outcome. However, as people get older, attitudes and relationships towards art and creativity often change. I have heard "Oh I can't draw", "I'm no good at art" so many times, whether it is when people are asked to draw as part of a game or during an arts-based research session. Similarly, it is common to hear people denigrating other artistic abilities: "I can't sing" or "I can't dance". At some point many people stop allowing themselves to enjoy the process of art-making and creativity for what it is, and instead critique and judge their perceived ability against others. This self-judgement and critique against internal standards of worth or others' accomplishments is part of rumination (see Lesson 1) and can affect people's attitudes to their bodies and their ability to enjoy movement and sport, as well as art and creativity.

Art intersecting with research

The philosophical meaning of what art 'is' has been discussed many times (Danto 2013; Lamarque and Haugom Olsen 2019). Art serves many functions and takes many forms. Alain de Botton and John Amstrong stated 'the modern world thinks of art as very important – something close to the meaning of life' (2013: 4). If only it were funded commensurately! De Botton and Armstrong described art as a tool that can allow us to become in touch with memories, and let people feel or access emotions such as hope or sorrow. It can allow people to find ways to rebalance or gain self-knowledge. Art can be designed to engage and facilitate growth, or to get an audience to notice and appreciate the world around them. It can also be used therapeutically, to 'correct or compensate for a range of psychological frailties' (de Botton and Armstrong 2013: 57). When it comes to engaging with or responding to art, a piece can be read in many different ways; for example, by looking at its technical mastery, political relevance at the time it was created or in the present day, appreciating its historical worth, or for its shock value. Depending on the reading that is being used, what comprises 'good' art from the rest might be something that has been recognised by the establishment as being significant, or utilised technical skills impeccably. It might have made a political point or be able to tell a contemporary audience something about the past. A 'good' piece of art might be able to shock the audience out of complacency. This idea of what is 'good' art and what is exhibited and recognised as good can be a stimulus for discussion – "I could do that". A therapeutic reading of art might define art as 'good' because it evoked a positive response for an individual (de Botton and Armstrong 2013), although as seen, therapeutic does not always equate to positive. De Botton and Armstrong focused most on visual art in their analysis – paintings, ceramics, and sculpture. However, art takes many forms and can include modes such as fiction, poetry, sculpture, theatre, film, performance, textile, dance, and movement. Each artform can be used educationally, therapeutically, and as a mode of and for research. The 'turn to the arts' in social research has popularised arts-based approaches and methods (Leavy 2015). These are more and more often utilised in social research (Kara 2015). However, artistic practice and Practice-as-Research (Trimingham 2002) are *not* equivalent to working with creative or arts-based research methods. While they may overlap, to claim otherwise negates the validity of what it means to be an artist or to research art. Arts-based research of this kind is postulated to be a betrayal of art itself (Jagodzinski and Wallin 2013). Artistic practice, arts research, and arts-based research are analogous, but not the same. Not all artists wish to research their practice, not all arts researchers will use arts-based methods, instead opting for more conventional forms such as surveys or questionnaires, and not all using arts-based methods are artists. There are many different terms for this type of work, which is potentially confusing and could provide barriers to learning more about how art and research intersect, as each term is likely to have a different interpretation and intention underlying its practice, and subtly different literature surrounding it (Chilton and Leavy 2014).

Arts-based methods can be used simply as a methodological tool to access or elicit 'richer' data. One way to avoid self-judgement around artistic ability is to avoid asking participants to draw. I do not think I am 'good' at

Figure 4: Collage of academic identity

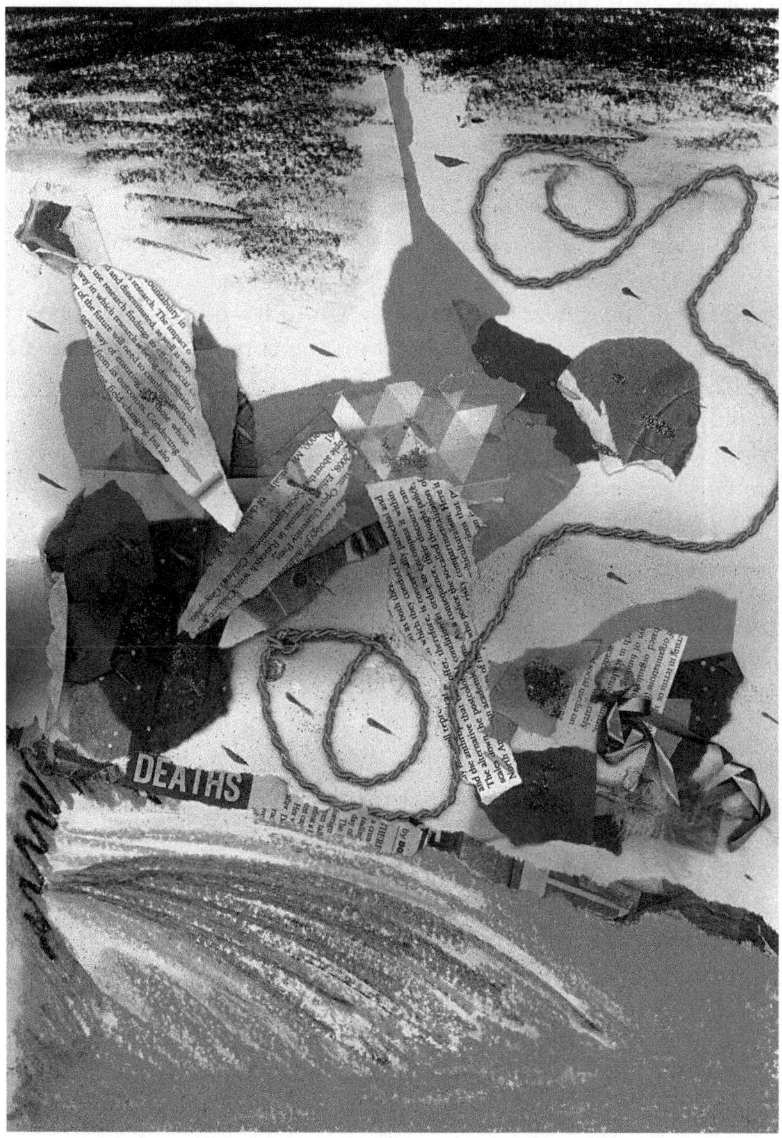

drawing, and this is one reason why I enjoy collage as a research method, where there is more emphasis on ripping, cutting, and sticking than line drawing (see Figure 4).

Self-judgement can impact on how and when arts-based methods can be used successfully in research (Brown and Leigh 2018a). In a study on academic identity that I will look more closely at in Case Study 3, I used a range of high-quality art materials and invited participants to create alongside me as a form of creative research (Kara 2015). The idea was to reflect and talk as we drew or made marks. Several participants, despite being aware before participating that the project involved arts-based methods, refused to pick up any materials for fear that they would not be any good. They seemed more comfortable in traditional talking-orientated processes of an interview. Another option is to use objects or images as metaphorical representations. These can be used to elicit stories, or as part of a sand-boxing exercise, where the objects and their placement becomes relevant (Mannay et al 2017). This type of relational work is also used in Gestalt Therapy. Another method that avoids drawing is modelling with Lego® bricks and pieces. Despite the popularity of playful research with Lego® for 'serious' research questions (Gauntlett and Holzwarth 2006; Gauntlett 2007), research participants, especially academics, can be put off by being invited to build with what they perceive as toys, feeling that the process is infantilising or trivialising what they have to say.

When drawings, photographs, and other visual materials are created as part of research, they also create *artistic* and *ethical* questions. Issues of ownership and empowerment in the use and analysis of visual materials have long been discussed in the social sciences. Jon Prosser (1998) addressed these in relation to the subjects of the study and the researcher. A participatory approach that incorporates co-creation, such as giving participants access to the researcher's camera or using their own to take photographs, allows them to take ownership of the images that are produced, and assent to which best represent what they were trying to say. The issue of the researcher as an 'outsider' is also less evident in co-constructed or co-created research (Dwyer and Buckle 2009). Participants and researcher can all take on roles of 'photographer', 'artist', 'documenter', and 'researcher' as appropriate. However, it is important with visual data (as any data) that an appropriate methodology is chosen to analyse as well as generate the data (Rose 2007). The analysis may differ depending on the research approach. For example, it is not appropriate to use an analytic approach such as compositional analysis when the research question is concerned with the meaning making of the photographer. If an artefact only exists to elicit a verbal response, it might be ignored. If it is thought to represent an experience, or could be considered more abstractly as a piece of art in its own right, then the most appropriate analytic frameworks need to be considered. Is it fair to analyse a drawing created in an interview by a young child with the same criteria as a piece of modern art? Is it fair not to? When visual materials include images of people, particularly of children and those taken by children, it is also necessary to consider ethical implications, as will be seen later in this section.

Academics exist within a context where criticality and excellence are prized over emotion (Bloch 2012). This is reflected in the difficulties associated with gaining recognition for modes of research that are seen as less conventional, or less rigorous. Whatever the artistic discipline, practice and experience can be fertile in terms of the practice and outputs of research, however they require time spent on reflection and preparation which can be hard to 'carve' out as an academic rather than as a practitioner. Practice-as-Research is now an accepted academic form within many arts disciplines including dance, fine arts, creative writing, music, and drama. The form varies depending on the discipline, and Estelle Barrett and Barbara Bolt edited a book exploring Practice-as-Research across creative disciplines (2010). It is common in theatre studies (Trimingham 2002) and creative writing (Leavy 2016) to include an exegesis or critical explanation or interpretation of the practice. Some modes of arts research, particularly those that focus on the written word, seem to fit naturally within a traditional research form, for example the use of fiction in education (Clough 2002) and health research (Stephens 2011). It is not surprising that a narrative approach with established philosophical roots as method, methodology, and mode of dissemination (Caine et al 2022) can appeal to a qualitative researcher (Moen 2006). Similarly, and possibly because of its connection to narrative, creative writing and fiction can easily be understood as being useful to illustrate findings from social research (Philips and Kara 2021), or forming part of a research practice itself (Leavy 2016). Words may be understood more readily than other forms of art by an academic audience. I used fiction as a research tool for dissemination following a collaborative autoethnography project with WISC. As I will share in Case Study 4, this was used to relate 'true' stories that were not 'real' (Leigh et al 2022c). It was important to protect my research participants and co-creators from the dangers of whistleblowing (Bjørkelo 2013), which they would have been likely to face had it been possible to identify their real stories within the relatively small academic community they came from. Narrative approaches are common in ethnography. One classic example that centres on the moving body is Loïc Wacquant's account of boxing in a Black neighbourhood (Wacquant 2004). Sensory ethnography intentionally brings in senses such as sound, smell, sight, and scent to record and 'listen to' life and lives (Back 2007; Pink 2009). Similarly, photography or film can capture research encounters or be methodological approaches in their own right (Harris 2016). The use of a camera in ethnography and anthropology provides another perspective or 'viewpoint', enabling a discussion of who wields the camera and what this implies about the reflexivity and positionality of the researcher (Ruby 1980; Postma and Crawford 2006; Poltorak 2019). Ethnography can feed into art production (Lyon and Back 2012; Bradley 2020). Art is becoming more recognised as part of a research process, with dedicated video journals and exhibitions of research outputs and artefacts. Nevertheless, art is still often found as an adjunct to 'real' research or as part of a related but less highly funded public engagement or impact project. The Dance Your PhD project ('Dance Your PhD' n.d.) typifies this. This annual competition for scientists promises 'geek fame' for short videos using interpretative dance to summarise the findings of a PhD.

I was lucky enough to have a long conversation about the nature of research with Melissa Trimingham, a Co-I on my second postdoctoral project *Imagining Autism* and one of the originators of Practice-as-Research in drama (Trimingham 2002), as part of a study exploring the experiences of researchers on an interdisciplinary project (Leigh and Brown 2021b). Trimingham was very aware that universities preferred more traditional research outputs, and that though drama research was the actual *doing* of the thing, it was only validated in the eyes of academia if it was reflected on in a conventional output such as an article or monograph. Regardless, she explained, "But I'm not sitting there … thinking I'm a researcher, I'm actually working with the child, I'm a drama person. 'Oooh a puppet', you know, it's like that."

One of the key differences I was aware of was the performative nature of drama as opposed to the internal focus of somatics. I asked Trimingham about the differences between performance research and Practice-as-Research:

> 'Well, no, it's exactly the same thing, how can I put it? When I first started doing my PhD, there were no Practice-as-Research PhDs, however there were precedents in things like music. So a friend of mine had got a PhD simply through composing music, very complicated music. It was all, I don't know, I presume an examiner looking at it would think, "Christ, this is so complicated, the guy must have understanding of music to PhD level". I don't know. But that's quite hard to translate into a kind of theatre drama PhD. How does a piece of practice be so sophisticated within drama that the examiner will think, "Gosh, this person is obviously working at PhD level practically therefore their understanding must be the same". Because a PhD necessarily for me does involve a lot of reading, you need to know what people's theories are around, the kind of thoughts that people have had to analyse this and you need to make your own selection in order to throw light upon this practice. The idea that practice throws up stuff that you don't understand, that you hadn't expected, although you might start with a hunch, you know, that, I was researching very obscure 1920s stage work where I had a hunch that it connected up with work I had done with Horse and Bamboo, to be frank, you know, working in masks, working in built-up costumes. And it did, but I didn't know how it connected until I did all the reading and all the analysis on the practical work that I did. That a student that I was

> working with would come up with a particularly interesting interaction say with a bit of stretchy cloth. It sounds absolutely ridiculous doesn't it but by looking at that, what is going on here, this is a body engaging with a piece of material and that's exactly what Schlemmer did in the 1920s, what's the connection here? What's the principle that underlies it, that's manifesting it?'

When I say that arts-based or creative research is not the same as artistic practice or Practice-as-Research, a key difference is this awareness of theory, literature, and analysis which is necessary for disciplinary research and yet is not a requirement for creative methods. Because my interest and background was in somatics, and the *Imagining Autism* project and Trimingham's prior work seemed, on the surface, very similar in terms of how she interacted with people (albeit the intent was different as Trimingham's was with regard to drama practice and not therapy or education), we spoke about how practices could be similar. Trimingham (2010) connected her approach to that of Oskar Schlemmer, an artist, sculptor, and director of the Bauhaus theatre:

> 'And of course it is somatic practice, it's to do with the body, brain, being at one and all the rest of it and that Schlemmer was no longer content with working on a canvas, he was also a self-trained dancer and he felt that the experience of space moving through space and engaging with materials while he did that, because he had a lot of built up costumes and so on, somehow told him more, gave him better answers to his kind of metaphysical questions actually because he was quite a spiritual soul. But better answers to how we perceive the world, how we made meaning. Which was very important within the Bauhaus because they were trying to set down rules about it and Schlemmer was always saying, "Why? I don't know if there's a rule we can make about it" because they tried to be very scientific about art and he kind of resisted that and it's because he was a theatre person. It's because he was more used to more fluid answers than the people around him were seeking or prepared to accept. So he was a real force for embodiment, if you like, within an institution that had probably never heard of the word never mind what it meant in the 1920s if you said embodiment.'

In my conversation with Trimingham, I speculated on the difference between practice and performance. Somatic performance, as exemplified by artists and academics such as Ben Spatz (2020, n.d.) focus much of their attention on engagement with the audience. My understanding is that performance is for others, whereas practice is more about the process and the moment. Practice can either be for oneself or in 'service' to another as in an educational or therapeutic type practice. I asked Trimingham whether immersive theatre of the type that she practised was more akin to performance or practice:

> 'Well, I would say that in Practice-as-Research, process is very much more to the fore but it doesn't exclude you presenting your work at the end as a performance and of course you might be researching audience response to something within a framed space. But you see there's a more fundamental divide I would start with even before you get to that which is the difference between, say, performance and drama. … Contemporary performance and the way that underlies our training methods and how it leads into performance art is very connected with a visual artists' approach to the world. All that is incredibly different to taking a script off the shelf, interpreting what the author might have meant and how you respond to it so what you want to say, you know like a modern Shakespeare or whatever and gathering a cast together and giving out your parts and everyone going into their mimetic, you know. To me that is a totally and utterly different beast to what I'm researching which I call performance. But it's really hard.'

I wondered whether the differences between performance and Practice-as-Research in drama were comparable to the differences between ballet and somatic-inspired dance. In the latter, there is an underlying philosophy around embodiment. There are dancers who embody this in a similar way to contemporary or immersive drama practitioners. However, it is not quite so simple. A contemporary dancer trained in a certain style will embody that form's particular movements, which would be different from someone coming from a somatic training. Even somatic movement trainings incorporated into dance programmes would result in differences between a dancing body that practised Skinner Release, Rolfing, or one that used integrative bodywork; and these would differ again from bodies trained purely in contemporary dance or ballet. Talking to Trimingham, I used the example of tenderness, or directness through space. The way a dancer expresses this as they are moving or holding themselves physically in space will be different depending on their background or training. Trimingham agreed, and countered with an example of playing a character in drama:

> 'I would say that a ballet dancer taking part in something like *Giselle* or *Swan Lake*, you've got a very strong narrative there, you've got character whether you like it or not, it's limited, it's a particular kind of spectacular style of dance. I think the difference within the theatre could probably be identified by this idea of the mimetic, you know. Because even in contemporary, like Sarah Kane's *Blasted* which is a

script-based thing which everyone says is highly contemporary, I think there's still an element of being somebody else in it, whereas the kind of performance techniques that we've been talking about that underlie the training, that underlie performance art, you're not actually trying to pretend to be somebody else, it's always to do with the moment. It's to do with, God it's so hard to define really. But I do think when you talk to somebody who knows nothing about drama research, nothing about theatre or anything, if you say, "I'm a theatre researcher" or "I research performance", they're probably thinking in terms of Shakespeare, your Gabler, your common conception of what goes on stage. I don't mean to be withering or condemning but I do think that many drama people like me, academics, don't realise that that is the shorthand that people have, a lot of people have for theatre. So that if you say, "Well, I do drama with autistic children", they probably think you may be putting on a play with them.'

This misconception of what drama research is, that is equating it with putting on plays, was one that I saw even among the research team on the *Imagining Autism* project. One of the evaluation team had told me that she had wanted to get involved with the project because she had seen a documentary about a group of autistic children and young people who put on a play with drama practitioners. There have been several projects like this that have been filmed and shared with public audiences. Generally, they show a powerful and positive effect on those involved – demonstrating the power of theatre that Trimingham described – and contributing to the misconception that this is what drama research or work must look like. The fact that this misconception was held by people within the evaluation team of an immersive theatre project contributed to challenges around communication within this interdisciplinary team (Leigh and Brown 2021b). I will look more at *Imagining Autism* and how the work approached the boundary between therapy and education in Case Study 2. Both Trimingham and I agreed that the challenge in somatic research, whether it is drama or not, is being authentic to what is going on in the moment, while retaining a separation and producing research that is seen to be valid and that counts for the metrics measuring productivity, performance, and quality. As academics, we need to meet these performance metrics or we fail to progress at best, or lose our jobs at worst. A further challenge is how to disseminate the work, and to produce outputs that meet those external validators of excellence, while holding true to the essence of the work that matters. It is 'easier' in many ways to focus on the external factors. For example, in *Imagining Autism* it might be the tangible equipment that the drama practitioners used and the timing of the programme, rather than the more esoteric nature of being present with the children and the immersive approach used by the practitioners that so reminded me of my own somatic practice and work with children during my doctorate. Trimingham agreed:

> 'If at the end of the day with all this, we don't get the psychologist to understand what we were doing … we've failed haven't we? Do you know what I mean? It's like if they really think that it's just this sort of theatre model. … How do we change things more widely if it takes that much work to get three people, four people to understand? There's just so much work to do. We've just got to get this published in a psychology journal.'

Another challenge for Trimingham and the other drama practitioners was the psychologists' inclination to reduce their work with autistic children to 'therapy' or an 'intervention' (see Case Study 2). In educational research, interventions are common. They are generally designed and used to address a problem – in other words they use a pathological model of something that needs to be cured or remedied. Educational interventions are often evaluated through an analysis of the outcomes of an experimental or intervention study, as in medical research (Hutchinson 1999). However, most creative research is not 'measures' based, but a phenomenological exploration. Trimingham and her team wished to transcend disciplinary barriers and use psychological evaluations to 'prove' their method worked.

My arts-based research

My doctoral research (Case Study 1) was arts-based and incorporated drawings, mark-makings, models, and photographs of and by children, in addition to movement. Children's drawings have value in research, just as in process therapy and therapeutic interventions (Driessnack 2005). Drawing and mark-making give an avenue for children 'to express their views and experiences' (Clark 2005). They can be a creative and fun method to actively involve children, and to discover what they believe to be important (Punch 2002). Fun can mean different things to people of different ages. Generally, children use the word 'fun' to describe their enjoyment of an activity, but it could also be 'a positive mood state associated with personal accomplishment and the ability to meet a challenge', a 'long-term intrinsic affect', or attributed to 'improvement, participation, taking control … interacting with peers' (Dismore and Bailey 2010: 503). Giving children the opportunity to draw or take pictures enables them to pay attention to sensory and internal cues more than traditional interviews or focus groups: 'when children are interviewed, the brevity of their verbal responses may actually relate more to their ability to retrieve information than to their knowledge or understanding' (Driessnack 2005: 420). Drawing can also help children relax, be a source of fun, and help establish rapport (Fargas-Malet et al 2010). Listening to children talk about their drawings can provide insight into their understanding (Clark and Moss 2005) because drawing provides a means to reflect on experience. Drawing is not only of value with children, David Hay and Simon Pichford used it as a means to encourage researchers and students to reflect on white blood cell recruitment, resulting in the identification of new phenomena (Hay and Pichford 2016).

In addition to drawing, I used movement as a research tool and process. I wanted to understand how attitudes were formed towards movement, and how children perceived it as 'fun'. What is important to note is that just as how enjoyment of the process of creating art can be destroyed by self-critical judgements about ability, the same is true for movement. Non-competitive and non-judgemental movement activities are more likely to facilitate a mind–body connection than competitive games or activities where ability can be easily critiqued by oneself or in comparison to others. If children are given the opportunity and experience to become more self-aware and attentive to how their bodies feel as and when they move, they might begin to experience 'flow'. Flow has been used as a concept to describe an inner experience that incorporates joy, creativity, total involvement, and an 'exhilarating feeling of transcendence' (Dismore and Bailey 2010: 4). The feeling of flow, possibly because it is pleasurable and associated with other emotions and experiences such as 'fun', is a motivating factor often associated with dance and other movement activities (Hefferon and Ollis 2006). The relationship between fun and physical activity has a popular association (Phillips and Stewart 1992; Alerby 2003; Dismore and Bailey 2010; Ford et al 2012). In my doctoral research (Leigh 2012), many children used the word 'fun' to describe their experiences within somatics sessions and again when they were given a later opportunity to reflect. Some appreciated the opportunity to be experimental:

> 'It was fun because like you could experiment, like what your body could do.' (C Year 6)

> 'It was fun just to see … just to make what poses you can make.' (T Year 4)

Others used fun to describe particular aspects or activities of the work, such as the way sessions were designed to be playful by incorporating balances and falling (that is, righting reactions) (Brook n.d.; Hartley 1989), embodied anatomy (Olsen 1998), and animal poses (Mainland 1998):

> 'It's like different and then when you balance you can fall over. It's fun.' (E Year 5)

> 'Well, the activities we were doing to like show the heart and stuff like that was really great.' (M Year 6)

> 'Because when we do movement and activities, it made me happy because it was just really fun that we were doing loads of stuff, poses, everything, and it made me a bit calmer.' (T Year 5)

Some of the children enjoyed the fact that they were participating in a movement session rather than working on other subjects, and that the sessions were co-operative:

> 'It was fun – got us out of maths and other work. It was fun.' (B Year 6)

> 'It's a bit fun sharing my ideas.' (C Year 4)

> 'The fun part was seeing everybody else.' (J Year 3)

> 'It was fun when we did that, because it was really just some certain people who were just chosen and we worked in a group.' (T Year 5)

> 'Doing it with someone else, also made it fun because like sometimes when I do things on my own even if I'm making it up or something, I prefer it if I'm doing it with someone else because then I have someone else to help me think about it as well.' (S Year 3)

For many, 'fun' was the answer when asked whether there was anything else they wanted to say at the end of the interview:

C: It was really fun, all fun, there wasn't any boring bits, I really enjoyed it. (C Year 6)

Me: Why did you like it?
Mi: Because it was fun. (Mi Year 3)

Me: Is there anything else you want to say about the stuff that we did?
M: I found it very, very fun.
Me: What was fun? What do you mean by fun?
M: Everything. (M Year 6)

One girl expanded a little on what she meant by 'fun', and related it to how she felt when she was caught up in both the work, and how it felt to be engaged by it – similar to the idea of flow.

S: It was fun. And exciting.
Me: Fun and exciting. What was fun about it?
S: Well, I think it was fun because we did lots of things, lots of games and things and our teacher made it very fun.
Me: What was exciting about it?
S: Well, exciting-ness was really because, well, anyway, well we had like things to do and sometimes – and making things up was exciting because you're like, hmm, what shall we do? Hmm, what shall we do? Hmm, what shall we do? (S Year 3)

The intersection of an individual's personal social construct (such as their age, gender, disability, previous experiences around movement and physical activity or education) will result in them having a positive experience or not. Fun, or physical pleasure, is often overlooked as a reason for participation in sport in favour of motivations for health, or other specific or extrinsic orientated outcomes. However, pleasure, and in some cases the blurring of pleasure and pain (Pickard 2007), is often cited by young participants as their reason for taking part in an activity. Creating a lived experience 'bank' of pleasurable moments, and having the opportunity to reflect on them, may allow children to learn how to enjoy their bodies (Wellard 2010). Movement needs to be enjoyable to encourage participants to continue, because how an individual feels about themselves affects how they move (Linden 2007). The children in my study expressed their sense of fun and excitement in the sessions to each other and to me, outside of the sessions in school or the playground, through their drawings, mark-making, writing, and in interviews. Some children enjoyed certain aspects more than others, though handstands and balances were almost always considered 'fun'. Being still, an aspect of movement and embodied experience I discussed in Lesson 2, could be quite challenging for them at times. However, no child expressed to me or to a teacher that they did not enjoy the sessions and did not want to join in.

In a study looking to explore how best to teach reflection and reflective practice to undergraduate dancers at the Rambert School of Ballet and Contemporary Dance, I, together with Phaedra Petsilas, Nicole Brown, and Catriona Blackburn, used a variety of creative research approaches to educate the students and, at the same time, capture their experiences (Petsilas et al 2019a; 2019b). This project was more of an intervention, as it was designed to address the superficial reflection that had been observed in the dancers. Even so, it was still phenomenological and exploratory in nature, rather than a project with strict baseline and endpoint measures, and our data gathering involved film, reflexive journals, and focus groups rather than any quantitative measures. The students were scaffolded through different theories of, and approaches to, reflective practice, and I drew on somatics and

Figure 5: Rambert students exploring reflection through the practice utilising principles of Authentic Movement

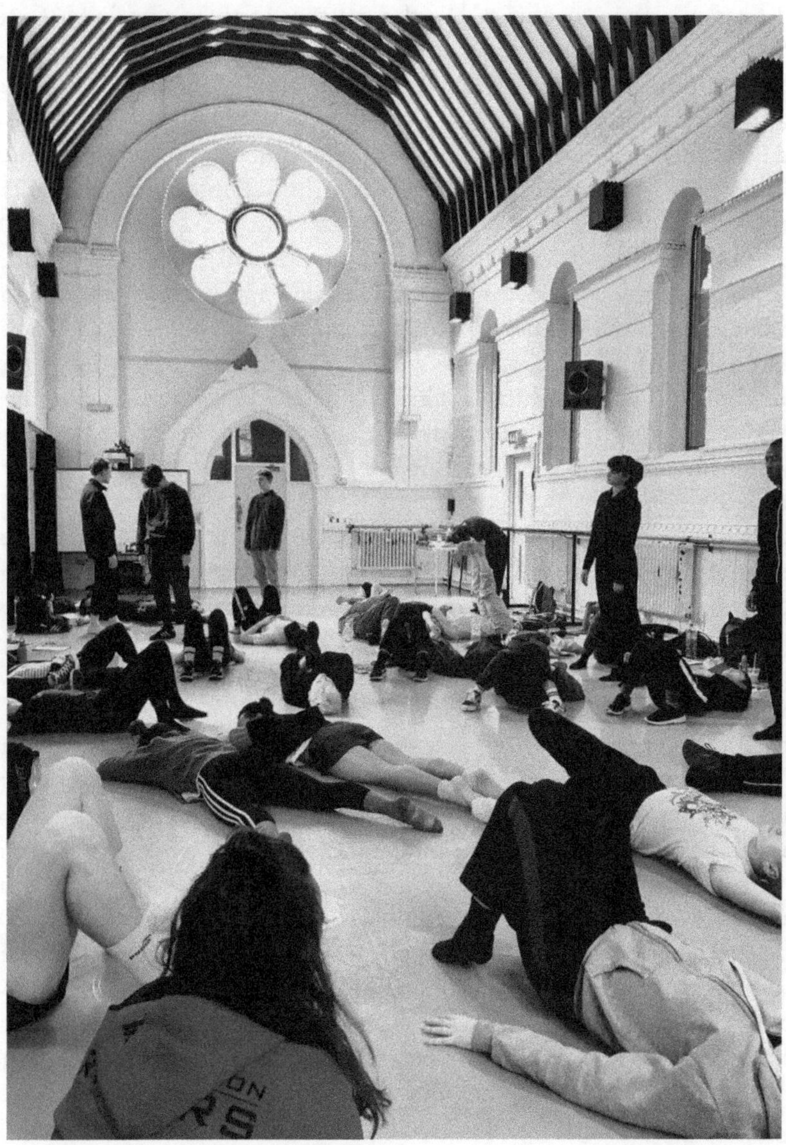

Authentic Movement (Adler 2002) to design exercises to develop internal and external awareness (see Figure 5).

Dancers are not often invited to reflect and pay attention to and express the sensations of their bodies as they perform. Ballet dancers in particular are expected to hide pain and present an almost inhuman sense of perfection

(Pickard 2019). Dancers who experience somatics can develop a new relationship with themselves, becoming sensitive to feelings, sensing actions, and becoming not an object, but the creators of their own lives (Green 1999). The somatics discourse comprises systems of thoughts composed of ideas, attitudes, beliefs, practices, and courses of action that carry power relations and construct truths that enable or constrain what can be done or said (Foucault 1963). Somatics promotes body awareness 'to allow individuals to make choices for their own well-being, thus counteracting the fantasy of an ideal body, which is so often removed from the concreteness of the lived body' (Fortin et al 2009: 48), and supports the development of an internal authority to construct self-knowledge and create states of more satisfying health and wellbeing. Although dance might be closer to somatics than cricket (Morgan 2006; Barrow 2008), a dominant dance discourse is around the ideal body, which is valued on the aesthetic criteria of slimness, virtuosity, devotion, and asceticism (Pickard 2007). The dance body may be 'alienated from the self, something to be subdued and managed' (Fortin et al 2009: 49).

It became clear that some of the students spent more time than others contemplating the tasks that they were set. For example, when leading a group sharing who they were as dancers by way of metaphorical objects, those shared included several water bottles, hair bands, mobile phones, and a ketchup sachet. This was not a problem, as the import of the activity was around the stories that were told, and these were unique to each individual. One student described their water bottle in terms of the structure and surrounding that enclosed it and kept the water in, just as the school and dance culture trapped them within a norm of expectations and careers. Another spoke of the water inside, and the flow and freedom to move, sharing how it made them think of the sea and open horizons and freedom. One young student spoke about their phone, though they had barely shared or spoken in a group context in the prior two years. The young student who shared the sachet of ketchup snatched up during their lunch talked about the best before date written on it, which led to an in-depth and touching conversation in the group around the short-lived nature of dancers and dance careers. The short-term nature of dance is one reason why Rambert offers degree programmes to people as young as 16, so that they can maximise their working life. Rambert do a lot of work to ensure their dancers have longevity in their careers, hence their desire to increase the reflexivity of their students, to make them more attractive employees for a dance company. What came out through post-hoc focus groups was that although we had designed the project to appeal to them by using movement, they perceived it as 'study' rather than dance. In addition, though they naturally saw myself and Brown as outsiders, as we were external to Rambert, they also put Petsilas in this role. Petsilas was the Director of Studies at Rambert, and taught theoretical components of their course. This meant they saw her as sitting outside their core study of dance, and as an outsider rather than an insider. As a consequence of the project, Rambert changed the ways that they taught and assessed reflection in the school, embedding creative elements into their programmes. In terms of where this arts-based research study sat on the borders, it was research designed to have educational outcomes. The cohort of students was large – the whole year group of more than 50 students were working in one large space. I did not feel as though I got to know all of the students individually, and the therapeutic potential of the practices they were engaged in was minimised. It was not easy (or safe) to attempt to establish a relational field or hold a therapeutic boundary in such a large and uncontained group. That said, as exemplified by the conversations about career length, and the way in which students felt empowered to speak when they had previously not felt safe to do so, there was obviously some therapeutic effect for some of the participants.

Lessons from science

According to the internet (so it must be true): 'the scientific method is the process of objectively establishing facts through testing and experimentation. The basic process involves making an observation, forming a hypothesis, making a prediction, conducting an experiment and finally analyzing the results' (Science Buddies n.d.). The scientific method is familiar to most of us, as it is the way children are taught to 'do' science throughout a school education. What is notable in the scientific method and the way that it is most commonly taught in schools is the absence of reflection, self-awareness, or the importance and impact of the relationship between the scientist and the world around them. Science is acknowledged as being 'hard', possibly because it is abstract (Millar 1991). As a result, science is seen as something worthy, and success in science something to celebrate (Frank 2012). This may be one reason why some social scientists aspire to be taken seriously as 'scientists' and hold fast to a scientific ideal (Flyvbjerg 2006).

One of the key tenets of the scientific method is scientific objectivity:

> The idea that scientific claims, methods, results—and scientists themselves—are not, or should not be, influenced by particular perspectives, value judgments, community bias or personal interests, to name a few relevant factors. Objectivity is often considered to be an ideal for scientific inquiry, a good reason for valuing scientific knowledge, and the basis of the authority of science in society. (Sprenger and Sprenger 2020)

Julian and Jan Sprenger continued:

> Objectivity is a value. To call a thing objective implies that it has a certain importance to us and that we approve of it. Objectivity comes in degrees. Claims, methods, results, and scientists can be more or less objective, and, other things being equal, the more objective, the better. Using the term 'objective' to describe something often carries a special rhetorical force with it. The admiration of science among the general public and the authority science enjoys in public life stems to a large extent from the view that science is objective or at least more objective than other modes of inquiry. Understanding scientific objectivity is

> therefore central to understanding the nature of science and the role it plays in society. (Sprenger and Sprenger 2020)

To paraphrase: scientific objectivity is ideal, it is approved, it has importance, and the more of it the better. No mention of the self or subjectivity that is valued and integral to qualitative research, art, or psychotherapy. Sprenger and Sprenger described four definitions of objectivity: a faithfulness to measured and quantified facts; a value-free ideal; the freedom from personal bias; and a feature of scientific communities (that is, that scientific experiments should be reproducible, and the community should be able and willing to criticise itself). Scientific objectivity is seen as a process of moving closer to absolute 'truth' in the sense defined by philosopher Karl Popper (1959). I respond to this by asking whether it is possible for scientists to be value-free, and if it is even desirable to seek an absolute truth?

It is probably easiest to examine whether science can be value-free by looking at how objectivity plays out among scientific communities. Aspiring to be part of a community that is not afraid to be self-critical and free from bias sounds like a worthy ideal, but is it attainable? If scientists are objective, free from values and personal bias, then it could be expected that the scientific community would be representative of the general population. However, this is not the case; there is an under-representation of many groups marginalised due to their sexuality, gender, race or ethnicity, disability, or socio-economic status, or intersection of these characteristics (Royal Society of Chemistry 2022a). Venus Evans-Winters stated that 'scientific jargon can be exclusionary, while privileging formally educated, middle-class, and Eurocentric styles and patterns of speech' (2019: 22). Despite concerted efforts to address gender imbalance and lack of diversity in science, little progress has been made (Rosser 2017; CRAC 2020; McGee and Robinson 2020; Royal Society of Chemistry 2022b). Barriers for under-represented groups cannot be considered in isolation, they have to be addressed intersectionally. I explained the impact of intersectionality on diversity in science in the book *Women in Supramolecular Chemistry*:

> Intersectionality is a term first coined by Kimberlé Crenshaw (1989) to describe the multiple barriers of sexism and racism faced by Black women. Intersectionality has since been co-opted to include other instances of compounding factors faced by individuals who experience intersecting marginalisation due to being BIPOC (Black, Indigenous, or a Person of Colour), having a chronic illness or disability, class, religion, sexuality, ethnic origin and the like. Within academia, the region of the world in which a researcher might be based might also marginalise them and their research. Women of colour (WOC) face a 'double bind' of racism and sexism 'the environments in which

> WOC STEM faculty must work are often not ideal … these sub-optimal environments often lead to faculty discrimination, intentional attrition (e.g. choosing to leave for a variety of personal or professional reasons), and unintentional attrition (e.g. not earning tenure)' (Cox 2020: 56). Women of colour are often victims of tokenisation (where they are differentiated from their counterparts in unfair ways, on display, expected to conform, be socially invisible, stereotyped and lack sponsorship), pioneerism (i.e. being the first minority in the department having to serve as the first or only representative of their gender or race), marginalisation (where their contributions are overlooked, ignored or minimised), and microaggressions (frequent intentional or unintentional derogatory comments) (Cox 2020). Science is not as democratic and meritocratic as it could be, though hopefully times are moving from when 'democratisation … applied itself only sparingly to people of colour and, to a significant degree, all women in science remain unreal to the men with whom they work' (Gornick 2009: 54). We must acknowledge that change in a world full of tenured positions is slow by default. If the efforts of the people trying to change things are not acknowledged properly or at all, they will become frustrated and stop altogether. This is the last thing we want. (Leigh et al 2022c: 55)

Coupled to the objectivity of the scientific community is the belief in meritocracy. A meritocratic scientific community would suggest that people achieve success or recognition solely due to their merit, and are not privileged by other factors:

> Meritocratic perspectives suggest that sociocultural norms in science education are rooted in the 'impersonal characteristics of science' (Merton 1996: 269) and produce objective sociocultural standards for communication of knowledge. Such perspectives align with positivist productions of scientific knowledge within value-neutral environments, positioning concepts of racialized or gendered microaggressions as subjective forms of preferential treatment. This value-neutral ideology protects inherited advantages, creates insider/outsider dynamics, and necessitates forms of cultural capital. Among students from traditionally marginalized populations, failure is viewed as an individual consequence rather than a reflection of systemic oppression. (Dubois Baber 2020: 19–20)

It seems that science may not be achieving its aim of objectivity or meritocracy and freedom from bias at the community level just yet. A study of over 25,000 professionals working in science in the USA showed that white, able-bodied, heterosexual men experienced more social inclusion, professional respect, career opportunities, and higher salaries than intersectional marginalised groups (Cech 2022). Out of the first 230 Nobel Prizes awarded for physics and chemistry, only 12 have been to women (Marie Curie won two), and none of those Nobel Laureates were Black. Half of undergraduate chemistry students are women, yet 81% of chemistry professors are men (Royal Society of Chemistry 2018). In March 2022, only one of them was Black (Royal Society of Chemistry 2022b). However, scientists:

> [h]ave a more difficult time than other kinds of workers do in perceiving themselves as discriminatory … science has a vested interest in the idea of the intellectual meritocracy. It is important to scientists to believe that they act rationally, that they do not distort or ignore evidence, that neither their work nor their profession is seriously influenced by politics, ambition, or prejudice. (Gornick 2009: 59)

It is possible to see evidence of prejudice and privilege much earlier in the education system, where children are not given equal chances to succeed (OECD 2018). Advantaged children perform better than disadvantaged children, with 74% developing a greater sense of belonging and achieving upward educational mobility compared to only 24% of disadvantaged children (Davies 2018). In order to address the lack of objectivity and build much-needed diversity within the scientific community, it is necessary to start by addressing inequalities and access to science careers (Mujtaba et al 2020).

Moving away from the objectivity of the scientific community, what about the objectivity of science research? Is it necessary to find out the truth? Richard Bailey has accused postmodernist, pragmatic, and social constructivist researchers of 'veriphobia' or a fear of truth (Bailey 2001). The reality is that science involves people, who are messier than numbers. People all have a history, context, identity, and story that impacts to a greater or lesser extent on their work (Latour 1999). This can be understood by realising that meaning and matter are interconnected, who people are affects what they can know; they are in relationship with each other (Barad 2007). Numbers can be quantified, ordered, and measured in a way that people cannot. To understand people, a different approach is needed. This is where qualitative research, intentionally subjective rather than objective, comes in. Rather than attempting to determine verifiable, measured, and generalisable truths, qualitative data seek to recognise patterns, and make sense of them to build a meaningful picture and increase understanding of the world:

> Norman Denzin (2010: 115), in his *The Qualitative Manifesto*, wrote a call to arms that said 'qualitative research scholars have an obligation to change the world, to engage in ethical work that makes a positive

> difference'. A qualitative approach allows us 'to improve quality of life … for the oppressed, marginalized, stigmatized and ignored … [and] to bring about healing, reconciliation and restoration' (Stanfield 2006: 725). Qualitative research can be used for both justice and healing: 'a restorative view of justice that is based on indigenous ways of healing, not scapegoating and punishing offenders' (Stanfield 2006: 109). Few would argue that it is time to make a positive difference, to improve quality of life, to bring justice and healing. (Leigh et al 2022c: 17)

In a discussion of Black feminism in qualitative inquiry, Venus Evans-Winters argued it is important to question both the objectivity and purpose of science, and that critical research paradigms are perfectly positioned to do this (2019). She continued: 'An ethics of care and empathy are important in qualitative inquiry and in the assessment of the validity of an exposition. The dichotomy between rationality and emotionality is obscured in Black feminist inquiry and data analysis' (Evans-Winters 2019: 23). Evans-Winters' approach has many parallels with my own work, with the emotional investment and presence of the researcher, and the way that it incorporates multimodal data to intentionally seek out emotive and authentic responses (Kara 2018). Ian Wellard joined a call-out of the 'tendency to accommodate calls for "objectivity" and … robustness through processes which separate the researcher from the researched' (Wellard 2015: 1). Qualitative research and subjective analytic approaches such as Reflexive Thematic Analysis are still often thought of as less valid than quantitative methods, even in social sciences (Braun and Clarke 2021b). This can lead to tension when working with scientists, as can be seen in Case Study 4. Qualitative research, and particularly embodied and creative qualitative research, demands that researchers are self-aware, and continually '[exhibit] reciprocity and vulnerability in the research process' (Evans-Winters 2019: 7). This allows the researcher to demonstrate the quality of their work (even if it is not objective). However, working in this way has ethical implications.

Science has to be creative and innovative, and ground-breaking science is often disruptive (Kozlov 2023) just as ground-breaking art or successful therapy is disruptive. Science and more creative forms of knowledge are often (and in my view artificially) divided. Understanding and humanising the stories, personalities, and people behind science allows a wider audience to connect with them and the work they do (Leigh et al 2022c). It also allows the scientific community to recognise and acknowledge the importance of diversifying and the barriers to achieving that (Caltagirone et al 2021b; Leigh et al 2022c; Slater et al 2022). Understanding the connections between meaning, matter, and discourse is key to uncovering new knowledge about the world (Barad 2007). Introducing more reflection and reflexivity into science will allow scientists and quantitative researchers to be more ethical (Kara 2018), and in turn help us to understand the representations and knowledge they create (Latour 1999). Scientific knowledge lends itself incredibly well to the creation of images, maps, and models that help to visualise, represent, and know more about the world around us (Myers 2015).

It might be easy to assume I am suggesting that people who are trained in the scientific method are less able to reflect, be reflexive, or self-aware about their sense of embodiment because 'the scientific mind is set apart from what is to be known' (Bordo 1986: 451). Susan Bordo postulated that this may be due to extreme masculinisation of a scientific mind, or a separation of the mind and intellect from the body and nature. However, scientific training in the inner workings of the body can be utilised to develop an inner awareness and understanding of the body that can be used to make sense of embodied perceptions. Personally, I have found that my scientific knowledge of the body has enhanced my embodied experience. I can use an example of how my bodywork training was managed. It was aimed primarily at dance artists and movers. The main component of the theory was anatomy and physiology of the living body. I found this element very easy, having studied biology and chemistry to a high level. Others on the course found this more challenging as they did not have a scientific background. Most of them would have described themselves as being intuitively aware of their bodily environment, but without the detailed anatomical knowledge that would enable them to visualise the internal workings of the body clearly. My scientific knowledge allowed me to create clear and detailed images of my inner body, which helped me to understand myself and work with others. Similarly, I use my knowledge of my body and anatomy to write fiction as art and science.

Fiction as art and science

> 9 years ago I remember being pregnant, and as my blood pressure increased I was travelling the 45 minutes to hospital first once, then twice, then three times a week to be monitored and have bloods drawn. The midwives saw the blanket my mother was knitting grow bigger alongside my belly housing the child it was intended for. One of them was better at getting my blood out the first-time round, and it came that when they saw my face in the waiting room they would direct me to her. She said my veins were fine, but they liked to hide a little. She always got enough to fill their specimen tubes until the last week when even she could not and so she sent me to phlebotomy to be bled by fingers more nimble than hers. Days afterwards a doctor apologised and told us I should have been admitted that day. But they

sent me home after having to calculate decisions based on available beds not medical need.

8 years 10 months ago I remember trying to stand with my just-born babe in my arms saying something's not right as my husband pressed the emergency alarm and blood poured onto the chair and the floor, and as people came in it pooled on the bed and the floor only stopping when a doctor past the end of her 12 hour shift literally put her hand inside me to stem the flow. My mother told me afterwards that as she sat in the corner of the room with my daughter in her arms she thought I was going to die. She watched me turn paler and paler as everything around me stained crimson. There was too much blood, and none of it was inside me. Enough blood to fill a thousand specimen tubes if you could only have scraped it all up. Later that day they had to send an anaesthetist with a tiny yellow butterfly needle, the size they use for premature babies, to grab more from my hand. My best friend, a medic, told me to refuse a blood transfusion as she saw too much damage as a result. Although when she saw me the next week still bloodless and weak she wondered whether she had given me the best advice.

Just now, *this* needle makes me cry. I don't cry at needles. Not when they are thinner than a human hair prickling my meridians like a hedgehog and not when they are five inches long and wide and stuck into my breast. I don't cry at needles. *This one hurts.* She had placed my arm on a disposable sheet and I had joked that it was in case she hit an artery. This is no longer a joke. My eyes fill with tears and emotions and my skin becomes hot and sticky and it is as though she is driving it into my nerves and my very being. I wipe my eyes, and a kind nurse comes over and pats my leg as the other nurse pulls the needle out. I live with chronic pain. I am used to pain, and to needles. But this one *hurts*.

She tries again. She is an IV team nurse, this is what she does day in and day out. This time she finds a vein, I feel it slide in and she fills bottle after bottle with my blood. I wonder whether the ward nurse will notice as she uses ones put aside for later. They come over, quietly replacing full with empty, they only needed one for a baseline. She picks up a syringe full of saline and the ward nurse fetches the doctor to 'consent me'. I consent for a procedure I have had before, that I read about on the internet, in medical journals, in their own hospital protocol. They have to deliver medicine into my veins, wait half an hour, and take more blood, then take a final sample after another 30 minutes. As the doctor is talking she notices that as the nurse presses her syringe the flesh on my arm is swelling and puckering. The blood came out, but the pay load is escaping through the other hole further up my arm and closer to my heart. They want to have another go, and I am wavering. They want to make the most of the IV nurse and her ultrasound machine. Let's just have a look they say. The IV nurse scans my arm as the doctor and ward nurses look on approvingly. 'There's a good one. Nice and big.' I don't feel I can say no. I don't want to have to come back again. This time the needle goes into my vein and the saline flush is a cold pipe up my arm. The kind nurse asks if I can smell it, apparently some people smell the medicine that is injected into their veins. I don't. As the IV nurse leaves she says if the cannula fails she does not have capacity to come back and fix it or take bloods, I was the first of 10 on her hand-over list. She is under-resourced and overworked. The medicine is finally administered by the ward nurses 50 minutes after the time zero base line. They say they will come back for bloods in 30.

It took me 2 and a half hours to get here, and I worked on the train. Travelling isn't that unusual. People often have a commute like this or longer to get to work, or they live half the week away from their families, being part-time parents. Others resign themselves to living in a different town, country, or continent from loved ones. There isn't much work, so you have to travel. If you have a job be grateful. Don't complain. It was the same journey four days ago. That time the kind nurse had organised the IV team to cannulate me, and I hadn't sat down long when a tall chap came in with an Infra-Red machine. It shone light onto my arm so he could see where the veins were, but not gauge how deep. I told him what the last person who had cannulated me had said – I do have a good vein but it's deep and right next to an artery. He had used an ultrasound, which let him know how deep to slide the needle. He got it on the first try. This chap doesn't have an ultrasound, he's not been trained on it yet. He has a go with his light but I can tell that he's nowhere near the vein. He inserts the cannula but neither of us are surprised when it will neither bleed nor flush. He tries the other arm, turning it over and aiming for the back. This time once the needle is in he digs around as though he's having a rummage. I'm not quite sure what he's aiming for, maybe he's hoping that if he scrabbles around enough he might get lucky. He asks to have a third go and the kind nurse catches my eye. She says I don't have to say yes, that after two attempts they can refer me to the anaesthetic team. I apologise to my chap and he leaves. I am left with a bruise that swells the back of my arm and turns the yellow, green, and purple of a sick twilight sky. I settle in my chair to wait, taking out my computer and plugging into the bank of sockets built for medical equipment. I jack in and crack on.

I work for the next 2½ hours, and then the kind nurse pokes her head round the curtain to say that she is going to have to call it. The anaesthetic team have not answered her bleep and there won't be time to run the test before she has to shut down the ward. She asks me to come back in four days and I look at my calendar – it is a research day. One set aside for writing, and only one meeting to cancel. I agree.

While I wait for the ward nurses to return to collect my blood I cannot work. My laptop stays in its bag this time and I ★only★ use my phone to answer emails, respond to messages on Teams too urgent to trust to email, and WhatsApp messages too important to trust to Teams. I read papers I have been sent, answer queries, send others. This is me not working.

I worked when I was admitted to hospital 8 months pregnant with my blood pressure sky high. I sat on the bed marking essays. I know colleagues who, post-partum, have written grants, responded to reviewers, attended interviews. My husband says I never stop working.

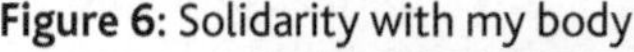

Figure 6: Solidarity with my body

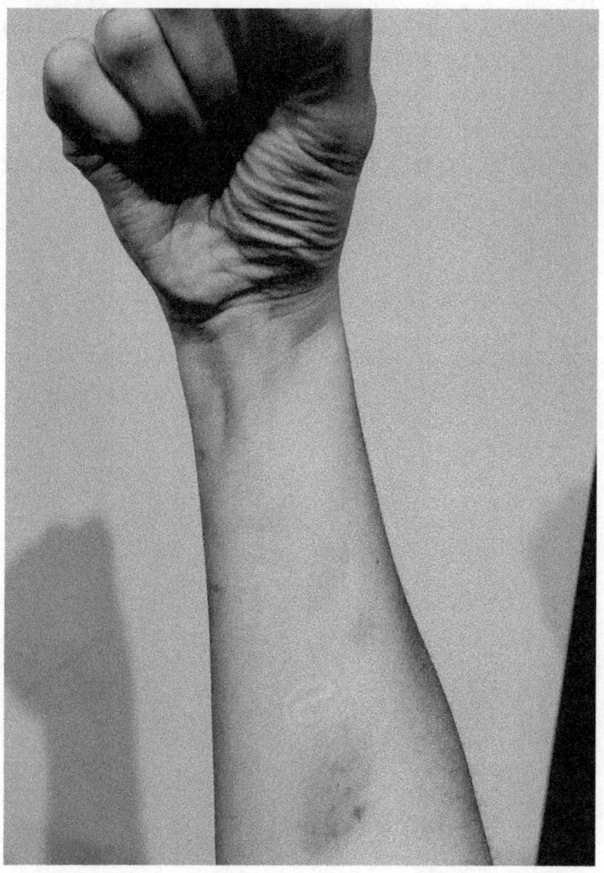

I just want to finish this one thing I say as he tells me dinner is on the table. There is always one thing he replies. There is so little balance in my life. When I work I am trying and trying and trying not to let people down, not to let myself down. When I am with my child I resent her stopping me from finishing this one last thing. When I am working I resent it preventing me from being with my child. I resent not being able to be present. There is always more to do. I am never enough.

The gentle nurse comes over to take my sample. She unclips and flushes the cannula and I feel the coolness. She then attaches a small syringe and sucks back clear fluid with a swirl of red. It's working. She switches the syringe for a specimen bottle, but the vacuum is not enough to pull my blood through the catheter tube. She calls to the kind nurse to come over, and while one massages my veins and applies a tourniquet, the gentle nurse uses a new syringe and pulls hard on the plunger to draw my viscous blood down. She empties what she has into the specimen bottle by hand, and takes a new syringe. She only needs 1–2 ml she tells me. Barely satisfied, she screws up the bottle and tries to flush the cannula again. This time it won't go, and she tells the kind nurse there is a clot. They don't want to force it into my vein, so they take the cannula out saying they will collect the last sample with a butterfly needle. As they are doing this the doctor wanders past, shaking her head 'but it was a big one ….' It stopped working. Maybe my vein was not big enough after all. It was not good enough to do what was needed. (extract from *Leeches* (Leigh 2023))

Lessons from ethics

Research, particularly research with the self or with people, presents many challenges and constraints. However, often the only mention of these and potential implications is within a formal university ethics approvals process. The requirements of these varies between institutions. Ethical processes are, for the most part, based around medical or clinical research. They are primarily designed to protect institutions from risk (Dingwall 2016), and do not take into account the same safeguarding elements as professional ethics (Hayes 2009). A real-world approach that shifts ethics from 'do no harm' towards a social justice perspective is advocated by Helen Kara (2018). She encourages reflexivity even in quantitative researchers to recognise and acknowledge positionality and bias, and a move from the view that science equals objectivity. Kara argued that researchers need a broader view of ethics, and should think of axiology instead as a 'wider term than ethics' (Kara 2018: 14). Axiology is a branch of philosophy that incorporates religion, aesthetics, ethics, and how these play a role in the construction of knowledge. Axiology implies the researcher adheres to values such as respect, reciprocity, and relational accountability (Wilson 2008). This in turn means they should be aware of how the research methods they choose can help or hinder the building of respectful relationships, and privilege some stories over others. Conventional Euro-Western research is non-egalitarian, with the researcher holding the power and making all decisions about what and who are researched, the methods used, and how data are analysed and disseminated. Research is done *to* or *on* a topic and participants are research subjects. The research is owned by the researcher, and they have control of it. Creative or arts-based, participatory, and embodied research can all challenge assumptions about participants in research and ethics processes with regard to ownership of co-created content, anonymity, and autonomy. Participants may not want anonymity, and might ask for their names or faces to be associated with their stories. They may want to choose which of their stories are shared, how they are presented, and who they are shared with. Research in these paradigms is *with* people not *on* them. Data are generated, co-constructed, or co-created, which means a consideration of ethics and axiology needs to continue beyond research design and data gathering, including reflexivity through analysis and dissemination (Kara 2018).

Lessons from art and science both highlighted the risks and vulnerabilities inherent in disseminating work of this kind:

> When we choose to use embodied research approaches on ourselves or others, we need to be conscious of the impact of shining a light onto these internal and personal processes whether we are collecting data from others, performing for an audience or sharing our innermost reflections. This process is necessary for me in order to be authentic to my background, my upbringing, and my experiences. However, I acknowledge that working and researching in this way can be considered riskier, particularly for those who are less established or working in environments which are more constrained or precarious. … Simultaneously we risk exposing ourselves, our vulnerabilities, and those of our participants in a judgemental and critical academic environment. …
>
> When I disseminate my work, when I sit down to write a chapter such as this, or show a film that has been born out of a research project, I have to figuratively and literally take a deep breath, release my shoulders from up by my ears, feel my feet ground into the floor, accepting the pain and tension in my right foot and ankle from old injuries and adjusting the balance of weight as I balance myself against an anticipated onslaught. And yet, I feel that it is worth the pain and the preparation because it is a way to be authentic and to share that authenticity with my audience. (Leigh 2021: 64)

In other words, when I use my self and my self-awareness as a basis for research, and whether that awareness is at the internal micro level, the felt systematic meso level, or the external and seen macro level, I need to be reflexive. I need to be aware of my positionality in relation to my research, my art, and my intended audience.

> It is only when I am honest about my own position on a subject that I am able to write in a way that is evocative and poignant for others to read. … I want my work to do the same: to evoke and trigger in those who have experienced similar stories, and to resonate with the imagination of those who have not. Whether I am writing about ableism, academic identity or other aspects of higher education, I want to be authentic to my own embodied experience, and by doing this, I hope and intend to touch others. (Leigh 2021: 62)

After reading my chapter 'Embodied practice and embodied academic identity' (Leigh 2019c), Ian Wellard reflected, 'I felt reassured that there were other people who were experiencing similar forms of (existential) angst about having to constantly defend and justify their alignment with embodied thinking' (Wellard 2019a: 171). He continued, 'Much of this anxiety is fuelled by the continued focus within academia upon the sciences and the separation of bodily practices from the mind'. Using an embodied and reflexive autoethnographic approach to research does not have to automatically privilege researchers with direct experience of an activity; nor does it have to assume that academics with the ability to put experiences into language necessarily have a greater understanding or knowledge: 'We only have to look at children engaging in play activities to recognise the multitude of embodied sensations and feelings they are experiencing. That they have limited ways of articulating these experiences in formal language convention does not imply that they are insignificant' (Wellard 2019a: 171). The state of embodied awareness about the lived and moving body is a 'specific orientation to the research process' (Wellard 2019b: 140). It encompasses temporal, spatial, sociological, and psychological contexts, and as such can be multidisciplinary.

The challenges of disseminating the experience of movement through language led Ben Spatz to set up a new journal: *The Journal of Embodied Research*. Spatz is a drama researcher, and uses their body along with audiovisual technology to explore the limits of using it as a 'laboratory' for research and performance (Spatz 2015, 2020). The moving body captured on film and in media helped stimulate Paul Bowman's interest in martial arts. He took an autobiographical or autoethnographic approach and described how he felt the absence of the body in literature while being drawn by his own movement experiences to write about cultural depictions around the body (Bowman 2019). He described the mixed blessing of embodied exercise:

> It is definitely marvellous to be 'in touch' with one's body, to become differently enculturated, enskilled, enabled, even emancipated from many problems that can plague people who are not 'in touch' with their bodies. But at the same time, we need to realise that our forms of embodiment can also become our bondage. (Bowman 2019: 21)

I resonate with Bowman's words as the 'innate healing power of our bodies, and the importance of healthy and strong bodies was grounded in me from early childhood' (Leigh 2021: 62). I struggled when my body was no longer able to keep up with the practice I had established:

> I rely on my practice of yoga to centre myself and orientate myself within the world. Missing practice impacts on my physical and mental health. I struggle during periods of illness, feeling disconnected not only from my body, but also my awareness of who I am, what I have to say, and how I can creatively weave together words into an authentic story. (Leigh 2021: 63)

The professional ethics that psychotherapeutic practitioners work to govern how they interact with their clients as well as the care they have to take of themselves. Therapists have an ethical duty of care to their clients (see Lesson 3). There are strict professional guidelines aware of the power dynamics in play, to safeguard both the therapist and client from harm. Similarly, educators are bound by professional values: such as the UK Professional Standards Framework developed by Advance-HE to ensure good practice and excellent student experience for higher education (Advance-HE 2022); or the professional values and standards of social justice, integrity, trust and respect, and professional commitment that lie at the heart of school teaching (General Teaching Council for Scotland n.d.). Therapists are required to have personal therapy at least through training if not beyond in order to safeguard their wellbeing and fitness to practise (Mearns and Thorne 1998). In contrast, institutional research ethics processes may make a nod to researcher wellbeing, but few mention this in detail (Boynton 2020). However, just like therapy, research requires emotional labour. There are 'real emotional risks to researchers' (Kara 2018: 161), particularly for those doing qualitative work. The ethical codes for conduct for psychotherapeutic practices specify regular clinical supervision (see, for example, the minimum supervision guidance set out by the British Psychological Society (BPS 2010)), and ideally this is separate from line management structures. A further complexity for researchers is that ethical considerations around self-care and care for others are unlikely to be prioritised within the context of overwork and unhealthy cultures in academia (Gill 2016; Clark and Sousa 2018; Boynton 2020).

Ethical and axiological implications

Standard ethical procedures for research in higher education institutions are set out in order to safeguard participants, and young children are deemed to be in more need of safeguarding than adults who are able to consent for themselves. As established, using embodied and creative research methods means research is more likely to approach the border of therapeutic practice, and therefore embodied and creative research with children can be considered a useful exemplar for ethical and axiological applications. Thankfully in social research there has been a move away from research that is *on* children rather than *with* them (Fargas-Malet et al 2010). Whereas children were once considered as objects, they are now much more likely to have their views and opinions sought out; although this brings its own methodological and ethical challenges (Mauthner 1997; Einarsdottir 2007). Different approaches towards research with children include:

> One which considers children as practically the same as adults and employs the same methods as those used with them

> One which perceives children as completely different from adults and uses ethnography (participant observation) to examine the child's world; and
>
> One which understands children as similar to adults but with different competencies, and which has developed a plethora of innovative and adapted techniques. (Fargas-Malet et al 2010: 176)

Children as young as four can provide important insights into their lives and experiences (Irwin and Johnson 2006). A researcher working with young children needs to be careful not to make assumptions about their capabilities, and to be reflexive about the internal images and assumptions they have about childhood that inform their approach, methods, and data analysis. Alison Clark (2005) recommended a variety of creative methodologies for listening to the views of young children (particularly those under the age of five). The idea is that actively listening to a child enables them to express their views; although this is relevant to participants of all ages (Back 2007). Listening is understood as an active process of communication involving hearing, interpreting, and constructing meanings, and is not limited to the spoken word. Active listening is necessary for participation. Rather than the extraction of information, participatory research is a dynamic process that involves the participants discussing meanings, while avoiding giving young children cues or assistance (Irwin and Johnson 2006). Listening means not trying to guess what children are saying (Mauthner 1997), and includes all the different verbal and non-verbal ways in which they communicate, which for my work included the medium of movement. Children need to feel supported in the research environment where possible, such as being somewhere familiar with trusted adults. Research activities should be fun, enjoyable, and varied, recognising that different children express themselves in different ways. The purpose of the research and the extent of participation that the children can have should also be made clear (Clark 2005).

When I was a research student I worked within the ethics processes laid out by my university. According to English law, consent for children to participate in research had to be obtained from the parents or guardians of the children, and not the children themselves (Jago and Bailey 2001). Legally, children were not deemed to have capacity to grant consent: 'it is widely recognised that in order to gain children's consent and involvement in research, one has to go via adult gatekeepers' (Punch 2002: 325). My research project took place on school premises and the sessions were run within the school day, so I first sought consent from the governors, headteacher, and class teachers at the school. I then asked the legal guardians of the children for their consent to participate and for permission to use images and artworks created by and of their children in my thesis and future publications. Consent has to be informed. In practice this means detailing the subject and nature of the research and what participation involves. For a project like mine this had to be accessible for the intended audience. I prepared separate consent forms for the parents/guardians and adult teaching staff who would all participate.

In addition to the legal consent required for university ethics process, I also worked to the ethical guidelines of two of my professional organisations, the British Wheel of Yoga and the International Somatic Movement Educators and Therapists Association. At times, on paper at least, the risk averse 'do no harm' institutional ethics were in tension with the more holistic professional guidelines. According to my professional bodies' guidance (and an axiological approach to ethics), it was ethical to ask the children themselves to assent. I wanted to give them the opportunity to verbally assent to participate in sessions and for their work and images to be used as part of my research, in addition to receiving formal and legal consent from parents or guardians. There was an implicit compulsion that the children would assent to participation, as sessions took place within the school day with approval from their headteacher, governors, class teachers, and parents or guardians. However, the fact that they had the right to withdraw at any time had to be made clear. Young children are used to doing what they are told by adults, particularly in an educational context (Punch 2002). Although the school had assured me that photographs taken of and by the children would be covered by the general consent given to the school, I decided to ask for additional permission, and until all consent forms were in I took no photographs. When I worked with older children (aged 9–11) they became interested in what I would do with the data, so I explained more about the process. The following extract from my field notes sets out how I explained the study:

> I started by sitting in a circle with the children and explaining a bit about the work. I said that the research was finding out about what children thought, felt about moving, and what it was like to be them. I told them that lots of adults tell them lots of things about what they should do, but that not many asked them what it was like to be them. I said that the permission slips would be going home in the newsletter and would ask for permission to take photos, that we could use cameras to take pictures (of themselves, and each other) and that those and their writing and artwork would be used for my research. I asked them if that was all right and they all assented to take part. Two children asked if it would get published in a newspaper, and I said that it might get published in special education magazines, called journals but none of their real names would be used. They seemed disappointed at that! (Field Notes)

Ethics of relationships

My study was participatory. One strength of participatory research is allowing participants to actively contribute and their voices to be heard and recorded.

The relationship between the researcher and participants, the methods they choose, and the way in which they then analyse the data are all important in a phenomenological approach (Larkin et al 2006). The concept of voice in the social sciences has different meanings. It can be taken to mean 'having a say' but can also encompass the language, emotional components, and non-verbal means used to express opinions (Thomson 2008). Children, just like adults, do not speak as one voice. They have different perspectives, experiences, and opinions. Individuals also use more than one voice. Pat Thomson identified five different voices that might be used by children or young people in research:

1. Authoritative – a representative voice used to speak on behalf of a group, elicited through surveys or discourse analysis;
2. Critical – intended to challenge the current state or portrayal;
3. Therapeutic – this is heard in safe spaces where difficult experiences can be discussed and supported;
4. Consumer – expressing preferences about lifestyle or culture and choices about identity; and
5. Pedagogic – a voice that is created by the experiences of being educated by particular kinds of people and regimes. (Thomson 2008: 4)

Within any research project it is up to the researcher to define which voice they are aiming to capture and the best methods of achieving this. Participatory research methods might facilitate situations where participants feel safe and able to say what they think without fear of judgement. However, young children can be reluctant to say anything they feel would displease the researcher. Participatory observations involve watching, listening, engaging with participants, and reflecting with them with regard to meaning making (Clark 2005). Thomson states children may 'feel more at ease in a pair or a group' (Thomson 2008: 6); however, in my experience this is not always the case. I found that it often took time for children to be confident in a facilitator's ability to deal with a situation so they felt safe, and knew that an opinion would not lead to ridicule or a negative impact within their peer group. This aspect of group facilitation draws heavily on establishing a secure relational field. I held a therapeutic perspective (Kirschenbaum and Henderson 1990) to create a space where the children were able to feel secure enough to express themselves physically and verbally, and trust that their contributions were recognised as valid. The children felt safe enough to explore emotional, open-ended, and challenging content with me and in front of each other. When research methods or questions have potential to result in emotional content or the capacity to affect participants deeply, as is the case with embodied self-awareness, I advocate being mindful and drawing on a therapeutic approach where possible. Participatory research methods may elicit the 'therapeutic' voice, but do not necessarily create or provide a safe relational field in which each participant can be supported and held within a therapeutic context. Not all researchers using participatory methods to generate data are trained in the skills necessary to establish a secure relational field. Data might be elicited for research purposes even though sharing that information in that moment was not in the best interests of a participant.

Ethics of touch

My work with the children involved hands-on touch, and I adhered to the Child Protection Policy of the school. Approaches that utilise touch positively have been shown to increase quality of life indicators for adults (Gregory and Verdouw 2005), autistic children (Cullen et al 2005), and children with additional needs (Cullen and Barlow 2003). However, touch can 'provoke anxiety' (Westland 2011: 20). Many people in Western society are ambivalent about touch, and afraid of the intimacy of it: the roots of this lie in how we were treated and how we continue to treat children (Piper and Stronach 2008). Often people working with children and young people are advised to avoid touching them at all; not because of restrictive laws but cultural pressures that have created a negative and self-sustaining no-touching culture (Piper and Stronach 2008: 10). And yet, touch is a central component of human interaction (Pink 2009). 'Many believe touch is essential for proper child development' (Piper 2003: 880), and attempting to comply with a 'no-touch' policy in early-years settings can result 'in a mind-body split' (Piper 2003: 881). Massage and other touch therapies have become more acceptable ways for children to receive touch. A reduction in the amount of positive touch a child receives in their early years may decrease their sense of body awareness (Bainbridge Cohen 1993). Body awareness can also be affected by processing and developmental disorders. Donna Williams, an autistic adult, described a disembodied sense of self in part due to her hypersensitive sensory awareness: 'I failed to identify with [my body] properly as "self"' (Williams 2003: 23).

As a student teacher I attended several different child protection trainings. One school told me never to touch a child. If I touched or was touched by a child, I was to report it to my head of department immediately. It can become problematic when professionals have become wary about touching children in their care – from putting an arm on a child's shoulder, to putting a plaster on their knee (Piper and Stronach 2008). Instead of being natural and spontaneous, touching children can become sanitised, organised, or only for therapeutic purposes. I decided that using touch would be safe and beneficial. I worked with groups of children who were always accompanied by at least one member of staff in addition to myself as the practitioner, and if a child showed any signs of discomfort or unease at being touched, that was taken as an indicator of them refusing consent, or withdrawing assent to receive hands-on work. In addition to touching children if I needed to draw their attention to a particular part of their body (for example, their toes or their back), on many occasions younger children would run up to me, want to sit on my lap, and hug me. If I had not allowed touch in this context these children would have experienced a physical rejection.

Ethics of awareness

Many people disassociate themselves from their body to one degree or another or differentiate between aspects of their body and consciousness, which, in turn, affects their perception of their body. Consciousness is, of course, a large part of who people are, and embodiment does not seek to annihilate the soul and only leave a body, as in the short story 'An Unfortunate Dualist' by Raymond Smullyan (Hofstadter and Dennett 1981: 383). Embodied self-awareness means that the thinking self is not seen as the totality. People can become 'conscious of thoughts, motives and emotions as well as sensory and perceptual stimuli' (Brown and Ryan 2003: 822). The children in my study were not asked to comment specifically on their perceptions of mind, consciousness, or Cartesian duality. Somatics, by its nature is 'embodying' and promotes mindfulness (Shapiro and Carlsom 2009) as it brings conscious awareness to the body, its movements, and processes. The bringing together of language, communication, and movement experientially reinforces a sense of an integrated body-mind. My presence would have implicitly reinforced this, as I used language that included all their feelings, emotions, and images as well as thoughts. However, these were children who had grown up in Western society, subjected to more traditional views of the body/mind split in most other aspects of their lives. Ethically, I had to give them space to tangle with challenging ideas and concepts and find a way to express themselves authentically rather than please me. MI, in Year 6, wrote in his journal about how he sensed the world around him and how that changed and was dependent on whether he was moving or still. He conceived his brain as an organ, his thoughts separated and differentiated from his body (see extract and Figure 7):

Me: This is all about finding shapes to be still. And you've written 'when I'm moving I can't see things. What I can see when I'm still. My brain I see is a big grey colour. And you've drawn a box and you've written I feel stuck. And I think the wood is like a maze. My brain is thinking a bug could be there'. So you've written thoughts and drawn pictures about the thoughts that you were having when you were still. That's what it looks like. Is that what it was?

MI: Yeah, I think so. (MI Year 6)

This drawing of a brain is of an owned 'my brain' seen by MI to be *part* of himself rather than the *whole* of his rational being. He wrote 'my brain is thinking a bug could be there', rather than 'a bug is there' which he may have done if he had identified solely with the thoughts originating in his brain. MI was developing his sense of embodied self-awareness through stillness and movement.

To think in movement is to experience a mindful body, and is tied to an evolving, changing situation. It is a way of being in the world, of wondering or exploring the world, taking it up moment by moment and living it directly in movement. It is the work of an existentially resonant body, where perceptions are plaited into movement and there is no 'mind-doing' that is separate from a 'body-doing' (Sheets-Johnstone 2010b). When I asked the children as part of a session on shapes to be still in, 'Can you still your mind?' there was a mixed response of yes, no, and maybe. When I asked them to tell me about how and why they moved, their responses gave an insight into how they saw their bodies and minds: 'How I move. I move gracefully, happily and joyful. Why I move. I move because standing in one place will get me nowhere. Things I do. I do birds, bunnies and tigers'

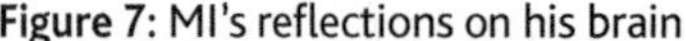
Figure 7: MI's reflections on his brain

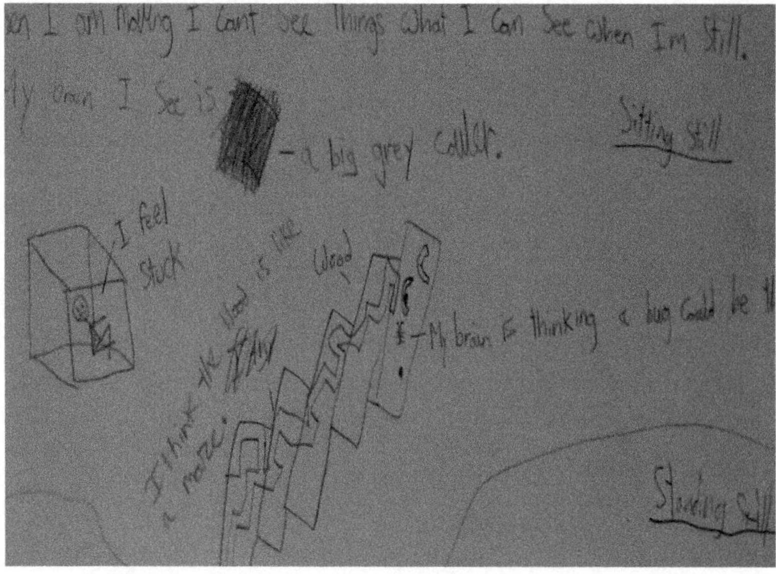

(C Year 4). Here, C seems to identify herself with a moving, natural world, and expresses a need to progress forward within it. An older girl, E, struggled to conceptualise her experience just through thought, but found that processing through other mediums allowed her to reflect on her moving self: 'I found that like quite hard to like think about it but then it was easier to write, to draw and write about it' (E Year 5).

The experience of the older children appeared to be that they were less comfortable considering this type of open and exploratory question. At no point did I try to guide them into giving me a certain type of answer, but allowed them to express what it was they felt, which included that sense of confusion at or 'not knowing', or 'hardness' that E spoke of. Some of the older children enjoyed the opportunity to consider this type of question.

Me: How did it feel when I used to ask you to think about what it felt like and to draw about it and to talk about it and to write about what it felt like to do all this stuff?
K: Sort of – there was – it makes me calm.
Me: It made you calm? What, thinking about how it felt made you calm?
K: Yes.
Me: Yes? Why's that?
K: Well, I think it's because you really have to think about it and be quiet. Sometimes you have to be loud and things. (K Year 5)

Being given time to consider questions like 'how does this feel?', 'how does this make me feel?' and 'how or where do I feel it?' was an experience that the children seemed to appreciate even though they were challenging, and questions like these were a fundamental part of the sessions. They were not just about the moving, creating body, but also about how that could be expressed.

Although gaining ethical approval for creative research can be tricky within a system designed for medical research, it can be incredibly valuable as part of a sense-making process for participants. K continued to talk about the journaling aspect of the work:

Me: What was it like writing it or drawing it as well?
K: It was very fun drawing and writing.
Me: Why was it fun drawing and writing?
K: Because you got to write how you felt and what you done and things.
Me: And you liked doing that?
K: Yes.
Me: Yes? Why did you like it?

K: Because people get to see how you feel.
Me: Is that important?
K: Yes. (K Year 5)

For K, feeling was not enough, her sense of self needed to be validated by those around her. She wanted to be seen to feel, to be witnessed, or observed by others. Evans-Winters described how a researcher might act as a witness to participants' experience (Evans-Winters 2019). Using creative methods allowed these children to be seen and their voices heard. Mk spoke about the drawing in the sessions as she reflected on the work she had done over the previous year. At the time of the interview Mk was aged 7 and in Year 2, although for much of the work she had been in Year 1 and Reception and so was one of the youngest children I worked with. This extract came at the end of the interview, after we had talked about writing and drawing about how it felt to move.

Me: Do you think looking back and remembering all of those months ago what you would have liked to have done more of?
Mk: More pictures.
Me: More pictures. Do you like drawing pictures? Do you like drawing pictures about moving and what it feels like to move?
Mk: Yeah.
Me: Why do you like drawing pictures like that?
Mk: Because it's fun doing that.
Me: Why is it fun drawing?
Mk: Because it's all colourful and I like colouring in the picture …
Me: Okay, so when you draw pictures of you how you feel when you move, you like drawing them all colourful?
Mk: Yes.
Me: Is that how you feel when you move?
Mk: Yes.
Me: You feel colourful when you move?
Mk: Yes. (M. Year 2)

The association of colour with movement by Mk may have been triggered by the use of vibrant oil pastels to draw within the sessions, or conversely, she may have expressed her enjoyment of using colours because of her internal experience of moving. These children were free to express what they felt in the way that they chose. One child reflected on a drawing of his mind in an interview about his work 'I used dark colours because I was bored at first and then light colours because I was happy and stuff because we had to use our brain and stuff to be still and concentrate' (Figure 8).

Another example of meaning making through creative methods came at the beginning of a session with the oldest children. I 'asked the children to

Figure 8: Dark then light mind

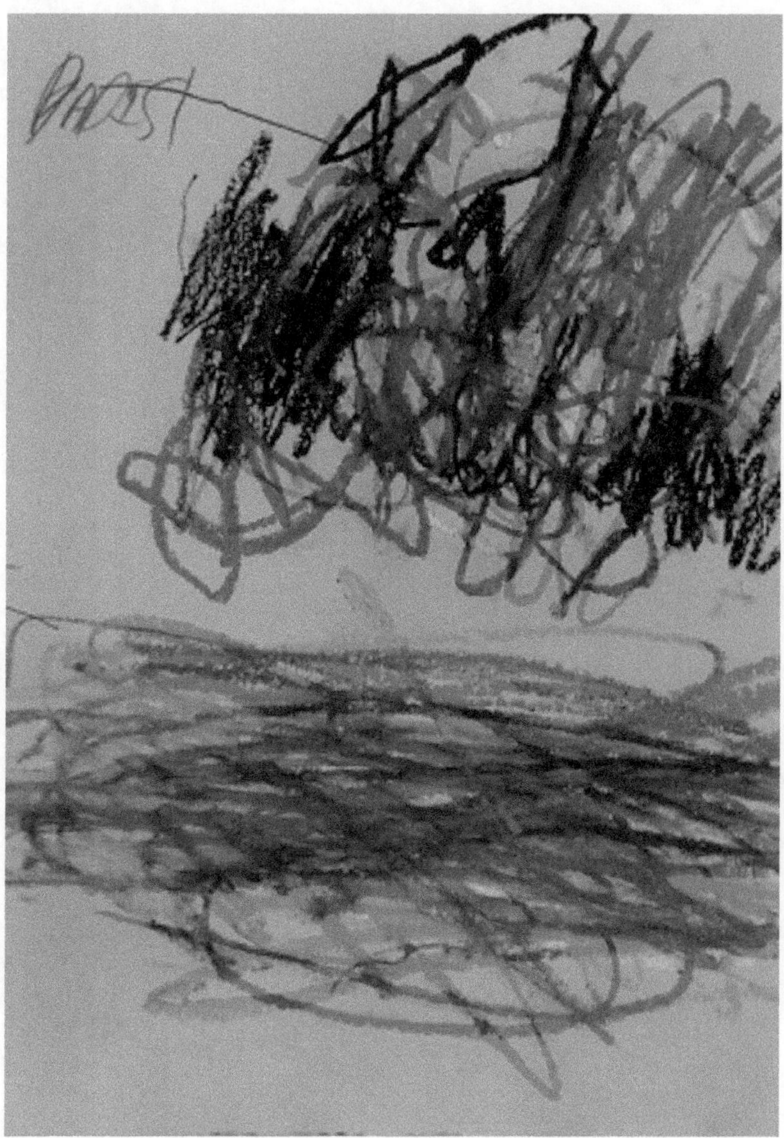

sit for one minute, then take two minutes to write/draw what it was like, what they felt. One child, L, drew her mind' (Field Notes) (see Figure 9).

As I said in Lesson 2, Sarah Pink described the meeting points between research, scholarship, art, and intervention. My study had 'thin' borders between research, therapy, and education which I explore in Case Study 1. For any research like this it is vital to balance the need to make an academic

Figure 9: L drew her mind

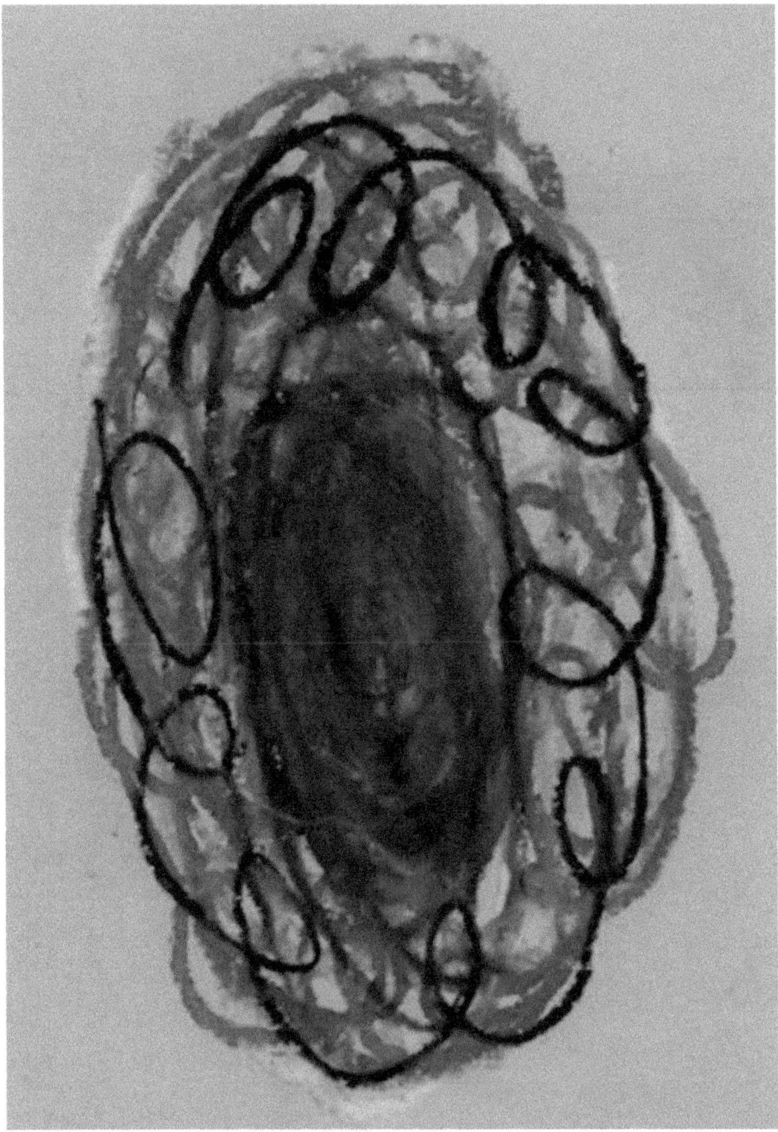

contribution as an output of performing a service or intervention, and the maintenance of professional duties of care. A researcher, whether they are nearing the border of art, therapy, education, or science, needs to be able to pick up on how, when, and in what manner what they do impacts on and affects the environment and others within, and to make conscious choices so they can work ethically and safeguard themselves and their participants. They need to be reflexively aware of how they feel and hold themselves in response to a given situation. This relates directly to my understanding and utilisation of embodiment. This does not necessarily mean they have to communicate this to their research participants at all times. In fact, that could be detrimental if participants are looking to the researcher to 'hold' the space for them. Although authenticity and emotional investment are necessary for research (Evans-Winters 2019), this does not mean a researcher has to expose all their flaws and vulnerabilities in every research encounter. For example, trainee teachers are advised to 'act' confident in order to control a class and establish discipline (Kyriacou 1998). It is possible to embody and project feelings of confidence while internally feeling less secure.

Part II of the book addressed the lessons a qualitative researcher or educator might learn from art and science, and the differences between a 'scientific approach' incorporating objectivity and meritocracy and one that might be more associated with qualitative, or embodied qualitative research. I briefly considered the lessons learned from ethics and axiology, and how research ethics meets or diverges from the kinds of ethical considerations and guidelines for therapeutic work. I used the example of working with children to explore ethics of conducting embodied and creative research which approached a therapeutic boundary.

PART III

Case studies

Introduction to Part III

Part III is comprised of four case studies in which I explicitly explore how my creative and embodied research bordered onto education, therapy, art, and science. Creative research may have more in common with a case study approach than interventions, which have been shown to be more suitable for in-depth, holistic research (Feagin et al 1991). Case study methodology is used to assess complicated phenomena within their contexts (Baxter and Jack 2008). Although my research is phenomenological, even phenomenology can be seen to be interventionist if an intervention is understood as implying an 'intentional action to bring about an immediate and effective form of beneficial change' (Edwards 2001: 3). Phenomenology may be seen 'as psychotherapeutic in its potential to bring about a whole new lived world', and of course, any research event 'essentially constitutes a form of intervention' (Edwards 2001: 3).

I have learned much through my research practice, and the case studies are intended to illustrate the ways in which different research projects have pushed towards the borders with art, education, science, and, most vitally, therapy. Those therapists who work in service to their clients (Rogers 1967) have a clear moral impetus, and the intent behind their interactions with their client is to help them. In contrast, researchers, artists, and educators may have many different and often conflicting intentions. The boundaries and guidelines of what they do and why are not always clear and transparent. For example, academics are driven to produce research outputs and research impact within a neoliberal climate that demands performance in a number of managerial metrics and a competitive job climate (Martin 2011; Fitzgerald et al 2012; Gray et al 2019). As such, there may be a tension between the desire to gather deep, rich, and emotionally honest data, and doing no harm to oneself or one's participants. If we as researchers want to engage our participants with the levels of engagement and interaction that creative research methods allow us, then I believe it is important to learn from a therapeutic approach.

Therapeutic training focuses on building rapport, trust, and developing a relationship and relational field in which a client feels safe and supported to speak. Researchers can learn approaches that enable our participants to open up more, to talk, and to share stories that result in deep, rich, qualitative data. Creative methods facilitate this (Brown and Leigh 2018a), however techniques from psychotherapy could be of value in any context where a researcher needs to build a relationship and trust. One aspect of this is learning to create and hold a boundary to contain participants' experiences so that they are not harmed in the process of sharing their stories, and are not left in the grip of reliving an experience that was emotional or traumatic with no tools to heal and transform. A second is a researcher learning how to protect themselves, process their own experiences of hearing stories that are personal, traumatic, or triggering to prevent vicarious trauma and the emotional and physical impacts of hearing others' stories. While the first point is concerned with protecting the participants so that they are not re-traumatised within a research encounter, the second is very much about protecting the researcher. Many qualitative researchers choose to investigate topics and areas that they are emotionally connected to through personal experience or empathic concerns. This is definitely true for much of my work. Becoming aware of this is important in recognising positionality and the extent of personal investment in the research. However, it is also vital to acknowledge and pre-empt any issues that arise, such as compassion fatigue and burn-out. Preventing these is a fundamental part of a therapeutic training, along with reflection and ongoing professional supervision. In contrast, academic supervision for undergraduate or postgraduate researchers is likely to be concerned with academic progress and not focused on how they emotionally process their work. Researchers beyond postgraduate study may not have any formal or informal arena where they could process such experiences.

Case Study 1

Working with children

I have already drawn on my doctoral research in this book, and am using this case study to illustrate how qualitative research can border onto education and therapy. This study took place over two years in a school setting. It comprised group somatics sessions timetabled to be part of the school day. The study was primarily movement based and used a range of arts-based creative methods designed to support children aged four to 11 to develop their embodied self-awareness, learn to reflect, and capture that process. This case study highlights the importance of intention to differentiate between educational and therapeutic content, and how therapeutic outcomes can be gained from research set within an educational setting.

Context

My doctoral research involved 26 children aged from four to 11 years old (Reception to Year 6) in a school setting over two years (Leigh 2012). The publications from this work have included the use of creative methods and journaling to facilitate children to develop a reflective practice (Leigh 2020a); children's experiences, perceptions, and self-regulation of emotion (Leigh 2017); and the connection between reflection, reflective practice, and embodied reflective practice (Leigh and Bailey 2013). I had worked with children in schools from early in the 2000s, offering after-school clubs in yoga at my children's primary school and others nearby. Teaching yoga and movement to children is different from working with adults – there are three rules to consider, which can be summarised in just three points:

1. children are not mini adults;
2. children are not mini adults;
3. children are not mini adults. (Bailey 2012: 21)

As well as traditional animal-based movements that appeal to children (Mainland 1998), I found that, depending on age, they also enjoyed faster vinayasa type sequences (Devereux 1998), and balances that related to developmental righting reactions (Brook n.d.; Hartley 1989). Introducing developmental movements such as hopping like a frog or rabbit (there is a difference – try it!), walking like a bear, or making shapes like a chameleon stuck to a wall were all firm favourites. I had also worked with autistic children, children with cerebral palsy, and physical and intellectual developmental delay. Although sessions focused on movement, as I showed in Lesson 2, part of moving is learning to be still. Whereas in an adult yoga class I would allow five minutes at the beginning and 10–20 minutes at the end in savasana or corpse pose (Iyengar 1966) to allow adrenaline and noradrenaline to leave the system and feel refreshed; for children it was a case of asking them to sit for one minute and explore different positions and gradually building up time. One pose I often used was child's pose or balasana (see Figure 10). I could see, and heard anecdotally, that sessions made a positive difference to their lives. I undertook my doctoral research to explore children's experiences in more depth.

My research was not designed to be part of the physical education curriculum. However, sessions were held during the school day and fit within a functional definition of physical education that includes all supervised and structured activities taking place within school (Bailey and Dismore 2004). The school perceived my work as fitting in with physical education, dance, and sport – 'these sessions help to meet the curriculum demands for dance and physical education' (Reflexive Journal). The children equated them with schooling, and they were viewed as 'enrichment' by teachers. Although the majority of scholarship in the field of the philosophy of education is concerned with the 'educational' value of physical activity and its place within the curriculum (McNamee and Bailey 2010), I was not attempting to establish whether my work had an educational benefit, instead I was phenomenologically exploring children's embodied experiences.

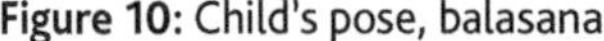
Figure 10: Child's pose, balasana

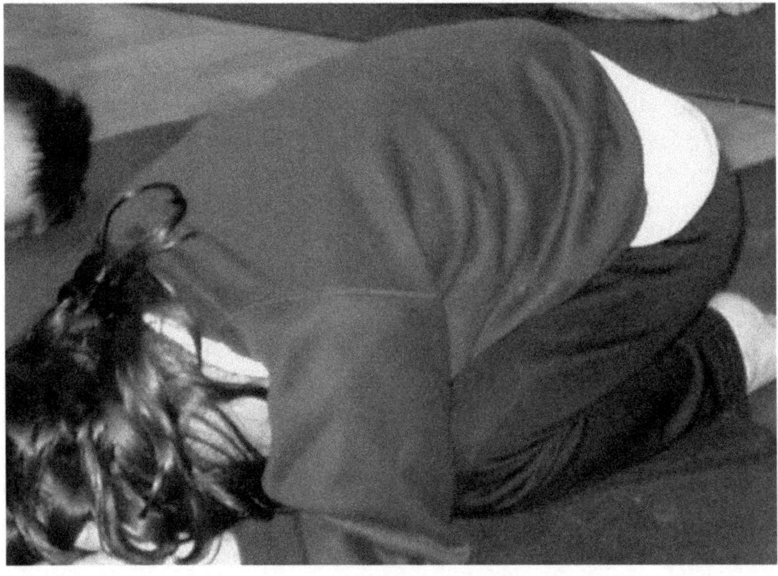

I worked within every class at the school at some point, and the relationships between the children, teaching staff, and myself built up trust and ease of communication which enabled the children to express themselves freely in a supportive and non-judgemental space. These were not children deemed in need of a therapeutic intervention but an ordinary mix of individuals, and the sessions were designed to be educational. However, as 'every educator … has some implicit understanding of what education is or what it should be like' (Biesta 1994: 299), my training and experience had implications for my view of what education should be. While my intention was educational, as I demonstrated in Lessons 2 and 3, I had to be aware of the therapeutic potential of the material, maintain a secure relational field, and 'hold' the educational space in a therapeutic manner (Rogers 1967).

Research approach

My research was phenomenological and participatory, and I used an interpretative and narrative approach with the 'power to reveal the embodied experience' (Stephens 2011: 62). I wanted to allow space for 'more complete and more naturalistic expressions of children's experiences' (Irwin and Johnson 2006: 826). All the children took part in sessions designed to be enjoyable and ensure they were recognised as 'the real experts of their lives' (Pearce and Bailey 2010). I 'allowed the young people time to think about what they would like to express' (Punch 2002: 54) by incorporating developmental play, yoga, drawing, mark-making, and modelling into three phases:

- The first involved working with all children in the school on themes of Finding Shapes, Organising and Moving On.
- The second focused on why, what and how we move.
- The final phase, with only the oldest children, explored emotions, sensations, reflection, and expression.

In addition, I undertook two case studies (Child A and Child M) to illustrate a single phenomenon within a general context (Kyburz-Graber 2004), that is, individuals in a class situation. My data included a mix of reflexive journal entries, field notes, session notes, drawings, models, images, and interview transcripts (see Figure 11). A multimodal analysis like this was 'especially suited to the investigation of affective phenomena' (Cromby 2011: 90).

Border with education

In a school setting children can be particularly vulnerable to suggestibility and may be influenced by the status of a researcher if they perceive them to be, or be equivalent to, a teacher (Greig and Taylor 1999). This affects

Figure 11: Sources of data

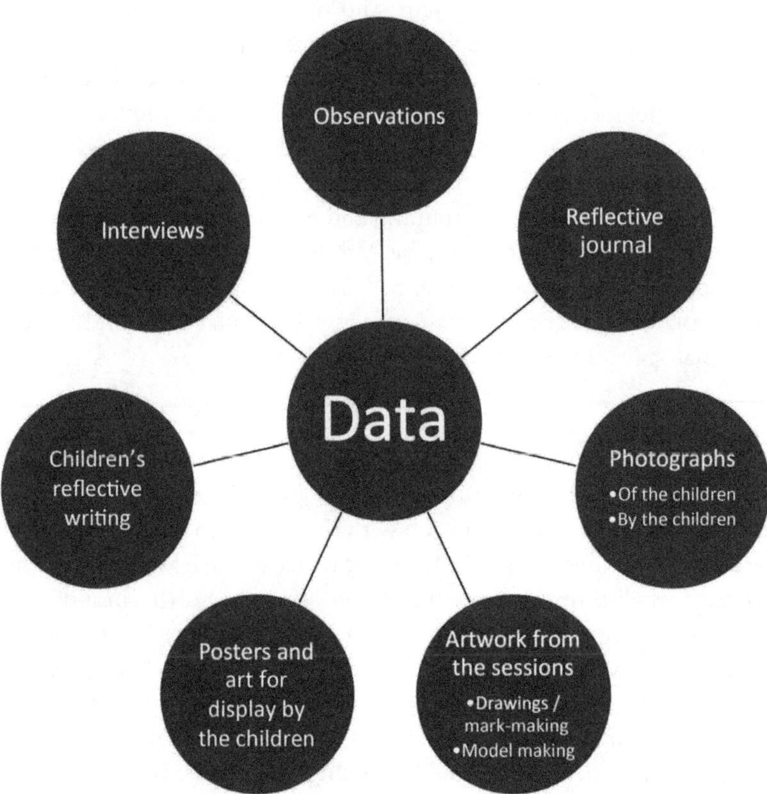

research findings as children may feel pressure to get things right or 'say what they think adults want them to say' (Fargas-Malet et al 2010). To combat this, I needed to create an environment that allowed the children to trust me enough to say what they felt and thought and not worry whether it was 'right' or what I wanted to hear. In my study only one child mentioned that they thought there was a need to be right. In contrast, many spoke of the freedom they had to choose, say, or draw. They were assured their experiences were valid and accepted. "No wrong answers whatever you said was true in its own way" (W Year 6).

I had a professional duty of care to keep the children safe and maintain behaviour standards, yet I wanted to establish an environment where they were secure and felt safe to explore. Observing the boundary between the need for an orderly (yet fun) class, and one that allowed students the space to be more experimental was not always easy:

> In some sessions I feel that I am having to focus more on behaviour-management and the drill sergeant 'copy me' style is then most effective,

> although this does not elicit, nor allow time and space so much for the children to explore their own experience. Partly this seems to be where there are more new children in the group who are less used to me and the way in which I work. (Reflexive Journal, Phase 1)

> Generally the class was noisy and active, though by the end producing really interesting and different work. Very clear difference to me with research as opposed to education – if I had been in charge of the class as their teacher I would not have wanted so much noise, but for this I want them to have the freedom to be creative and expressive. Interestingly one of the loudest groups were actually working very safely. (Reflexive Journal, Phase 3)

I reflected on behaviour management a lot. My main tactic to elicit positive behaviour was positive encouragement, and this worked well: 'Lots of verbal positive encouragement "I like how Aj is using her face …"; "look at how J is being a twist snake". J did not want to join in until he became a standing up twisty snake which was fantastic' (Field Notes).

In Phase 1, I worked in the school for three afternoons a week which proved challenging both physically and emotionally. I was very aware of the difference between working as a research student compared to a therapist or educator:

> I realised that one difference between this work (as my doctorate) and my normal therapeutic/educational work is that it is a lot more challenging to let go of this. In part this is due to my working habits – fitting it in around everything so that it is an intrinsic part of my life it feels as if there is always a part of my brain working, analysing and churning it about. … This is not particularly useful for the letting go part that is necessary in normal therapeutic work! (Reflexive Journal, Phase 1)

I felt the edges of my roles as educator, therapist, and researcher: 'the data collection part of the project is separate to the education aspect – it is a phenomenological account/study/exploration of children's education in "embodiment"' (Reflexive Journal, Phase 1). I also had opportunities to witness the children in different scenarios:

> Observed an out of school choir – aware of differences due to context? Within the school day even if children have to assent to take part reality is that they are in a mode of doing what their teacher wants. They have to choose to go to an after school club so those children who are less willing, who may be more distracted/disruptive not present. If they do not behave they do not get to go. Also a child that 'needs' more

> support may not get the chance to go as the parent perceives that they would not be welcome? (Reflexive Journal, Phase 1)

In Phase 2, I gave each class in turn three sessions. I wanted the children to begin to notice their moving bodies and become aware of different ways they could move and how that would be perceived by others. This was designed to enhance the inner awareness; 'the dialogue between inner and outer experience in relation to the whole person' (Olsen 1998: 11). Andrea Olsen describes the capacity to listen and be sensitive to our body as something that closes down as we grow older. This was borne out in the session on 'why we move' with Year 3 and 4 children (age 7–9). I noted 'some were confused/wanted to have more direction – interesting as the littler ones were happy just to draw a picture of why they moved' (Reflexive Journal). The 'natural' embodiment of children is in part due to their physical interaction with the world around them. Joseph Tobin (2004) discussed how the body, and children's experience of their bodies, is threatened by societal emphasis on the importance of words rather than physical expression, resulting in children who have less access to contact and bodily movement in early childhood educational settings. Touch is an example of this. As shared in Lessons from ethics, I did use appropriate touch in the sessions, as contact and adjustments were an integral part of my yoga and somatics trainings: 'an awareness of ourselves through skin contact of some sort does seem to be important for an on-going sense of self' (Westland 2011: 21).

Phase 3 was only with the oldest children, aged 9–11. I was in class one afternoon a week for six weeks, giving the class teacher extra time to get on with her work. Although present, she did not participate or assist with behaviour management unless at my explicit request. In the past, some teaching assistants had sat out, however most joined in and all had participated with behaviour management when necessary. I had also, apart from on one occasion, always worked with half the class at a different venue at my request. This fostered a sense that the sessions were different from normal classwork and gave the children freedom to share, speak freely, and explore the material in their own way. This was no longer possible. We worked in the children's usual classroom with tables and chairs pushed back. The space left was narrow and the children were quite cramped. I wanted to introduce concepts that would encourage the class to think about their experiences and reflect. We explored ideas of stretch, pain, happiness, and recognising emotions in ourselves and others; thinking about meanings of words as well as sensation. We explored showing, expressing, and recognising emotion, and how stories are told through words and pictures, fitting with ongoing literacy themes on characterisation, emotion, and expression.

The following term we worked intensively over three days on a display for their classroom. These days were very child-led, as apart from a structured warm-up the class worked individually or in small groups to produce posters. They were free to choose any aspect they wanted to. Some shared work on understanding what made them (and their friends) happy. Others drew yoga poses or wrote poetry. A theme for many groups was balancing on top of each other. Although not something I had taught them, I supported their freedom to move as they wished within the bounds of safety: 'Because of all the balancing and stretching do a longer a warm up … Enforcing again the need to be aware of each other particularly when balancing or climbing on each other' (Reflexive Journal). The days looked slightly chaotic, yet nearly all the children were taking very good care of each other. One child was in a group that appeared to be very loud, but were in fact being very safe. I asked him to speak to the class about 'what it was like to be hung between two friends – said he felt safe, trusted them not to drop him' (Field Notes). However, not all children were paying this much attention, and I noted that two who had joined the class after the earlier phases of the study were least aware of themselves and their peers. I spoke to the teacher:

> This is different to 'education' [there is a] need for more creativity and freedom but [it] has the edge of being less in control as a teacher. She agreed and said they were enjoying it. They need in this research to have the freedom to express what they want and not what they think I want. (Reflexive Journal)

Several groups chose to write and draw about emotions: how they showed, shared, and perceived them. This indicated the value they placed on exploring and identifying emotions in themselves and others: 'emotions and feelings can be treated as elements of embodied process that feed into and through social interaction' (Cromby 2011: 87). Some found it easy to 'read' others' emotions from movements and faces, whereas others seemed to need to practise and learn (see Figure 12). B recognised the effort that her partner put into showing his emotions. "It was realy [*sic*] easy to tell D's emotions, he put a lot of effort into it." B was also clear about which emotions she enjoyed seeing: "I like seeing peoples [*sic*] emotions if they are happy." B implied she did not enjoy seeing other people's emotions if they were not positive, which could be because she did not enjoy the feelings evoked in her own body as a result. Her partner D, did not find it as easy to show his emotions, nor to see his partner's: "It was more easyier to take a photo than pulling a espression. … It was harder to pull a espression of your feeling. … It was very hard to see what someone else was [*sic*]."

Recognising another's movements as expressions of emotion can result in increased empathy (Sheets-Johnstone 2010a: 112). As self-awareness increased and norms changed, the ability to empathise with others increased: "because I wouldn't have known what would have made them

Figure 12: "Very easy if you look carefully ..."

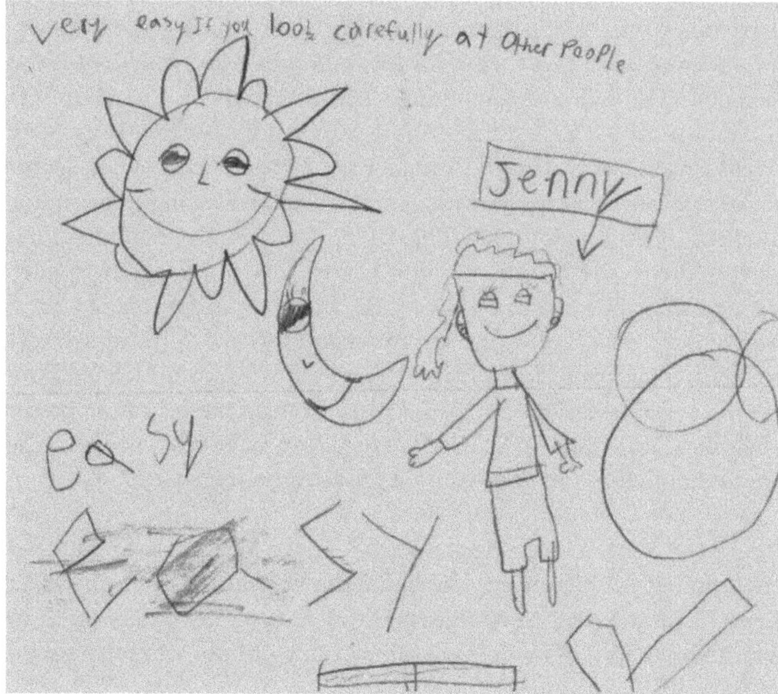

really excited but I would now" (M Year 6). Empathy is not always connected to movement: 'the common understanding of empathy … is grounded in static images' (Sheets-Johnstone 2010a: 115). Empathy is developed as a child grows and plays games of pretence with others, which is a key developmental stage necessary for learning to recognise different mental states, developing a theory of mind, and learning to engage in the social interactions that form part of society (Keys and Bailey 2006). An absence of pretend play and a later absence of empathy have traditionally been seen as markers for developmental disorders (Bailey 2002).

Border with therapy

The border between the therapeutic and educational contexts of somatics overlapped at times as individuals processed information about themselves, their bodies, and their sense of embodied self-awareness. This was most evident in the Phase 3 sessions with older children. The trust that had been built over time meant many felt safe enough to express deep feelings and emotions. I needed to remain aware that issues had to be contained within the group, and that some children needed more therapeutic holding.

I encouraged the children to relate their emotional experiences and awareness to the physical and moving sensations of the body. This was in order to 'ground' the emotions. By this I mean that the emotions were, when possible, associated with a particular movement or sensation within the body, remaining tangible and 'real', and easier to express through language: 'emotion and feeling are being treated neither as wholly biological nor as simple manifestations of language' (Cromby 2011: 82). This was in the framework of Authentic Movement, where the moving experience (of emotions, sensations, or images) is expressed through verbal and written language (Adler 2002). As well as moving, learning to be still was integral. Being still, often in mouse or child's pose, was practised often. We usually began by being still for a minute, and finished in the same way, perhaps for a little longer. It was remembered by the children in interviews.

Me: What do you think you learnt?
A: That if times are hard and that just to actually do a mouse pose or something to help relax. (A Year 5)

One girl, C, said "It was very peaceful, it sort of felt like the minute was just going to keep going." However, it was more challenging for some:

Me: Did you find it easy to be still?
E: No, not really.
Me: Are you glad that you tried?
E: Yeah.
Me: Why?
E: Because I don't normally try and be still. It's just you move around. (E Year 5)

E went on to describe how she used mouse pose to gain autonomy over her emotions.

Me: Is there anything else that you want to say about the stuff that we did?
E: And how to get calmer.
Me: How to get calmer.
E: By doing mouse pose.
Me: Is that something you'll remember?
E: Yeah, yeah. Because if you're angry you can always do mouse pose to calm you down.
Me: It's all right to feel angry as well but it's good to be able to change how you feel if you want to. (E Year 5)

Self-awareness has a flexible relation to emotional intensity (Silvia 2002), and E demonstrated using her self-awareness to regulate her emotions. As part of a session on emotional regulation, one girl chose to write about what she did when she felt sad, instead of how she moved or where she felt it: "When I'm sad I go to my bedroom and cry lots, and lots. If I'm at school I usely [*sic*] keep my sadness inside me, not many things cheer me up just my animals" (ML Year 6). In this session we used a technique to explore things that made us feel happy in a way that could be seen physically (for example, eyes shining, shift in facial expressions, and posture). Although the instructions had been to think about things that excluded people and animals (as ideally happiness should not be dependent on others), this child said nothing in her life made her happy except for her cats. As I talked to her and she described how they also walked away from her when she was sad, she became more upset. The aim was to find actions to regulate emotions to become more self-reliant and not base happiness on others. Within a therapeutic setting I would have liked to explore this so she could begin to find and recognise emotional states other than sadness. However, in the classroom setting there was only room to reassure her as best I could, continue to check in with her in sessions, and talk to her teacher.

I had similar moments working with developmental movement patterns, aware they could only give children an experience of choosing between different modes of locomotion and noticing which came more naturally. Therapeutic work would explore a pattern in depth, re-patterning where it was initially inaccessible (for the process of re-patterning in somatic bodywork, see Hartley 1989; Bainbridge Cohen 1993). Although the sessions were not designed to highlight developmental issues, nor was I attempting to link developmental patterns to academic attainment, teachers commented in amazement that children most challenged by movements such as hopping also struggled with classwork, particularly literacy. They told me they were surprised how the children were able to improve throughout a session by focusing and concentrating, and that they were able to focus more easily in class afterwards.

There were two children, brothers I shall call A and M, who stood out for me as in need of a more intentional therapeutic approach. A was in Reception (age 4) when I first met him. Initially he isolated himself from the class, and as he grew older he began to be more and more disruptive. He was on the special needs register for children with special educational needs (SEN). I was told this informally by staff, however I was not allowed to see his records, nor was I told his official diagnosis if one had been given, as I was not at the school as an educator, but conducting research. I recognised A was likely to be autistic. Autism can affect perceptions of the self and embodied self-awareness: an autistic woman described: 'I found it very hard to hold onto the concept that my body was part of me' (Williams 2003: 23). A was in a relatively large class which had a few children who were disruptive and had a pattern of egging on his challenging behaviour. His teacher, Miss W, and I had been working to integrate him into group activities while ensuring his behaviour was not disruptive to others, and that behaviour in general was not an issue. The more I worked with A the more his behaviour struck me as out of the range of normal.

> More evident this year that ?something? is not quite right. Last year A was also different but very happy and engaging and eager to be part of what was going on, just not always so able. This year he is less willing to make eye contact. In out of school contexts if he hears an answer he doesn't like he breaks eye contact and the interaction (e.g. I walked the dogs to school with my daughter for a few days – when I saw him one afternoon he asked me with eye contact where the dogs were and I said that they were at home he looked down walked away very abruptly, not interested) feedback from Miss W is that peer relations are less good this year he is starting to get angry and it is hard with new children in the class. He needs more attention. (Reflexive Journal)

I ensured he was not left out in sessions as the differences between his behaviour and that of the others in the class became more pronounced.

> Played game with ball and names but this time asked the children to balance the ball, say their name then throw and sit. Most did very well, no one threw to A – I did – he was placed at the other end of the room so I walked nearer as I wanted to ensure that he would have a good chance of catching from a soft easy throw and I can't throw that far accurately... I did the same for R who was last as I didn't want to make it different for A. (Reflexive Journal)

Sometimes he would join in, but often he would not.

> Stand sit, clap balance on bottoms – some children really watching and listening, others not. Lots of playing with mats. A was circling the class throughout this. (Field Notes)

> A had laid down and wrapped himself in his mat and stayed still – occasionally making noises. (Field Notes)

> Asked class to get into pairs – there was an even number, and J was to work with A, but A did not join in. (Field Notes)

At times although he said he wished to join in, he still did not. 'The pairs showed their poses, all clapped. … A chose not to however he had asked earlier if we could play the game where we show and tell' (Field Notes, Phase 1).

There was progress, and A chose to join in with activities more and more, although often this was at my prompting or encouragement.

> A was being talkative and fidgety and the TA [teaching assistant] got up and took him from his mat. I asked A if he wanted to share my mat and he came to mine. (Field Notes)

> I started to show them the organ doll. I showed the brain, then opened the shirt to show the ribs. I asked if they could feel their ribs and they did. A said that he couldn't feel his so I showed him. (Field Notes)

> J and A chose to continue modelling. L and K took a while to model, so only had a short time to draw. I asked A if he wanted to play show and tell and he did and I asked if he wanted to go first – on his own or with somebody else. He wanted to go on his own first. When we gathered back A went first, then most of the children went in pairs, some on their own. (Field Notes)

I made sure I fed back to Miss W, who was pleased A was joining in. However, his contributions were not always positive: 'A is challenging in this group which is large anyway. In part this is because he commented on what the other children were doing or saying negatively. He may be better in a smaller group, or ideally one-to-one before reintegration into the larger group' (Reflexive Journal).

One session particularly demonstrated the importance of trust and relationships in supporting SEN children. Miss W was absent and a supply teacher came with A's class to the space. The school generally engaged supply teachers for periods of illness or long-term leave, so they knew the children. This teacher was new to the class and me.

> As the group came in I asked them to take off their shoes and socks, and I saw that A had gone straight to sit on the beanbag and was looking over at my things. I went up to him and said that he had been doing such a good job of guarding my pipe-cleaners last week that I had wanted him to look after my things again and thanked him. Miss W had said that being in a circle was hard for A, so I had placed the beanbag behind me so that I was a protection/shield. I wasn't sure how much support there would be from the teacher with me. I was very glad that I had done this. (Reflexive Journal)

Rather than allowing A to join in where he could and take time out if needed, the supply teacher expected him to behave like a 'normal' or neuro-typical child.

> We then came to a circle with A behind me, and I asked them to vote on a story. The children chose on a bear hunt (Rosen and Oxenbury (Illus.) 1989). They all knew the story so I asked them to find a space so we could go through the animals/ways of walking. Most of the children were joining in and enjoying themselves. A picked up the beanbag in his teeth to be a bear – as I was asking him not to R tried to bite it too.
>
> I was with A and enjoyed seeing him join in and move with the children. The supply teacher came along and spoke very harshly to him and told him to behave or come and sit down next to her. I didn't particularly like the way she spoke to him. Some of the children sat down near me, others were moving about being the characters. She tried to get the children to sit in a circle, but I said that they needed space to move if they wanted to. A was sitting in front of me in a group of children which I perceived to be good progress. (Field Notes)

Afterwards I reflected:

> Class was different this week with the supply teacher who did not know the children. She seemed to have an entirely different style of relating to them – more old school – which I did not see them respond to well.
>
> She was less able to support me and the class in terms of an exploratory context – i.e. allowing them the freedom to explore the material. However she also did not seem to have the authority to enforce behaviour when that was required. In contrast the children looked to me at the end of the class for discipline and maintaining the line and comfort. (Reflexive Journal)

Integrating SEN pupils, whether their needs are physical, emotional, or behavioural, into mainstream lessons can represent a challenge for teachers in all subjects, and can be a 'daunting task' in physical education (Robertson et al 2000: 5). Teachers often have concerns that including such pupils could have a detrimental effect on the rest of the class (Morley et al 2005). David Morley and colleagues found teachers believed that SEN pupils who were given assistance in other lessons were often left to cope in physical education, which is not in line with inclusive education if it is 'concerned with minimizing the number of pupils who, because of the nature of the curriculum, have negative experiences' (Vickerman 2007: 389). However, children with SEN do not all fit into neat categories. Those with physical disabilities or motor difficulties need a different level and kind of support from those with emotional or behavioural difficulties, learning difficulties, and sensory impairments.

Children exhibiting behavioural difficulties were reported as being the most challenging to work with and plan for (Morley et al 2005). I reflected on a struggle I had in Phase 3 managing behavioural difficulties with the oldest children, as some children went through a particularly difficult stage in class with their teacher and with me. I became very conscious of the differences in managing challenging behaviour as an authoritative teacher figure, a therapist, or a researcher.

> I am aware that by not allowing them to participate this exacerbates the feelings of exclusion, of not being wanted, of messing things up, but as a teacher needing to retain control of the class I want to send them out, I need to show them I am in control and that disruptive, dangerous and unacceptable behaviour cannot be tolerated.
>
> Where is my role as a researcher in this? To be honest, it would be to work only with a small group of 'good' children who would be able to listen, to work, to express themselves … or as a therapist with the 'difficult' ones to work individually or one-to-one. M is a child who, along with his brother, has been identified by me as a possibility for this type of work. (Reflexive Journal)

M was A's older brother, and was in Year 4 (age 8) when I first met him. I was told informally he had a diagnosis of ADHD. He was very talkative and could be disruptive in class. In the first sessions at the school before this study started, I found he responded well to vigorous exercise and space to be quiet and still. Again, I was told informally that his behaviour in class improved after sessions. At some point I was told he had been put onto medication, however the class teacher and teaching assistant felt it was impacting negatively on his behaviour. By Phase 3, M was in Year 6 (age 11). Although very bright, he was getting into more and more trouble in class and was presenting to me as a very unhappy child. In the session on self-regulation:

> M did not want to join in said the only thing that made him happy was dying. I said it was about being able to tell when someone else was happy. I checked in with the class teacher and told her that M wanted to die. She said this isn't unusual for him. (Field Notes and Reflections, Phase 3)

Figure 13: 'Mad' and 'lost'

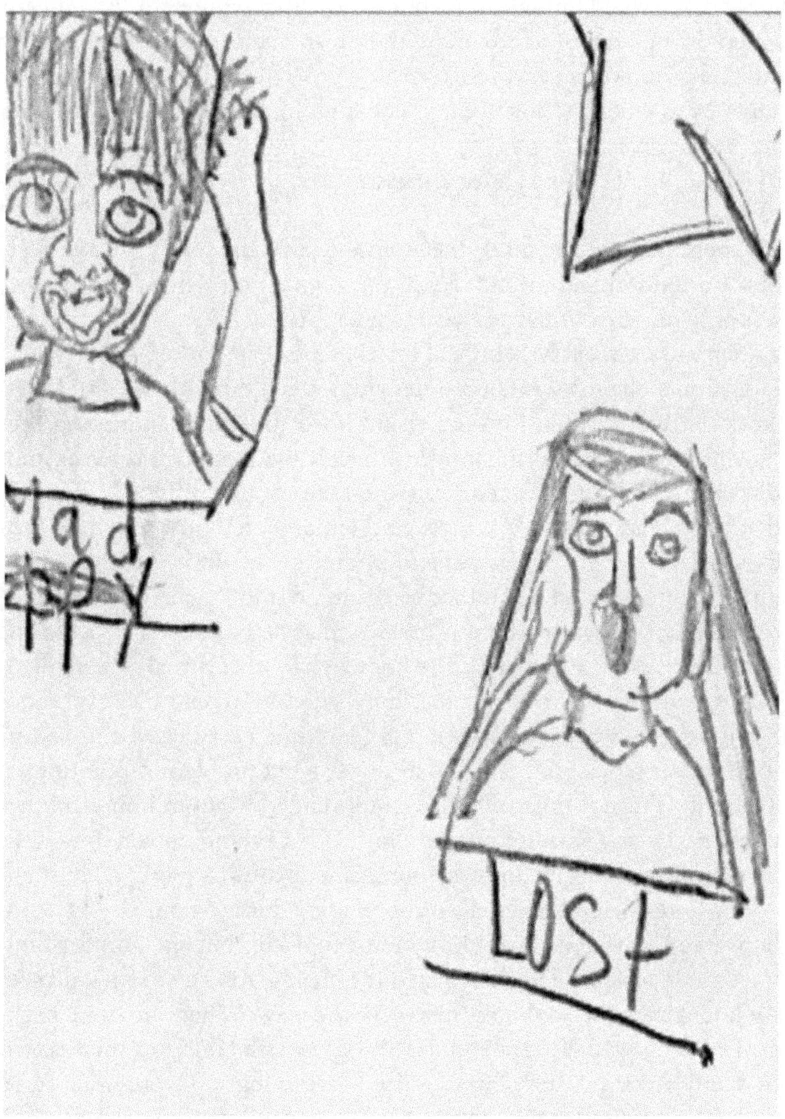

Obviously, it is not healthy for an 11-year-old boy to repetitively speak of dying as the only thing that would make him happy. This, along with his other behaviours, marked him out as a child who would benefit from one-to-one therapeutic intervention. In addition to this incident, he could be quite disruptive in this phase of sessions. He was sometimes excluded by other boys in the class, and his behaviour meant he was excluded from some activities. However, at other times they did include him; 'R did a great job at including M into a 3 with himself and B' (Field Notes, Phase 3).

I found the situation with M quite hard to handle. I was presented with a child who described himself as 'mad' and 'lost' (see Figure 13). As a therapist I wanted the opportunity to work with him and help, but it was not possible within the group or as part of this research project. In addition, I was unsure whether I was willing to involve myself with him, his mother, and the school in yet another role.

One time, I talked to M after a session:

> The behaviour of M and Aj meant that during the session a large part of my attention had to be focused on them – and when it wasn't (or was only on one of them) an accident happened. Afterwards they have golden time, except M who had lost that privilege earlier in the week. He sat on a chair. I wrote up notes and looked through the children's work. M had written how much he liked stretching and doing the moving, and remembering how much he had got out of it last year, and focused so well and worked so hard I went to talk to him. I told him that I had read what he'd written and remembered how much he had liked it last year, particularly the fast bouncy stuff and asked him if he knew what he could do so that he could do it lots again this year. He told me that he wished he was normal, that he had problems and was stupid and silly. I asked him if he knew what was normal – he replied that everything was not normal, he wished he would die, everyone hated him, he was a 'prat', he lost golden time every week and began to get upset repeating again and again 'I've got problems,' (pointing at his head) 'I'm not normal.' I had not intended to upset him – on the contrary, I was wanting to let him know that I remembered how well he had done and give him encouragement to do so again. He then got up and stormed out. [His teacher] asked him to come in. He said he wanted time out to think, which I told her, but she said for him to come in at once. He did, kicked the chair across the room, and she took him out. I stayed with the rest of the class. When she came back I asked if he was all right – she had told me straight after the session that he'd had a very bad day yesterday – screaming and kicking all day – she said she found it disturbing that he says he has problems and that he wants to put a knife in his heart, he wants to die, he's not normal, and said that it is his mother who says all these things to him as she wants a label for him. I explained what he'd written, and what I had been saying to him before he kicked off, and she said that he is just a normal boy – being told he has problems and issues does nothing to help him on a day-to-day level. (Reflexive Journal)

From my training (Sumar 2007) and experience working with SEN children, I was aware that parental acceptance is key to allow space to develop. If a parent expects and perceives their child to be 'normal' then offering a therapeutic intervention may be counter-productive. I deliberately used activities designed to enable the class to begin learning how to recognise and regulate their emotional states. Because of the difficulties the class had been having as a group, they were able to use this to impact positively on their friendships. In his interview M spoke about this:

M: I wish we had done more of the emotion stuff, because I quite liked that.
Me: Okay. Why did you like that?
M: Because it made me understand about other people's feelings and stuff.
Me: Okay. That's quite a big thing to be understanding. How did it help you understand about other people's feelings?
M: Because sometimes I just do stuff and don't realise I'm hurting other people's feelings. So that sort of helped. So I knew to try not to do something that would hurt someone's feelings.
Me: Did it help … we did a lot about recognising what other people were feeling as well, was that helpful?
M: Yes.
Me: And I remember …
M: Very helpful. (M Year 6)

M verbalised what he felt about expressing his emotions through the creative methods:

M: I quite liked drawing about it because I liked doing drawings to explain my emotions and stuff.
Me: Okay. Do you find that helpful? Yes? Why is that helpful?
M: Because I enjoy doing drawings and when I draw it sort of calms me down. (M Year 6)

He demonstrated that he had begun to take responsibility for himself:

> 'I learnt how when we'd … whatever we do, how much we stretch, we always need to be careful of ourselves and everybody around us and if it's … if you're asking us to do something that's stretching us too far, we should always just do it as far as we can but not so much it hurts.'

In the sessions I took a lot of care to link ideas of pain and stretch beyond the physical and hoped that this learning would stay with M. The exercise that asked the class to identify what made them happy and recognise accompanied changes in facial expressions and brightness of eyes is drawn from trauma work (Trippany et al 2011). M had used this to self-regulate his emotions, identifying that listening to music made him happy:

Me: Was that a useful thing, so that if you're feeling sad you could do something that would make you feel …?
M: Yes.
Me: Do you still use that?
M: Yes. (M. Year 6)

Although I had perceived M to be getting something positive from the work with me, I was not aware of the extent to which he had internalised his body awareness, awareness of others, and the responsibility for regulating his own feelings by listening to music. M's words and experience have stayed with me, as they demonstrated the positive therapeutic impact this kind of work can have on an individual even when the intention is for it to be research or education. What M gained from these sessions meant more to me than the successful completion of my doctorate. M expressed how he was able to regulate his own emotions more effectively and recognise emotions and feelings in other people, which helped him interact with his peers in class and get in less trouble as he was no longer acting out. M showed he was able to take the educational context of the sessions and use it to his own therapeutic advantage. He embodied the stages of therapeutic treatment of lost embodied self-awareness defined by Alan Fogel (2009: 23–24). He used the sessions as a resource, allowed himself to slow down and become more aware of his body, verbalised his experiences, made links and boundaries with those experiences and the rest of his life, and was starting to self-regulate and re-engage. Work with A highlighted the importance of trust and having good communication to fully support a child whether you are a researcher, teacher, or therapist. Both case studies, along with the rest of the project, demonstrate why it is essential to remain aware of a therapeutic context and its potential implications within a research or educational context.

Case Study 2

Working with artists and researchers

This case study draws from work project-managing the research component and later following up researcher experiences of the multidisciplinary research study *Imagining Autism*. This brought drama practitioners and researchers together with an evaluation team from psychology. It exemplifies the borders of qualitative research where it meets with art, education, and therapy. While I was positioned within the evaluation team, I was very aware of similarities between the improvisational drama and my doctoral work with children. This case study also highlights the ways in which researchers reflect and position themselves in their research.

Context

Imagining Autism was a collaboration between a team of drama academics and practitioners and two teams of psychologists. The drama researchers had a long history of using improvised drama and puppetry with autistic children and children with other special educational needs. They had seen how their approach had a beneficial effect, increasing capacity for and willingness to engage in social interactions and imaginative play. They had heard from families and teachers about how their work 'ameliorated' some of the challenges the children faced day-to-day in allistic society. The two leads were both parents of autistic children and had personal reasons for their interest. However, they were unable to 'prove' in the scientific objective sense that what they did had an impact, or establish why. As drama academics they were used to using Practice-as-Research (Barrett and Bolt 2010) which is, rightly or wrongly, often not as highly regarded as other research approaches or methods within academia (Mårtensson et al 2016). They decided to collaborate with psychology researchers to evaluate the impact of a programme of improvised drama to 'show' that what they did was of benefit and had value. The study was designed to be systematic and rigorous, involving standardised tests of IQ, numeracy and literacy, momentary time sampled observations of the children in class and at play, and regular ADOS (autistic diagnostic observation schedule) tests. The study involved 27 children aged 7–12 years from three schools in the UK over 18 months to allow for improvements in testing due to developmental changes. The improvised drama was delivered in a specifically designed environment called 'the pod', which was a black-out tent-like structure the practitioners erected in a suitable space in each school. They delivered sessions for 10 weeks in each school. Their findings were published (Shaughnessy and Trimingham 2016; Trimingham and Shaughnessy 2016), along with the feasibility of the study to assess and evaluate the intervention as a treatment for autism (Beadle-Brown et al 2018).

The language used to describe the work – for example 'ameliorate', 'intervention', 'treatment' – is not in line with that preferred by autistic people or indicated by the social model of disability (Oliver 2013). Unlike the medical model of disability, which suggests that disability results from the impairment of the individual; the social model suggests it is the environment that is disabling. To give a physical example; a wheelchair user who cannot enter a building is either disabled because the deficit is with them as in they cannot walk up the steps (medical model), or because the deficit is in the environment and society that surrounds them – the building is lacking in the ramps/lifts that would make it accessible for them because it was not seen as important (social model). In terms of autism, an accessible environment would avoid sensory overload and negative perceptions about the capacity and capabilities of Autistics. Diagnosis of autism is made against criteria set out in the latest version of the *Diagnostic Statistical Manual* (DSM) (American Psychiatric Association 2022), or the *International Classification of Diseases* (ICD) (World Health Organization 2022). The DSM-5 defined Autism Spectrum Disorder as 'persistent difficulties with social communication and social interaction' and 'restricted and repetitive patterns of behaviours, activities or interests' including sensory behaviours that are present since early childhood to an extent that they 'limit and impair everyday functioning' (American Psychiatric Association 2022). The literature around autism largely positions it as a disorder or disease and often highlights parental challenges (Escalona et al 2001; Bromley et al 2004; Kern et al 2006). Gaining a formal diagnosis for autism is gendered and racialised (Mandell et al 2009; Mallipeddi and VanDaalen 2022). I have had a clinical psychologist say to me that if an adult is able to hold down a job, have friendships, or a relationship, then they cannot be autistic. These damaging assumptions and societal perceptions that Autistics lack humour or playfulness and the capacity to emotionally or socially engage and communicate with others persist.

In *Imagining Autism*, the drama and evaluation teams were blinded to each other's work. 'Blinding' in this context means the content of the work of each team was hidden from the others, designed to be analogous to a clinical trial where the research team do not know which patients are in test or placebo groups. I was not part of the drama team but was aware of huge similarities between the improvised drama approach and my doctoral work. My role as project manager of the evaluation team meant I was in schools conducting observations, assisting with standardised tests (some of which I was not allowed to administer as I was not a psychology graduate), conducting ADOS tests, gathering information about behaviour and capacity from parents and families, and conducting interviews with teachers and parents. Over the 18 months I had a lot of contact with the children and families involved in the study, and it was important that they felt safe and supported when I met with them, as some of the standardised forms I was asking them to complete with me asked for very personal information that was often accompanied by harrowing stories. The interviews I conducted with parents and teachers after the study made it clear the project had had a positive impact on some children. I heard parents talk about increased use of language and play, and positive behaviour changes.

Research approach

Following the study, I completed a small follow-up project and interviewed the Principal and Co-Investigators and members of the drama and research teams to find out about their experiences (Leigh and Brown 2021b). After ethical approval, and with transcription funded by a small internal grant, I contacted as many members of the teams as I could. Each interview was one-to-one and lasted between 40 minutes and 2½ hours. They were conversations that acknowledged I was a participant as well as a researcher, and was conducting the research from an insider's perspective (Oakley 1981; Brinkmann and Kvale 2014). One key tension was around language, which is probably no surprise. Definitions of words such as 'therapy', 'education', and 'intervention' were different between teams, as were understandings of what constituted research. The drama practitioners saw their work as valuable but not therapeutic, while the psychologists were evaluating it for its therapeutic effect. Another tension was around the support, time, and training given to the drama practitioners. Some had prior experience working with autistic children and others did not. I will share extracts from conversations with two drama practitioners (DP1 and DP2) and reflect on how they and I negotiated borders of research between science, art, education, and therapy.

Borders with art and science

I was interested in how the artistic drama practitioners began working. DP1 explained how her theatre and arts background led to a breakthrough:

> 'We were in a playroom with these children and we were working with some students and it was all a bit chaotic but what was happening was the children were getting distracted because there was so much stuff in this playroom so that, for example, one child who is into pica [eating things not normally considered food] just wanting playdough because he knew it was in the cupboard. And it was very hard to

get any kind of concentration or sustained interaction with these children. And I said to [DP2], "What we need to do here I think" and I was going back to my experience with theatre, "is we need to block off the space, put up some black drapes all around so we've got a concentrated space and they can't see all this distraction and then in that space I suggest we put something like I used to do … we'll make an outer space environment, UV light, just a cardboard cut-out, puppets in bright colours, somebody in a spacesuit, minimal lighting", there wasn't even a roof to the thing.

So I got hold of the caretaker and begged and pleaded could I put some hook eyes in the wall. I knew you could do this, I've done it so often transforming spaces in various arts centres and god knows what else. So he let me put these hook eyes in and I put ropes through and I literally just strung these drapes, enormous black drapes that we'd borrowed and it just worked incredibly well. Each week we spent some time getting some really rudimentary sort of props together. It really was poor theatre, there wasn't any proper lighting but we managed to get a UV light and then we did an arctic, it was like Christmas and we put a Christmas tree up in the corner, made a kind of living room with a fireplace Father Christmas came through and at the other end was the snowy environment, just in a square. And the first week it seemed to work really well getting the concentration of the kids and the responses were just like up 100% and one of the teachers called the head-teacher along to start filming it because it was so amazing.'

She went on to explain the reasoning behind collaborating with the teams of psychologists to evaluate their work:

'DP2 asked [one of the psychologists] to come along and said, "Look, do you think we're onto something here?" and she said, "I think you might be" because she watched and so it was from that that we put together the much bigger bid for the Arts Council. The idea of evaluating it just seemed a real step forward because having worked in the arts we all know as arts practitioners that this stuff works, we know it but you can't convince a psychologist unless they've got their evaluations. And you will ask any practitioner who works with special needs children in the arts and they will say it works, you know, ask parents, but this is all anecdotal evidence.

So we decided to stick our necks out and say, "Yes, let's get it properly evaluated" and I think I was a bit naive about it. I was so convinced that something would show up on the test but DP2 was going, "My god, what if nothing shows up, what are we going to do?" and in fact she doubled the contact because originally we were only going to do five sessions and she doubled it within the budget as well which was really great that she did that to try and maximise the exposure because it really wasn't very much. It was like 40 minutes a week for like 10 weeks and we were expecting these children to have advanced on these quantitative scales within that time.

I don't think I had any idea what it was going to be like, those evaluations. I think that's one of the reasons I was so naive about it and then you realise they're going to be stuck in a room with a table and doing all this sort of ADOS stuff and all the rest of it. I might have been a bit more frightened if I'd realised at the beginning.'

The word, 'frightened' is quite telling. DP1 had no idea what evaluation might entail or how it would impact the children. She struggled with a 'scientific' and quantitative approach rather than one that was phenomenological or experiential:

'I began to realise that the only thing that the scientists were going to, or the only thing that was going to have some sort of impact perhaps within the more scientific community were changes that could be identified very clearly, a lot of in a quantitative though not entirely quantitative way, that were lasting and that as [a second psychologist] kept saying, could be replicated again and again. In other words that you could come up with some kind of a formula, a simplification that could be duplicated, that other people could administer.

Because the point was it's no good if it's a few genius drama practitioners who are, you know, delivering a highly effective intervention but you can't deliver it to lots of children, you know, you can't make it more universal. I actually totally disagree with him on that because if you have managed to identify through a form of an intervention, something that works, I'm not so concerned about the massive duplication, I'm just very interested to know what this tells us about the way we educate autistic children, the more fundamental principles underlying our methods. You know, can they be replicated within education, within the care system, within the way the parents treat autistic children? Not can we come up with something like ABA [Applied Behaviour Analysis] that you can, "flog" to loads of parents or schools or so on.

I suppose what worries me is that, it's also very exciting but I don't think I could achieve it, I don't know how we go about bringing about a root and branch revolution in the way that we understand the importance of somatic practices basically within the education and upbringing of autistic children. Or should I just say "children"?'

DP1 was arguing against the predominance of scientific objectivity discussed in Lessons from science. At this point in the conversation I broke in:

> 'Yes, I think you should just say children and I think this is where my heart is completely and utterly with you in that it's not about the pod and it's not about the puppets, for me it's about the approach, the practitioners and the way – the mind that they go into that space with the children and the presence and the awareness that they have and the way that they interact with them. And it could be a drama practitioner or it could be a somatic movement practitioner or it could be a play therapist or a play worker and it's not about what they do.'

DP1: Could be a visual artist doing a painting.

Me: It's about how they do it and the mind and the intention with which they work. And that, to me, isn't something that's very tangible, particularly if you're looking to record it in the kinds of tests that were employed because, you know, autistic children in particular have very spikey profiles so that the results that you get may not actually in any way represent their abilities, it just represents their willingness to engage at that particular moment on that particular day with that particular person.

We agreed that in essence the work was about finding a way to meet children where they were and communicate with them there, rather than forcing them to meet and communicate on other people's terms. "If you're saying that an autistic person isn't communicating with you, no, they're not communicating with you on your terms but that doesn't mean to say that they're not communicating" (DP1).

The art of *Imagining Autism* was using drama as a way to meet the children where they were, which naturally had a tension with a scientific *need* to prove and quantify affect.

Border with education

Education equates to an intention there will be learning. *Imagining Autism* took place in schools, with the aim of giving autistic children space and environment to learn about playful engagement. DP1 described this in terms of being with children, and playing rather than teaching or researching:

> 'Within the pod, when I was doing it, I wasn't thinking about research, I'm being, I'm just with this child and trying to communicate with them or trying to find out what it is, what's the way into their world

> and having fun actually. Because [DP2] and I were watching this footage the other day of me in a dog costume trying to break into one child's world. He was with his camera the whole time, she said, "You're just like a couple of kids the pair of you". But that's what it is, you're just playing, just in the moment and responding and the joyful moment when he'll do something with you or pays attention to the thing that you're looking at and so on.'

She then described a reflective or hermeneutic spiral identical to that associated with reflective teaching (Brookfield 1995):

> 'This iterative model, you know, this idea that it is a constant spiral but you're also kind of moving on in your understandings so you jump into the spiral with all the knowledge and the baggage that you have. You have this practical experience and then you come back to analyse it and then you've moved on a bit and then you do it again and again and again so it's kind of what you call the hermaneutic spiral because it's kind of, the spiral is limited by your own experience and knowledge, what you read along the way, what you experience, you know, what you come across. So if you're a dancer and you jump in the spiral, you're going to come out with dancer-y answers and if you're a drama person, you'll come out with more drama-based, if you're a psychologist, you might come out with more psychology-based answers. But the idea of practice, this model is trying to integrate it into the reflection because the reflection alters the practice, and the practice alters the reflection.'

The intention behind the project was to scientifically evaluate the impact of the improvised drama approach. However, the research design did not factor in the impact of the evaluating team. I explained to DP1 that while the drama practitioners only worked with the children for 40 minutes a week for 10 weeks, the evaluation team were going into schools and were present in each for one to two weeks a term over a period of a year and a half. As a result, we formed strong relationships with the children, not only the ones in the project but others in their classes. We worked with them individually, and were in class and the playground doing observations. When I interviewed the teachers at the end of the project, one commented on a child who had hardly entered the pod at all and yet had had a marked change in behaviour because he was better able to deal with transitions. Whereas he would have got very upset moving from room to room or doing something different, by the end of the project that was easier. The teacher put that down to the fact he had got used to being taken out for the project and all of the assessments and tests with the evaluation team. Although they were standardised and children had to sit at a table, we tried to make them as fun and engaging as we could within the constraints. The additional one-to-one attention (or two-to-one for many tests) also had a positive impact. This child ended up showing some of the biggest advances in the standardised tests, even though he only minimally engaged with the drama practitioners. He engaged with them enough for them to be able to realise he was hypersensitive to light and darkness and needed haptic pressure. Once recognised, this allowed the school to control his environment more effectively. I explained to DP1 how the need for haptic pressure might be connected to his developmental delay, and what it might mean:

Me: It would be a sense of not knowing where you end and when the world begins. It's about boundaries, it's about skin, it's about knowing that there's a choice between touching something or not touching something. About this is me and this is other. If you think of a newborn baby and you take their clothes off, they think that you're removing part of themselves. It's that. So from a developmental perspective, it's a very, very, very early thing.

DP1: Jesus, yes, how interesting. When you were speaking, I was just trying to think about that. There was some very early work, if you read someone, I think it's Paul Schilder who was writing as early as the 20s, I have a 1950s edition and he took in a very early kind of embodiment but basically saying how when you touch something, you've got a stronger sense of the extent of your body because, it's very basic stuff but obviously, that sort of sense that you suddenly feel the division between the tips of your finger and what you're touching. If you can imagine that's a bit blurred, this would be really a very scary world really, a very scary world.

Me: Yes, because there's no control. There is no sense of this is me and this is other.

DP1: Yes, that sense of identity, as you say, very, very early kind of experience that's not. Yes, the way the baby feels more, we always feel more vulnerable on our front and that's something that happens throughout our lives, goes on throughout our lives. Possibly from that experience of lying on the back.

Me: But that's also to do with the Moro reflex, startle reflex and if you have stimulation on the front of your belly, so if you're lying on your front then you can feel much more safe and much more protected. Again, this is developmental stuff. I think this kind of, the way that you're speaking and the way that my background is why I feel quite strongly about all of this and I think, for me, there was a lot missing from, you know, the

> ideal project is of course going to be more than what there is in reality but I think in the terms of working with these kinds of children, there is so much that can be done but there is so much that is always lost in the realities of day to day. Particularly a school like [redacted] where they've got so many children with so many different needs and the classes are really big and they have up to 20 people in each of those rooms sometimes with all the children and all the teachers and all the teaching assistants. And again, these are the bits that we saw that you perhaps didn't see.

This conversation demonstrates the different theoretical approaches we had to reach the same conclusion, as well as the ways in which the different relationships we formed with this child could have allowed us to support him better earlier had we not been 'blinded' to each other's work or allowed to reflect as a group on our experiences working with the children. One of the struggles other drama practitioners had had throughout the project was the lack of time to reflect on each session within their team and to process what had happened iteratively and learn from it (Leigh and Brown 2021b). Although reflection was part of the formal evaluation of the project, this was not embodied reflection as set out in Lesson 1, but a process that required the drama practitioners to complete a weekly reflective form. DP1 told me they used to argue about who was to do that, as there was no time allocated for them.

Me: But even those forms, I've written about embodied reflection, those forms, for me, thinking about that, they're just tick-box … and they're not very … there's not much value in there because you're not asking the right questions and you're not asking in the right way … also I think the understanding needed to ask the questions depends on the practical experience.

The implications of practical experience and understanding for effective reflection was a really key point for me. These forms did not facilitate effective individual reflection, effective reflection for the drama team, and the separation of the evaluation and drama teams meant that we as evaluators were completely excluded from any reflective process. However, when the children talked to us about what they were doing, which they did because they had built relationships with us during the time we spent observing and evaluating them, it took me less than half a minute of conversation before I had a very good idea of what the drama practitioners were up to. Admittedly, not the specifics of each session, but the intention and ethos behind what they were doing. However, when I later interviewed other members of the evaluation team who were part of the same conversations with the children but had different backgrounds (that is, not in somatics), they did not pick up on these cues and the work of the drama practitioners was very much hidden from them until the project had finished.

Border with therapy

I realised that I negotiated the definition of 'therapy' when I was talking to the psychologists and the drama researchers. My somatics training was the same whether I was to work as an educator, therapist, or artistically. In psychology, therapy describes a range of approaches and frameworks that intend (or result) in a therapeutic effect (see Lesson 3). In contrast, drama therapy tends to refer specifically to Psychoanalytic drama therapists (NHS n.d.). Drama therapists would have a training and approach very different from that of a somatic movement therapist or drama practitioner, particularly one versed in improvisational techniques.

DP1: Very often what people think we did in *Imagining Autism* was a kind of drama therapy, it becomes a shorthand that's actually totally incorrect and it doesn't identify what are the key elements in the project.

Me: No, but the psychology team do refer to it as drama therapy and intervention.

An intervention in the psychological sense is something introduced to enact change or fix a problem. An intervention does not have to be therapeutic, though it can be. In the case of *Imagining Autism* the psychologists saw the 10-week drama programme in the pod as an intervention, though the majority did not recognise the impact of the evaluation team on the children as an intervention as well. After a conversation about somatics, the ways in which therapy is defined, and how somatic practitioners are supported to conduct therapy (or education, or art), DP2 related how in her view, *Imagining Autism* did border onto therapy. She was clear that the approach of the practitioners in the pod was not Psychoanalytic in style, but the study had been designed to measure whether it had had a therapeutic effect. She explained:

> 'So our orientation, I guess, was therapeutic to the extent that we were trying to ameliorate some of the symptoms – if you regard autism as a clinical condition. Now it is a clinical condition that can cause distress, and therefore I'm very cautious about using the term drama therapy because it's predicated on psychoanalysis. What we were not doing was trying to access an inner child or return children to pre-symbolic states or anything like that.

We have elements of speech therapy, we have elements of music therapy, we have elements of play therapy in what we're doing. What we did do was return the children to play. …

So in terms of therapy I think where you're in a situation where you are trying to positively address or reduce things that might be symptoms and not being able to communicate properly and not being able to recognise your emotions or the emotions of others are symptoms. So to some extent there is a therapeutic element, but it's not drama therapy.

I mean we've talked a lot about this word therapy and I actually feel a bit uncomfortable thinking that what I was doing was therapy. Even though I've just written, as I said, an article about the explosive power of this kind of work and how we have to be ethically responsible. …

But even as that, I was thinking of ourselves as drama practitioners that theatre is a powerful medium and we need to be aware of that and I still would hesitate to describe myself as a drama therapist, I wouldn't describe myself as a therapist, I really wouldn't. …

A therapist within your definition perhaps I am doing that work but I haven't had the kind of training that you talked about which was to do with protection of yourself and others and so on. And no one's ever thought it necessary that I have it or neither have I thought it necessary that the practitioners should have it so maybe that's an area we need to be looking at quite urgently.

But it is tricky because you move away from being a drama practitioner who is learning to respond in different ways perhaps, you know with all the training that we're talking about. You seem to move into a much more medical kind of area. Am I right? Or a more, um, perhaps a less creative, less arty kind of interpretation of what you're doing. Very difficult, sorry I'm thinking on my feet as I go really, it's very interesting questions of the boundary because while I'm very happy to describe myself as a theatre person, a drama practitioner, I'm not a therapist because I can't throw off that, the implications of that word even though you're telling me what I'm doing is therapy.'

It is clear that DP2 struggled to identify as a therapist in any sense, yet she was aware of the power, as she put it, of the theatre work she was doing, and this created a tangle inside her. I explained:

Me: No, I'm not telling you what you're doing is therapy, I am saying that there are similarities to what you do and the approach that you use to what other people might call therapy. And I think again it comes down to area-specific understanding of terminology.

So, for example, a lot of the people I trained with are dancers, but Dance Movement Therapy, again, is a very specific narrow way of working so I know a dance movement therapist who also trained as a somatic movement therapist but for her they were very separate ways of working and separate ways of being. …

And one of the problems in the somatic field is that it originated a lot in America and in different parts of Europe and it has kind of unfortunately become a victim of the need to copyright and trademark and to create even more silos within silos, you know, the heritage of what you do.

I went to a conference and met these people who were doing some kind of dance developmental movement work and they sneered at me because I wasn't trained in the same way that they were and I went home and I looked it up on Google and theirs was like a month course and I had six years of training and, because it's not what you do, you're discounting it because it's not using the phrases that you use. … I think this whole kind of work should be very holistic and very encompassing and very organic and yet it's very fractured.

DP2: The silo mentality I think, very telling, silos within silos if you're not careful, yes.

Me: So I'm not saying that what you do is therapy. I think it has therapeutic outcomes but I think there's dangers of going into that pod saying, 'I am doing therapy' because that isn't going in with the intention of 'I'm meeting you where you are and we're going to play and see what happens'.

DP2: Yes. Play, we haven't even said that word but yes, it's a playground.

Me: Yes and it's about from that play, things may arise and things may improve, you know. I just, I don't know, I really struggle with how it's delineated in literature, partly I think because by experience people who can do this work in practice, very rarely write about it in academia.

DP2: Yes, I think that's very true.

Me: That's what I've learned from talking to people because for me the terms are used almost interchangeably and it's much more about the practitioner's intent. In that in somatic movement you actually just tick a box whether you want to be down as an educator or a therapist or both, the training is the same. So it is how you are intending on working. So when I wrote these questions on all of my thoughts that … I wasn't really aware of all of the background of drama therapy and what that has for you as a drama practitioner. But I do come back to the question of, I think you were working with therapeutic intent, but the drama practitioners didn't have any kind of a therapeutic training or support system in place.

The lack of therapeutic training for the drama practitioners was something I felt very strongly about. I asked DP1:

> 'Do you think it would have been better or it would be something to think about in the future to have in that training more of the awareness of the therapeutic role? And I'm really hesitant about using the word therapeutic because all of the connotations of drama therapy, and I'm not saying that you should approach it from the Psychoanalytic perspective but, thinking very much about my training, the therapeutic element for me is about having that awareness of all of your shit and not bringing that into the space when you're working with that group or with that child or with that person for whatever reason and to be able to hold the space safely and to be aware of, you know, the process that's going on within that space and also the fact that they have to go out and carry on with the rest of their lives and all of the transference elements that might occur.
>
> So the fact that you might be working with this child and it might trigger something in you for whatever reason, and that you have the support and the backup and the space to take that and to process it because one of these things I think came up in the [workshop for drama practitioners working with autism].
>
> And from your drama practitioners I've talked to, two of them mentioned it that it's incredibly emotionally tiring doing this work and I think if there was the acknowledgement that you're not going in there to do therapy, but this kind of work has a therapeutic effect or it can have the potential to have a therapeutic effect and to safeguard the practitioners, would having an element of therapeutic training be useful?'

DP1: Well, because I've never done therapeutic training I don't know. I mean all that you just said to me now, I thought, 'Ooh, yes, that's interesting' because no one has ever held my hand in that way and said, 'We know this is emotionally tiring, you need to protect yourself' or what have you. I'm afraid that's quite new to me. I've never trained as a therapist in any way.
So you're saying to me that normally that would be part of the training of somebody who was undertaking some kind of a therapy?

Me: Yes. So my mum is a psychologist and a counsellor, counselling psychologist, and a supervisor and she did all of that training when I was a teenager and when I was doing my movement work and that training, she was looking at the syllabus and looking at the content of what I was doing and saying, 'This is the same'.

At that point, she was teaching on a counselling course. So the processes and procedures were very, very similar and the structures of it were very similar. The content was different as it wasn't talking therapy. I wasn't training as a talking therapist, but the need for supervision for example, so that you know that whatever goes on in that session, you have to take that elsewhere and you have to have a supervisor and it has to be regular so that you have a place to process everything that's going on.

The awareness that it's not just about what goes on in that interaction and with movement work and the kind of work that you do, even more than talking counselling, there's a certain amount of preparation that has to go on. If you need to be physical in a space, you can't just go in there cold, you have to have years, months, weeks, the moments before making sure that your body is prepared and ready to do that, otherwise you can hurt yourself and you can hurt that other person.

So it's kind of taking all of that awareness into that work. And it doesn't necessarily change the work that you do. When I was in private practice I could work therapeutically and I could work educationally with children, and I worked with children with special needs, but I also worked with musicians and dancers who would just do it because it was nice and because it helped their creativity.

You know, it was the same work and it was the same training but throughout it all there was the kind of support for training and the structures that were in place around it.

I think for me when I hear you talk, it sounds so similar in what you do, the approach you use, but in some sense it lacks that safety net for the drama practitioners which worries me I suppose.

DP1: That's interesting. 'It's drama, we don't need to have special training like that', but talking to you, actually we should have thought of that but we certainly didn't. I didn't. I think I was aware, I think we were all aware it was absolutely exhausting, you felt exhausted at the end of the day, but it's like I suppose in all my life, I've done an awful lot of work with special needs, with [my theatre company] when I was there, nobody ever sort of, it was never described as a therapy, it was always described as doing drama.

Me: Yes and I think the therapy word, it has all those other implications, especially if you think in the context of *Imagining Autism* where the psychology team probably did think of it as therapy because for them therapy is something that has a positive effect and that's what they were looking for.

So for you to say, 'But this isn't drama therapy, we're not drama therapists' but hang on, you're using drama for a therapeutic effect therefore you are a drama therapist without any of the baggage that drama therapy comes with, psychoanalytical and all this, and you work in a very specific way.

DP1: Well, what I would say, I wouldn't like to give the impression that I was irresponsible, that we were irresponsible in any way because, well not irresponsible, what I mean to say is we are all aware I think and the article I was bringing up for you was talking about the potentially explosive effect on the children of this kind of work and how absolutely essential it is that we recognise the power of the instrument that we've got, you know and that this is an ethical responsibility basically, it comes down to ethics and it's not something that you rush blindly into.

Equally, one of the things that we've only latterly recognised is the effect upon the practitioners in the sense that we were busy recording change in the children and all the rest of it but this enormous blind spot that [DP2] recently identified was that we have not, did not, measure change in the practitioners. Which is a pretty glaring omission when you think about it. But we all learn as we go along but I think it's not a mistake that we would make next time.

Me: I'm not saying that you were unethical in any way, that's not what I'm trying to imply, I suppose it's more kind of …

DP1: … gap in the training, what you're saying?

Me: I'm not sure whether it's a gap in the training, I think partly it's to do with the fact that you have this kind of work going on in silos. So there's work going on in dance, there's work going on in somatics, there's work going on in drama, but they don't necessarily talk to each other and there's no awareness of what's going on in all of these fields, so you have people thinking that they're discovering it for the first time rather than learning from the body of work.

DP1: It's really true, isn't it, one of the things I often say at the beginning of articles is we're not the only people who are working in these ways, you know?
That they share, like I was saying, the common core of the thing could be replicated across a number of different art forms, approaches, therapies. And that we can get too hung up on, 'What's the *Imagining Autism* formula? What's it about *Imagining Autism*?'.
It's like [psychologist] saying, 'We need to find out is it the puppets? Is it the masks? Is it the attitude of the practitioner?' or whatever it is, and it is no one thing.

These conversations were part of what kickstarted my thinking that I needed to write a book to address this gap, and to bring awareness to the ways in which different types of research (and art and education) can border onto therapy. They also demonstrate how disciplinary silos can inhibit researchers from placing their work in a wider context. The drama practitioners' understanding of what constituted a 'drama therapist' was a barrier, though they readily acknowledged they would benefit from the training that therapists received. The issues of transference, countertransference, and burn-out were the same in improvised drama as in psychotherapy, but the drama practitioners were just expected to deal with it. Likewise, supervision (when it was available) was for academic research, and not for the interpersonal processes associated with it. In my edited book *Conversations on Embodiment across Higher Education* (Leigh 2019a), I was struck by the number of different theoretical justifications and bodies of literature that lay behind work that was, on the face of it, very similar in purpose, intent, and affect. The disciplinary boundaries of what constituted research shaped the psychologists' view of the 'therapeutic intervention' and the questions they asked about it – wanting to find out exactly what was having an impact, how, why, and whether it could be replicated. Similarly, disciplinary differences in understanding the boundaries of what constituted art, education, and therapy resulted in barriers to researchers in accessing training and support more common to therapy for their artistic emotionally draining work that had, and was intended to have, a therapeutic and educational effect.

Case Study 3

Working with embodied academics

This case study highlights issues around positionality, anonymity, autoethnography, ownership, and dissemination in research, and exemplifies the boundaries of qualitative research with art and with therapy. It draws from a study funded by the Society for Research into Higher Education that used a range of creative approaches to explore embodied academic identity. It will explore questions around positionality and visibility in the process, the challenges and opportunities of taking an autoethnographic approach, as well as considering the outcomes of research such as dissemination and the conflicting pressures on academics to produce outputs that 'count' and are not messy.

Context

This study came about from a personal need to explore the tensions that I felt about being an academic. I worked in educational development, with responsibility for supporting others to develop their own sense of academic identity. The idea of what an academic is or should be is not always made clear to an early career researcher.

> Being an academic is something that is often bound up with a fair amount of mysticism and misperception. In movies and books, academia and campus life can be portrayed as some kind of halcyon idyll, with young people willing to learn, experiment, and have fun under the benevolent guidance of wiser men (and they very often are assumed to be men – a Google image search of 'what does a professor look like' displayed 29 white men in the first 22 images returned by this search in June 2021). However, in more recent times this has changed, with academics portrayed as 'the bookish but socially challenged swot or the egomaniac self-publicist that communicates his or her elevated status at every available opportunity' (Back 2016: 68). Les Back goes on to say 'Academics themselves don't much like other academics, and often feel a deep estrangement from their colleagues as people. Perhaps part of the problem is that our forms of self-presentation are tied to the modern academic desire to be taken seriously – that is, the embodiment of entrepreneurialism, "being smart" and "world-class" braininess.' Back, along with other commentators and researchers, blames the

> shifts seen in the 'modern academic' on the neoliberal university, which captures academics' dispositions towards hard work and achievement and overlays them with demands. Back states 'Academics should see themselves first as teachers' (Back 2016: 46) but this sentiment is at odds with advice given to early career academics to focus instead on their research, grant income, and markers of esteem in order to attain success (Fanghanel 2012). Teaching, whilst an integral component of the kinds of professional and educational development courses found for early career researchers in the UK, Australia, and parts of Europe, is not recognised nor rewarded in the same way as conventional research outputs or cold hard cash (Prondzynski 2014).
>
> The current accelerated pace of the academic world is sometimes termed 'fast academia' (Vostal 2016). Work is experienced like a treadmill (Rosa 2010) with the associated symptoms of overwork and illness endemic (Acker and Armenti 2004; Gill 2016). Universities have to run as businesses, with the purpose of higher education changing from individual transformation to producing goods and workers for the knowledge economy (Williams 2013). Squeezing budgets to maximise profit results in a need for academics to increase the speed and productivity of their work without losing quality – though as Bourdieu says 'you can't think when you're in a hurry' (Bourdieu 1998: 28). Speed and acceleration of this kind is tied to the political economy of capitalism (Vostal 2016). (Leigh et al 2022c: 33)

This speed and acceleration of academic work has led to an increase in the expectations of what an academic should produce, which in turn has resulted in overwork and harm to academics (Gill 2016). As I shared in the introduction, my journey was not straightforward or conventional, and I found academia to be very critical, cerebral, and judgemental. Indeed, criticality, and the idea of being able to think critically, is a key quality long associated with 'good' students and 'good' teaching (Brookfield 1995). The demands of academia to work at an accelerated pace and to be hyperproductive (Kyvik and Aksnes 2015), and the idea that taking time for oneself (or even one's work) was shameful (Shahjahan 2019) was in stark contrast to my embodied practice. The ethos of my somatics and movement practice was to be non-judgemental, accepting, and present to myself and others in the world around me. My background in embodiment and therapy rather than a more traditional or respected discipline caused me another point of tension as I sought to develop my own credibility as an academic (Leigh 2019d). I did not feel that my practice was valued in education as much as it might have been in a field such as dance or drama where Practice-as-Research is accepted (see Lessons from art). My research was described as 'bleeding' rather than 'cutting' edge by a research director, due to my emphasis on the unspoken and creative ways of connecting with participants and disseminating my research. I am thankful that as I have progressed through my career my approach has been valued more by those who are senior to me, specifically because of the way in which creative and embodied methods can allow people to share and voice what would otherwise remain unspoken. However, when I was developing the research idea for this particular project, the tensions between my disciplinary background, research approach, and the 'norms' of academic research and careers were very pertinent. Nevertheless, my practice still formed the bedrock of my work and informed my research approach and writing. I felt more authentic when I allowed myself to be truer to my background rather than performing what I thought an academic 'should' be or 'should' write. Part of my journey in designing the study was reaching out to academics who seemed to be exploring similar tensions in their own work, which resulted in the edited book *Conversations on Embodiment across Higher Education* (Leigh 2019a). A large part of that book had been bringing people into conversation with each other by inviting each author to respond to another's contribution.

Another layer to the tension I felt between my practice and academic identity at that time was due to my experience of ill health and chronic illness after I gave birth to my youngest child. When I returned to work following maternity leave I was unwell, but at the time did not realise how much this was affecting me and how I had internalised my own ableism. Illness and disability are not easy to navigate within academia (Brown and Leigh 2020). While the proportion of people in the general population with a chronic illness, disability, or neurodivergence is estimated to be at least 30%, in academia disclosure rates are around just 4–5% (Brown and Leigh 2018b). Disciplines that have pronounced gender inequality (such as a high proportion of men to women or other marginalised genders) tend to have disability disclosure rates that are even lower. Disabled staff do not fit the hyperproductive norm of academia (Navarro 2017). I followed the study I share here by exploring embodied experiences of ableism, invisible disability, neurodivergence, and chronic illness (Finesilver et al 2020; Leigh 2021). I keep a reflexive journal, and shared part of this in a book chapter on internalised ableism. This extract exemplifies the tensions that I felt as I did my best to perform the role of an academic while feeling the pull to honour my own experience of ill health and lack of wellbeing.

> *Coming to terms, 2015*
>
> So I'm feeling very emotional. The ramifications and consequences of being ill seem to be looming larger than ever.
>
> It feels like I am having to prove myself three times over to make up for being ill. As though I am being punished for being ill. As though living it is not enough.

What's the line between bullying/discrimination? Being treated differently? Made to feel as though I wanted to be ill?

They call it 'brain fog' – for me it was a complete inability to process. I could hear but not understand what people were saying. I was disorientated, confused. This made me anxious.

It was only when I began to feel better – when I started on the correct medication – that I realised that not only was my brain fogged, but my body also.

My research is about embodiment, about being in the body, and not only could I not think, but I could not feel into my own body. Moving was painful. Exhausting. Where once it had been a source of energy.

The invisible illness/disability aspect of this is so pertinent too. Am I protected? Who protects me? I am fighting to do my job to live my life and every thought is a struggle. But other people can't see it. I don't feel like 'me'.

But they don't know who 'me' is. They assume/think I don't know what. I'm slacking? I want to be like this? It's an excuse? That I'm trying to get out of teaching to do research?

I was told to concentrate on what I could do – research, writing. I could do this – slowly. But not creatively. No original thoughts. Yet when I did this it was seen as an easy option?

I remember applying for conferences – but it was vetoed because it would upset the team if I went to a conference when I wasn't teaching.

Complete lack of understanding.

Thing is, it's only now, when I am feeling so much more like myself, that I can conceptualise it and write more, express what it was.

But I'm not in it any more.

That said, I'm not yet out of it either. Am I disabled?

I have a disabling condition.

Where does that sit with a marginalised status?

Or not?

It is hard to have a voice if my mind is not processing my body isn't working.

I need to move tomorrow to prepare.

To protect.

Am I subject to more scrutiny than my peers? It feels that way.

New normal, 2016

I used to feel an expert in my own body and my ability to read others. Now I don't. This brain/body fog that inhabits and pains me obscures my sense of myself and my confidence is shaken when it comes to anyone else. I don't inhabit or represent what I believe and

I feel I 'should'. How can I help anyone else or educate them when they only have to look at me to see how I am lacking?

This inability/unwillingness to accept how I am as a new normal does seem to be driven by the need to produce, to drive around, when in fact in my body I am crying out to do nothing but rest and breathe and heal. I need to heal so much. Then I resent this academy that keeps pushing me to injure myself. I feel broken but I don't know if they can see or if they care.

Broken academy, 2017

I want to acknowledge the structural issues such as overwork or casualisation that are endemic in the academy. Recently I found myself delivering a session to postgraduate research students at my university on 'balancing research, teaching and life'. I was struck by the irony of this, as my co-facilitator and I had been exchanging emails about the session at 11 pm and 5 am in the previous days, and I arrived for the session itself hot and out of breath, having run from nursery drop-off to meeting after meeting to get there. How can we preach the need for wellbeing when we model anything but? When we are driven to do anything but? Is this an environment I would want my daughter to be in? I'd want her to have her eyes wide open. Why do I think of it as a win when a PhD student tells me that they are looking for a career outside academia?

Being perfect, 2019

Today I taught for 5 hours. I was in a room full of people who needed and expected me to show them how to teach, while also expecting the day to be a waste of time, and not wanting to be there. I sometimes feel like I am a performing monkey. I have to be upbeat, I have to have energy, I have to be engaged, I have to be good. I have to be the teacher they dream of being. I have to deliver the right message. Teaching is fun. Teaching is worthwhile. Last week I was teaching a different full-day course and I was so aware of the cost it had on me. I hadn't been practising, I didn't feel strong in my body and I was hyper-aware of how hard it was even to stand. My pores were tired, I wasn't able to hold the energy in the room without leaning or sitting, and yet the room layout was such that I couldn't sit and be seen by everyone. When I would normally perch on a table the table tipped up. I wasn't on my own. I don't think anyone else 'noticed' and the feedback we had was good. But I knew that to get through this week and next, teaching for five hours at a stretch day after day, I needed to be more in my body. This means that for the last four days I have got up at 6 am to practise, to be more in my body, to feel whether today

I am stiff (always) or off balance, or where I need to be gentle with myself. And yet I end today with iron behind my eyes clamping them down because I know that I can't rest and recover and recuperate ready for tomorrow, instead I have to sit and write and think and be creative because this manuscript is due in. I cannot take the time I need and it is costing me. My teeth hurt, I am so tired. I don't have it in me to put in the hours in the evening, at the weekend, that I need to do to get it all done. Others would. Others do. But I can't. I am only one day into this teaching load. The pressure is relentless. And still, in the classes, I am continually putting in more content, asking my students, my would-be teachers, to consider the needs of their students, to consider their own needs as teachers, to be aware of the pressures of overwork and hyper-productivity. I asked them to think about what it means to be a good teacher, while modelling being one, engaging with them, conducting the class, as one said, as an adaptive stand-up comedian. She didn't mean that I had a comedy routine, but that I had to adapt and change what I did to fit the needs of the room. Which is what a good teacher does. But a good teacher doesn't flake out or fade out when her students are talking. I did. A good teacher isn't counting the minutes until the class ends so she can get on with something else, something that counts more. I did. And should a good teacher be a role model? I think so. But I did not tell them my story even after a conversation around disclosing aspects of your identity as a teacher and acting as a role model. At the end of the day we talked about the things every teacher should know. I said 'don't be a dick'. It covers a lot. And they said 'a shitty session doesn't mean you're a shitty teacher'. I feel shitty right now, what does that count for?

Seen from the outside, 2019

Good job on handling the late student and demonstrating professionalism.

I expected to fall asleep in 5 minutes but it was very interesting.

Really well-led talk, managed to keep attention for a long period of time.

I loved the fact that you refer to what you did earlier in the workshop as an example of group management.

I really enjoyed this … Pace of the lesson was great and was an excellent example of the kind of teaching I'd like to do. (Leigh and Brown 2020: 165)

This highlights the performative aspects of teaching and being academic as well as the differences between reflection as a mirror, reflexivity as an embodied process, and being seen by others. The evaluations and feedback I received did not resonate with my inner experience.

I designed the research project on embodied academic identity in 2015. I carried it out over a year – 2016–17 – and continued to analyse and write about my findings through 2018–19. Ultimately, I wanted to find out whether I was alone in feeling opposing pulls from my embodied practice and academic work and the need to perform as an academic, and if I was not, how others managed these along with their own sense of wellbeing.

Research approach

The project used a variety of arts-based creative research methods as a form of Embodied Inquiry (Leigh and Brown 2021a) in order to encourage the participants to reflect on and to share their experiences of reconciling an embodied practice with their academic work. I asked academics who self-identified as having an embodied practice to take part. It was a sample of convenience in that I asked people I knew who had embodied practices or whose work I had read and enjoyed, and they cascaded this out to their own networks. After full ethical approval I met with 12 academics individually for between two and four hours, and they all shared their practices with me as well as reflecting on aspects of their embodied and academic identities. The practices they shared included dance, yoga, martial arts, meditation, Alexander Technique, and climbing among others (see Figure 14). The academics came from a variety of disciplines including mathematics, dance, drama, anthropology, music, and education. The meetings all took place

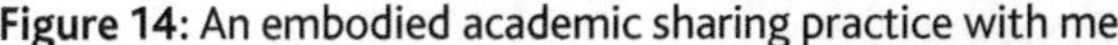

Figure 14: An embodied academic sharing practice with me

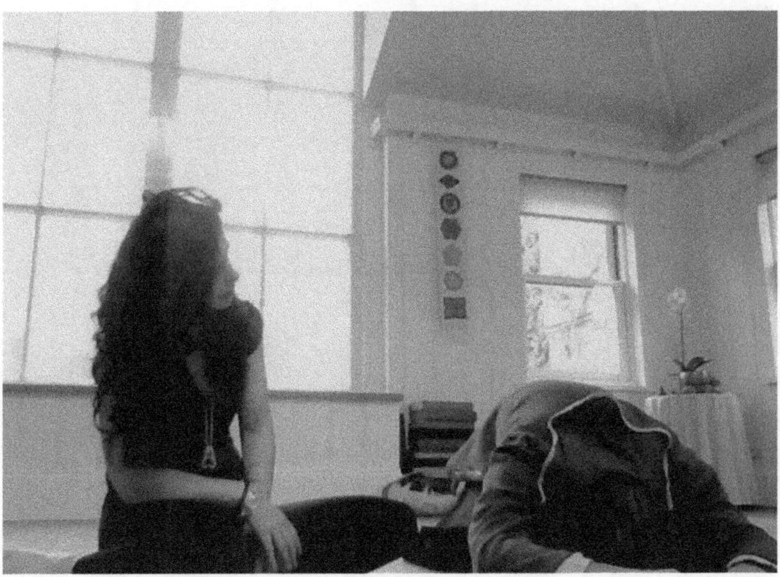

in studio spaces away from the academic office, and the participants had access to high-quality art materials to use at all times. The meetings were recorded audially as well as filmed on my laptop. The audio recordings were transcribed, and the video footage was later edited together with an academic film maker to produce a video essay (Leigh and Blackburn 2017). The research showed how important their embodied practice was to these academics' sense of wellbeing (Leigh 2019b), and the tensions that they experienced between the two aspects of their identity (Leigh 2019c).

Borders with art and therapy

This project generated a lot of art. Some was created by participants as they reflected on questions and the embodied and academic aspects of their identity as a form of elicitation. For example, Figure 15 illustrates one of several drawings created in response to the question 'How do your embodied and academic practices affect your sense of wellbeing?'.

Although wellbeing had not been a main focus of the study, the way that nearly all of the academics related their embodied practice to their understanding and sense of wellbeing was one of my key findings:

> Wellbeing is a funny concept, apart from a lack of consensus over how it is spelt, there are many discourses over what it actually means. The UK National Account of Well-being (2012) defines it as a dynamic

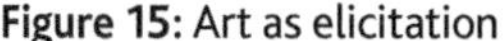

Figure 15: Art as elicitation

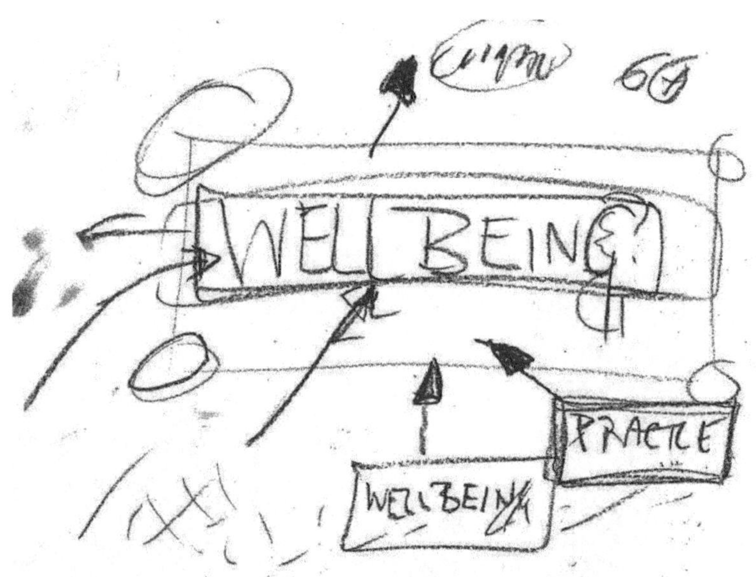

> thing, a sense of vitality that people need to undertake meaningful activities, to help them feel autonomous and as if they can cope. However, as Richard Bailey puts it, 'many of these discussions take it for granted that wellbeing equates to mental health' (Bailey 2009: 795). In turn, mental health seems to be conflated with being 'happy', or with factors that are personal, and to do with whether life is going well for the individual or not. Griffin (1996) explicitly connects wellbeing with happiness, similar to Aristotle's idea of it being the fulfilment of human nature (Barrow 1980). Philosophically, wellbeing can be associated with either a hedonistic 'desire fulfilment' whereby it is achieved when an individual has sated their desires, or as a more objective theory which judges whether things are good for people or not (Parfit 1984). This latter view is one which sometimes results in lists of factors that indicate wellbeing or quality of life (Nussbaum 2000) and quantitative measures of wellbeing (Sen 1999). However, quality of life should be seen as a dimension of wellbeing rather than be conflated as the same thing (Dodge et al 2012). Practices that increase awareness and the quality of consciousness have been reliably shown to have a significant role in increasing wellbeing (Brown and Ryan 2003). Embodied practices such as yoga, mindfulness, and Authentic Movement, a structured dance form that draws on Jungian principles (Adler 2002), contribute to wellbeing through enhancing this sense of present awareness and a wholeness of mind, body and spirit (Bacon 2015). Wellbeing is often measured quantitatively, and yet if we are looking for embodied answers to research questions, how should we go about collecting data? (Leigh 2019a: 224–25)

My embodied approach seemed to allow for the capture of what wellbeing meant to my participants.

Ownership of art created as part of research is not always clear-cut. The data that were generated as part of the project 'belonged' to me. Part of the consent process had been that the participants agreed to let me keep and use their art – their drawings, paintings, mark-makings, and the like. The participants also consented for me to use their images and recordings, though I went back to each person who was featured in the video essay to ensure that they had an opportunity to assent to being included in the film as well. Research ethics processes often prioritise anonymity, however this is not as easily achievable when using video, and in the case of the film output each academic asked for their name to be shared in addition to allowing use of footage that showed their face. As well as encouraging the participants to reflect using the arts-based materials and talking, I also used movement as a research tool. Part of this was by asking the participants to share their practice with me. Where their practice overlapped with my own practice of Authentic Movement (Adler 2002), I was also able to use this directly as a research tool.

Rather than sharing the overall findings from the research, in order to illustrate the border between research, art, and therapy I wanted to reflect on two meetings with one participant. She shared a particularly harrowing journey as she attempted to establish her own academic identity through her doctoral studies, as well as some of the art that was created by her and in response to her story. I do this to demonstrate the emotional containing and holding necessary to support her. This participant, given the pseudonym Kimberley, shared her story of both her embodied practice which gave her immense satisfaction and joy, and her academic work, which, at the first time we met consisted of over seven years of a PhD including periods of intermission that she was struggling with. She did not identify as an academic, she said, 'I always feel like I don't measure up'. At that point she was not sure whether she wanted to finish or not:

> 'Finishing it, well one way or another it's going to get off my back because I've got a time limit and I've got to either decide that I'm not going to finish it which is a whole process in itself and it's quite a difficult thing to do … it was really messing me up big time and I just felt, "I can't do this".' (Kimberley, 1st meeting)

There was a lot of emotional content for Kimberley around her academic work – "I'm going to probably cry a lot in this because I cry every time I talk about this" – and yet she wanted to talk about it: "It's probably good to talk about it although I'm not saying anything new. But yeah, I've put so much energy into not just the work that I've done but trying to work it out, work out why I'm doing it, work out whether I should be doing it." Kimberley went on to say:

> 'I know there's a lot of other stuff tied up in the PhD which I've tried to work through or I've sort of been working through and sometimes I feel like I'm just making excuses, though I suppose the thing is that … my dad was an academic and for him, I mean I've talked to my mum a bit about this, you know, she said really it's just that he couldn't imagine other ways of having pleasure through your work and so for him, an academic career was always going to be what he aspired to for us. He died on the day that my MA [Masters's degree] started, which was also at my university, so it's almost like that's really tied up with the whole kind of academic process, especially there.' (Kimberley, 1st meeting)

Kimberley drew an image that represented her embodied identity (Figure 16) which showed use of reds, oranges and yellow colours, and bold strokes that

Figure 16: Kimberley's embodied identity

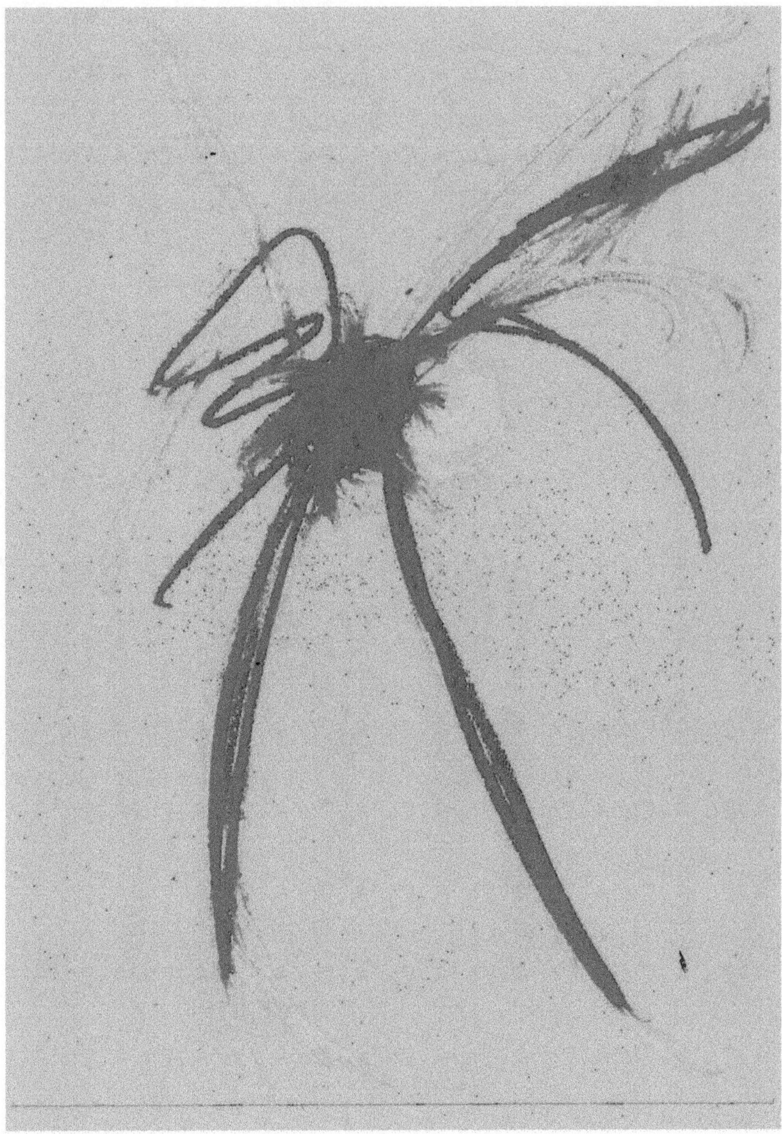

indicated movement and energy moving the figure off the page. In contrast, the image Kimberley drew of her academic identity was dark and forbidding, with a large rectangular building looking over her small figure and crushing her to the ground. The doors to the building had jaws that threatened to chew her up, and she positioned her supervisors, the academics, at the top of the ivory tower, and other PhD students inhabiting a liminal position half in and half out the tower (see Figure 17).

Figure 17: Kimberley's academic identity

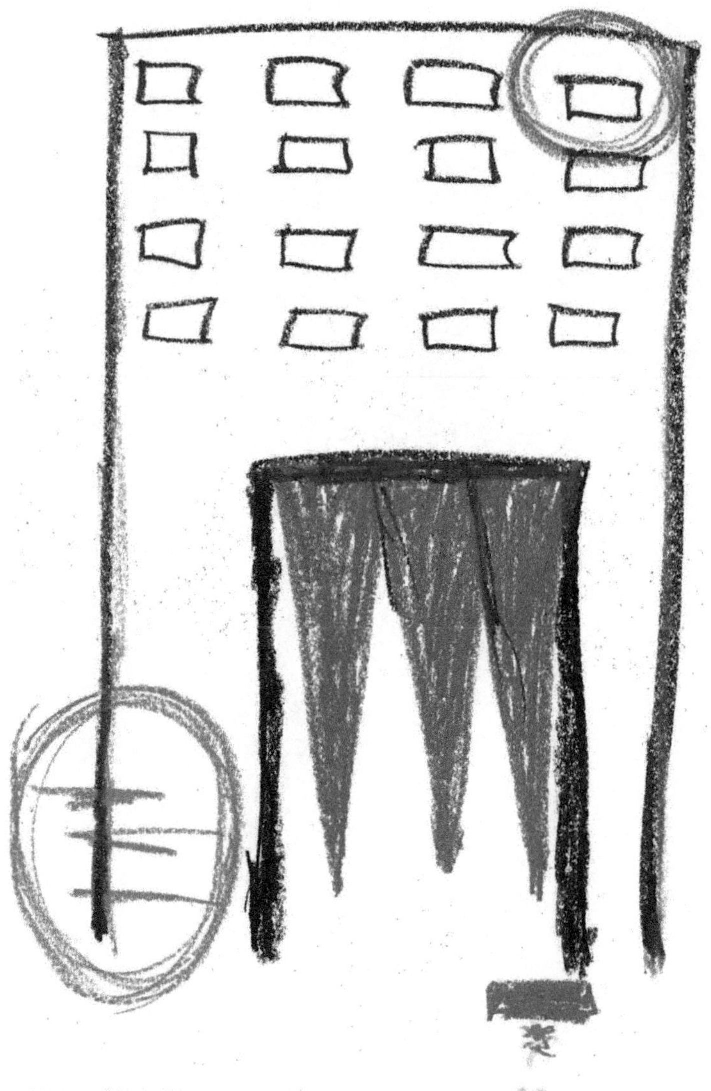

Kimberley shared her dance-based practice with me, demonstrating an exercise that she used with students. I was asked to close my eyes, and she led me round the room, up, down, over, touching and interacting with various objects she found. This playful exercise allowed Kimberley to traverse the connections between her academic identity and embodied identity, and how they did not necessarily need to be in opposition with each other. As we talked after this exercise, I made marks or drew in bright colours on a

Figure 18: Responding to Kimberley

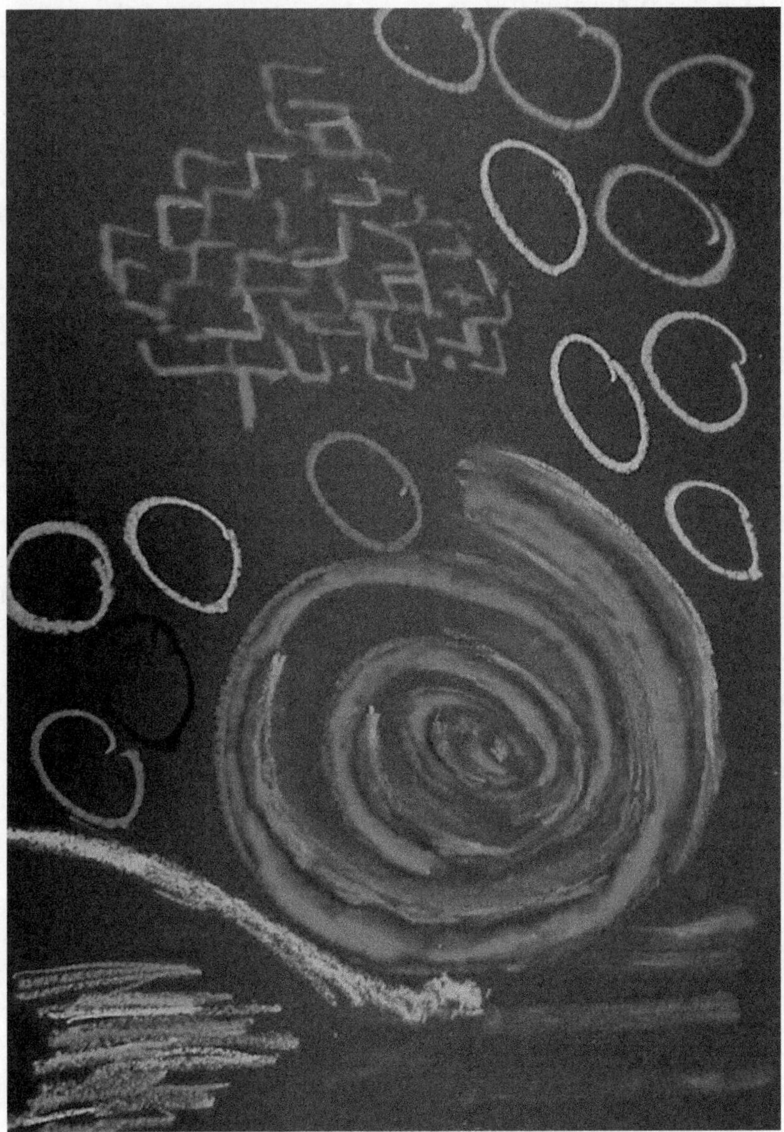

black piece of card, inscribing bubbles, interlocking puzzle pieces, as well as a spiral tunnel (see Figure 18).

This first meeting lasted two hours. Kimberley found the process emotional but helpful, likening it to a therapeutic encounter, and asked to meet again. Kimberley was the only participant in the study who I met with twice. At our second meeting she said, 'I've got a final, final deadline for this PhD … and I still don't quite know whether it's going to happen or not'. We used Authentic Movement as a tool this time, as both Kimberley and I had practised the form in the past.

Authentic Movement is termed as process work and draws on Jungian archetypes (Hartley 2004). It can be used therapeutically in order to allow a mover to process their experiences, as well as a method for research (Bacon 2015). When practised in a pair or dyad here, two people work together. The witness is responsible for providing a boundary, which can be equated to establishing a secure relational field. This equates to keeping the time that has been agreed, and ensuring that when they speak, they do so 'in service' to the mover. This means that the witness, like a therapist, has to intentionally choose how and what they say – for example, if a particular movement pool made them imagine pain, death, or a traumatic image, it would not necessarily be helpful to share this. There are many variations to the form of Authentic Movement (Adler 2022). A dyad often allows mover and witness to swap roles and take turns moving and witnessing. It can be practised in a large circle where people move into and out of the space, taking roles as mover or witness as the impulse takes them, though this usually requires one person to act as an anchor or witness for the whole time. When used more for therapeutic or process work as here, only one partner of the dyad moves and the other holds the space and boundary for them to do so. Usually a mover speaks first, and the witness responds to them, and the form is that both use the present tense to differentiate it from other ways of speaking (Adler 2002). Kimberley moved while I witnessed. Kimberley described her movement pool:

> 'Curled up on my side in the sun and I get sun on the back of my neck, I really enjoy that, I'm crying and I just want to howl and I feel like I can't, like I can't just let all this out. So I'm kind of … just feeling that kind of tension between wanting to let it out and how I'm holding it, which is kind of. … So then I turn onto my front, it's easier to have my face in the sun but it's not quite worked because my face has changed as well, so I'm probably just trying to get back to where that was … I'm lifting my head away from the floor and I can feel the wetness of the floor from the tears underneath my cheek … I just need to howl and again I'm sort of stopping myself and I start biting my lip quite hard … I'm really feeling all of this tension in my body because I suddenly think about yielding and then I think well I'm full of all this tension and then I think well, I wanted to move and I haven't really moved so I kind of lift my left elbow up into the air and then sort of start moving my arms but especially feel my elbows, like my elbows seem to be leading this movement and there's a lot of effort in it and I'm actually really enjoying the effort … when it stops and I come to rest on the floor, I feel much, much calmer.' (Kimberley, 2nd meeting)

I witnessed her moving and said back to her:

> 'I see you on the floor and my eyes are really drawn to your ribs … I'm really aware of your breath and the way that your ribs and your chest are expanding in three dimensions, the whole of the back of you and everything is moving with your breathing and then it kind of stops and starts and I can't see your face so I don't know if you're crying but I'm very aware of the stopping and starting, your breathing and the way that you're breathing with the whole of your body … even though it's not smooth and it's not easy but all of you is breathing and I see you breathe and I'm breathing as I see you breathe.
>
> I'm aware of the context of here and that feeling of … making space and feeling constrained and feeling constricted and whether that's from this whole academic thing and that process of changing, changing what is there to make room and to change, so that you're not, this is my imagining, my wanting for you not to feel constricted but to make space and to change what is around you so that it has space and there is room for you to be whatever you want to be and when I see you resting again on the floor, lying on your side, still curled up away from me, I see your breathing is quieter and stiller and as I said, I'm imagining you more at peace and there's a contrast at the beginning, you were curled towards me actually and one arm's towards me, your right arm is towards me and it was almost as though you were cradling, I see you cradling yourself or someone and that tension that you speak of, seems to resonate in my body and less so at the end.'

Kimberley responded, 'I really like that image of making room, that feels very satisfying. Because I didn't really have many images forming, I was just … there was the emotion that really felt like grief.'

Kimberley and I both drew and painted images after she had moved and been witnessed (see Figures 19 and 20).

What is striking in these two images is the way that both contain references to the sun, which seems to symbolise a sense of hope, growth, or renewal in response to the idea of making room. However, both also have references to blocks or barriers. Kimberley's image has interlocking lines or frames, woven at points with what could be red wire, wrapping about a young tree stem. Mine is more abstract, with regular vertical lines backed up with dots, or contrasting colours and shapes. I shared the transcript of our session with Kimberley, and she used this as well as our meetings to invigorate the remainder of her studies, which she did successfully finish later that year.

As can be seen from these extracts, Kimberly went deep into her emotional process in both of our meetings and utilised them as therapeutic encounters. Had these taken place in a conventional interview scenario or using a

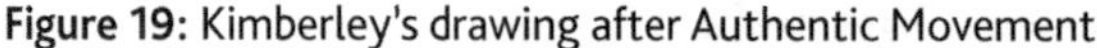

Figure 19: Kimberley's drawing after Authentic Movement

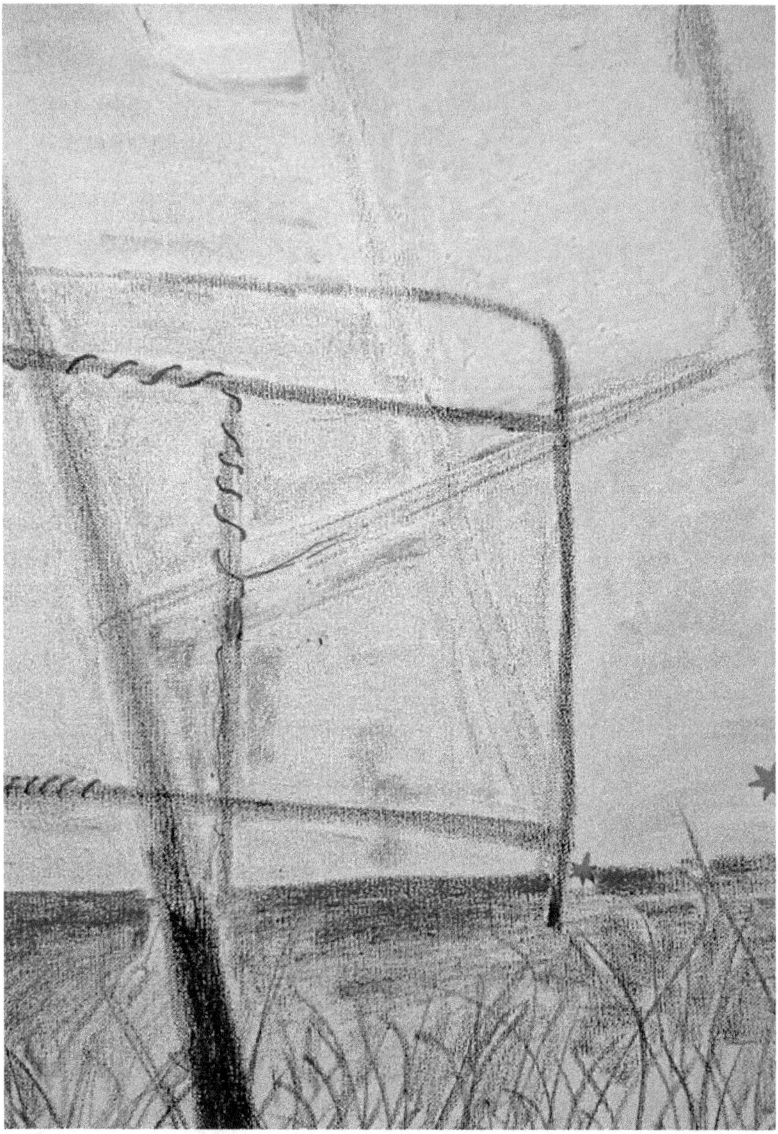

conventional research approach I do not think that she would have shared so much of her own emotional story and grief or been able to turn them to positive effect. I provided Kimberley the opportunity to express her thoughts through creative methods and create representations of words that had before been unspoken, bringing up into consciousness the schism that she felt between her embodied and academic identities and recognising where the root of this lay. Interweaving movement, used artistically and within a

Figure 20: My response to Kimberley after Authentic Movement

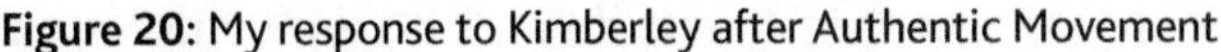

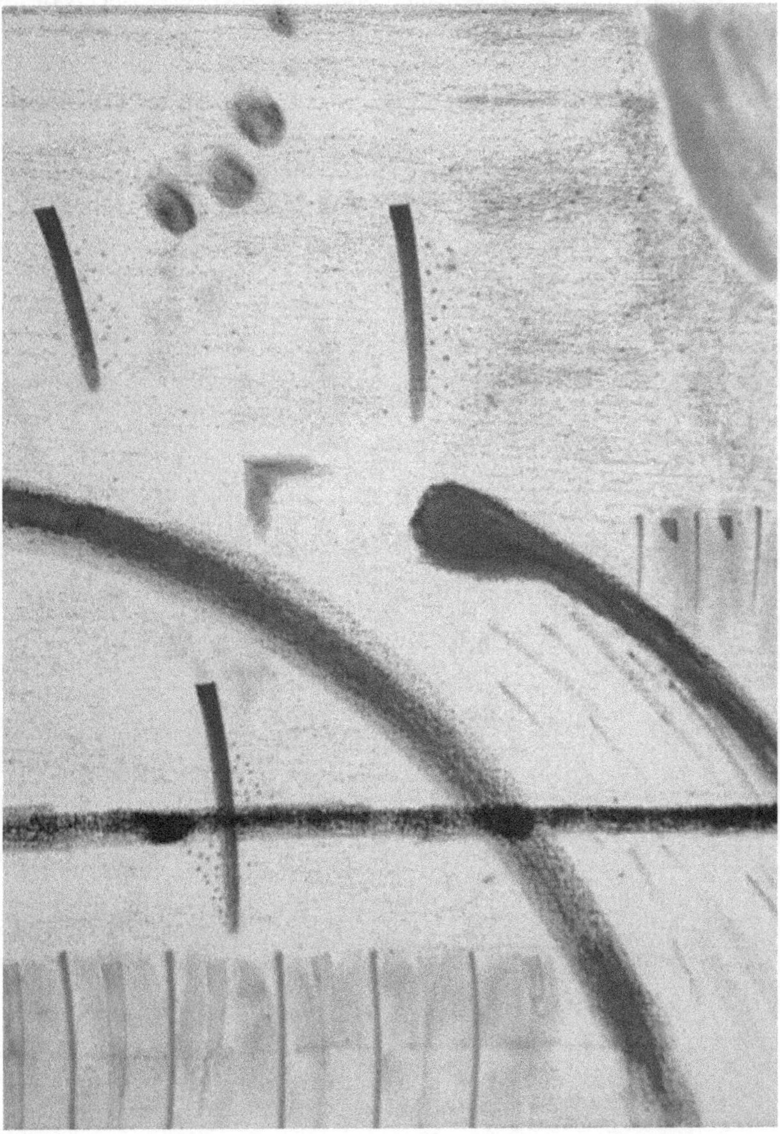

context and form that Kimberley recognised as boundaried enough to allow her to process her experiences, facilitated a breakthrough – a moment of sunshine pooling on the floor through a window – that broke through her grief and allowed her the impetus to continue with and ultimately finish her academic journey with her PhD. These meetings with Kimberley went beyond research and moved towards therapy, though it must be noted that this was not true about all the meetings I had with participants in this study. Many shared with me that they found them valuable, being given the opportunity to reflect and make connections between aspects of their identity and lives that they had always thought were separate, but that does not make them therapeutic encounters. Kimberley was very vocal about the value she saw in our meetings, and the ways in which they helped her to untangle her identity and relationship with academia, and ultimately how they supported her to finish and submit her doctorate. I was very present to the need to hold space for Kimberley, to allow her to process and to start her journey towards acceptance and change. Faced with her need, my intention was in service to her, and not focused on data collection. I was able to do this because of my therapeutic training and background, and yet I am aware that other researchers without this experience and knowledge might not be able to hold space for their participants in the same way.

Case Study 4

Working with scientists

This case study of my work with the international WISC network exemplifies the borders of qualitative research with science and therapy. Integrating and using qualitative research methods – explicitly embodied, creative, and reflective research methods – with scientists and in a scientific context allowed us all the opportunity to reflect on the ways in which research approaches and dissemination are defined by disciplinary boundaries. My work with international Principal Investigators and research groups felt at times like either teaching or group therapy, and definitely required my full set of therapeutic skills and holding, particularly as the bulk of the work was undertaken online throughout the COVID-19 pandemic.

Context

In the very first chapter of this book, I shared the story of how I came to qualitative research after initially studying chemistry at both undergraduate and postgraduate levels. That I ended up leaving science is unfortunately all too common. Women are marginalised in chemistry (Royal Society of Chemistry 2018), with the largest attrition occurring post-PhD (Royal Society of Chemistry 2019a). Although I left during a PhD and not after completion, I contribute to the statistics around the lack of retention for women and other marginalised groups. Those that choose to stay continue to have challenges. The Royal Society of Chemistry (RSC) recognised that women in the chemical sciences face barriers in publishing (Royal Society of Chemistry 2019b), which can be thought of as akin to microaggressions as defined by Sara Ahmed (2017). Even before the COVID-19 pandemic impacted women academics to a greater extent than men due to uneven loads of caring responsibilities and work distribution (Gabster et al 2020), the RSC stated that the rate of change meant gender parity would never be reached (Royal Society of Chemistry 2019a). The chemical sciences are not unique in this. The scientific community is not known for its diversity with respect to gender (Greider et al 2019), race (Makgoba 2020), sexuality (Smith 2020), or disability (CRAC 2020). Of course, the barriers that face an individual with a protected characteristic are intersectional (Crenshaw 1989) and compound.

The international WISC network was initially created to support a small group, before being scaled to build an intersectional sense of community supporting the retention and progression of women in the field. It began with a group of four women in the UK and Europe who began to meet every two weeks on Skype to ameliorate their feelings of loneliness and isolation, and to find peer mentoring and support (the full story of how WISC came to be formed can be found in the open access book *Women in Supramolecular Chemistry* (Leigh et al 2022c)). When Jennifer Hiscock, Cally Haynes, Claudia Caltagirone, and Anna McConnell began to expand their model of peer mentoring and support to the wider community, they wanted to make sure that the network was community-led. Although they thought that a mentoring programme would be useful for others, they wanted to survey the community to find out whether there was a need or desire for this, and other kinds of activities that they wanted to engage in. I had become friends with Jen H in the years after I had met her as a student on a course I was teaching. Then, she had been a new lecturer, and part of a cohort taking the introductory module of the Post Graduate Certificate in Higher Education. Now, she me to take a look at the draft WISC survey, knowing that I also taught research methods and research design. When I looked at the survey I quickly saw it was not fit for purpose and would not find answers to the questions they wanted to know. I rewrote it for them, and Jen responded by co-opting me onto the WISC Board and making me Vice Chair (Research). We launched the survey in November 2019, and in the year it was open collected 100 responses.

WISC employs an area-specific approach that 'calls in' the community to support its own (Caltagirone et al 2021a, 2021b). In addition to a programme that included mentoring, webinars (in collaboration with the RSC's Macrocyclic and Supramolecular Chemistry Special Interest Group), in-person skills workshops and events, and resources collected within a website (WISC 2020); WISC utilised my qualitative research and expertise in equality, diversity, and inclusivity to develop a research programme. This resulted in research disseminated to the chemistry community that explored the community's need for support (Caltagirone et al 2021b), their experiences doing and managing research through COVID-19 (Leigh et al 2022b), and life as a woman in STEM (Leigh et al 2022a). WISC have also published a series of articles as comments around families for *Nature Reviews Chemistry* (Leigh et al 2022a, 2022d; Slater et al 2022) as well as book chapters on the importance of community (Leigh et al 2023) and creative data analysis (Leigh et al 2024b).

WISC created a community and place where I was able to integrate myself and capture stories and experiences so that they could be shared. What is most novel is that I was able to give these women the means and tools to do this from an embodied perspective, using the skills I had developed through my therapeutic practice, and sharing qualitative research methods including collaborative autoethnography (Bochner and Ellis 2016; Chang et al 2016), and creative methods (Kara 2015) such as video (Harris 2016) and fiction (Leavy 2016).

Research approach

WISC formally launched in November 2019 with that first online survey (Caltagirone et al 2021b). Jen H and I had been working in the background, writing an element of creativity and reflection into her UKRI Future Leaders Fellowship (FLF) application to explore her evolution as a leader, and developing the idea into a separate bid for a British Academy (BA), Royal Academy of Engineering, Royal Society, and Leverhulme funded interdisciplinary BA APEX application (BA 2021). The BA APEX study was to explore the impact of creative and reflective methods on the lived experiences and scientific careers of women Principal Investigators (PIs) and how they ran their research groups. In chemistry, as in many disciplines of science, in order to progress in your career it is necessary to obtain a PhD and often to undertake one or more fixed-term postdoctoral research posts working for a PI before applying for independent funding in the form of a fellowship or grant. Many of these early career fellowships allow for the starting of a group, which would be composed of a combination of undergraduate and postgraduate students and/or postdoctoral researchers. The jump to being independent is a recognised challenge for all those who wish to remain in academia, and particularly so for those who are marginalised (Caltagirone et al 2021b). We proposed setting up a collaborative autoethnography group (Chang et al 2016) for six women PIs across the UK and Europe, which would allow them to share and reflect on their experiences, as well as to conduct rhythmanalysis (Lyon 2019) in the spaces where their research group worked in order to find out more about how they moved through spaces and interacted, with the overall aim to increase communication and collaboration. We also proposed working with a UK research group, directly involving them in creative and reflective activities. In 2020 we found out that not only had Jen H been awarded an FLF, but that we had also won funding for our BA APEX study and were given the opportunity to apply to an additional public engagement fund.

The COVID-19 pandemic changed the nature of our study. Laboratories were shut, and even when they re-opened numbers were limited. Given the priority to support the research group, it was not appropriate for me to take up space to film and conduct a rhythmanalysis, if that meant taking a place from a research student with limited access due to strict number limits in rooms. The lab groups were not able to use the space in the rooms in the same way that they had pre-COVID-19, and the value of conducting a rhythmanalysis seemed somewhat dubious. In addition, there was a lot of anxiety from students and staff about the presence of cameras, in case we 'caught' them not complying to rules around distancing, masking, or the like. These rules were constantly shifting and changing, and the institutional priorities were obviously on supporting and educating students and adapting to remote work and study. The collaborative autoethnography project had always been intended to run online. However, the pressures of living and working through a pandemic led to an increase in mental health issues for many academics (Abbott 2021), and gender disparities were quick to emerge (Flaherty 2020; Gabster et al 2020). There were additional challenges for mothers and those who were responsible for caring for others, as in academia they were often expected to continue working from home responding to the demand for online delivery, as well as supporting remote schooling for children. Pressures for academic mothers are well known (Evans and Grant 2008), and the specific challenges faced by women scientists and mothers are not new (Monosson 2008). However, through the pandemic scientist mothers faced additional penalties (Powell 2021). Due to this, the collaborative autoethnography group expanded. There was a real need and desire for support, and we felt very strongly that we wanted to ensure as much as possible that anyone who asked to participate in the group when they heard about the project was welcomed in as far as we could make possible. By the end of the BA APEX funding there were 16 members in the WISC collaborative autoethnography group from across the UK, USA, Europe, and Japan, in both academia and industry. On top of this I was asked to support and create additional collaborative autoethnography groups, including ten women PIs from South Africa (predominantly bioscientists), and women bioscientists across the Eastern Arc universities collaboration. These groups were all designed to meet for an hour a month, and I would only suggest a topic for reflection for the first session. After that each session naturally led from the last with a consensus on what people should think about and prepare.

My work with the research group also had to change as a result of COVID-19. As well as not being able to begin the rhythmanalysis and visit different research groups led by women as planned, everything had to be online instead of in-person. Originally I had planned to facilitate conversations by bringing in a variety of creative materials to in-person meetings, including building Lego® models (Peabody and Noyes 2017), using arts materials for drawing, mark-making, and collage (Kara 2015), and using metaphorical representations through the use of objects and images (Lakoff and Johnson 2003). These were all designed to explore and develop their ways of working and communicating with each other and to facilitate group communication, using play as a means to stimulate creativity, elicit authentic stories, and establish emotional connection (Brown and Leigh 2018a). Instead, still working closely with Jen H, I ran bi-weekly sessions online which, as I will share, at times bordered on group therapy sessions. This was almost certainly in part due to the format and the way in which group interactions online are not as free-flowing or natural as an in-person conversation around a table in an arts-based workshop (McMillan 2015). The pandemic added to the stress that the students were experiencing, not only because of anxiety about their research while labs were shut or their individual experiences and worries about their families and loved ones, but because of the vicarious trauma the entire population was experiencing (Prideaux 2021). Jen H and I wanted to use the time we had for the group and support them as much as we could. One of the topics in the collaborative autoethnography group that was discussed a lot was how to support research groups and students. One of the international PIs who joined shared that she was really struggling with her group, who were not working productively or communicating with each other. I offered to work with them in a similar fashion, and began meeting with them online regularly as well. Jen H talked about this work, and as a result I was asked to develop a more structured programme based on the work with these two research groups which was piloted in a Doctoral Training Partnership (DTP) to address issues of attrition of PhD students. While there is normally some attrition in such programmes, COVID-19 had exacerbated this, particularly for students who were marginalised in any way. For the pilot I trained two facilitators who then worked with small cohorts of PhD students across the three campuses of the DTP. Based on my experience and the specific needs of the DTP, we identified six session topics they discussed in turn throughout the calendar year. The DTP and its funder were keen to embrace a new approach to support their students, embedding reflexivity and creativity into their induction processes for new students in addition to expanding on the pilot programme.

My approach to WISC's research foregrounded collaborative embodied approaches to capture lived experiences through the collaborative autoethnography and work with research groups, triangulating these with data from a series of online qualitative surveys, and in-person workshops directly with the community at events. In addition, my work on intersectional identity and marginalisation in academia and science (Brown and Leigh 2018b, 2020; Leigh 2021; Slowe et al 2023) led to projects on accessible labs (Egambaram et al 2022), disability and inclusion in science (Leigh et al 2024), and raising the visibility of Black women in chemistry and Science Communication. The main WISC survey research topic changed each year, with foci derived from including the community's desire and wants for and from WISC, experiences through COVID-19, and 1st Gen. 1st Gen is a catch-all term to describe people who are the first generation in their family to enter higher education or university (Allen et al 2015). Multiple barriers for 1st Gen students have been identified in the literature (Uche 2015). These include a decreased sense of belonging, fewer interactions with faculty, increased anxiety over money, a tendency to choose universities based on location and proximity to home rather than research reputation or excellence, a lack of networks and 'know-how' about how the system works in academia, and imposter syndrome. 1st Gen students face an attainment gap (Zalaquett 1999). These challenges are not restricted to 1st Gen students, and not all 1st Gen face them. As might be expected, there is a correlation with 1st Gen and students from minority ethnic backgrounds (Black and Brown students), low socio-economic class, and poverty (Nguyen and Nguyen 2018). In addition, 1st Gen is not always a clear-cut definition. For example, as I shared in the first chapter, my mum has both an undergraduate and a master's degree, so by definition I am not 1st Gen. However, because she attained her degrees as a mature student, part-time, and for her undergraduate studied remotely through the Open University, she had not had the typical experience of going to university. When I came to apply myself, neither she nor my father were able to advise me on the processes of applying or negotiating the choices that I had to make. In some respects I identify with 1st Gens because of this. In contrast, when my daughter aged 15 decided she wanted to read computer science and was not sure whether to continue studying computer science or make different A-Level choices, I invited a Professor of Computer Science out for coffee and got his advice that she would be better off taking maths and further maths, which she did. My knowledge and connections, or in other words my privilege, gave my daughter better advice than she would have received at her school, and enabled her to gain a place to a top-ranked university.

The plan for WISC's research is to continue to focus on topics that have been collaboratively identified by the community itself. In order to demonstrate the efficacy of the approach and the value of bringing embodiment, creativity, and reflection into science in a way that scientists will find more easy to recognise (Kara 2022), in addition to the qualitative focus in our publications to date, we intend to conduct a statistical analysis to show quantitatively the impact that the collaborative autoethnography group has had on participants' scientific outputs and achievements.

Border with therapy

This project was not set up to be therapeutic. While I described at length in Part I how and why my therapeutic training influenced my approach to qualitative research, when I shared this case study with some of the scientists who participated in the project, they told me they felt uncomfortable with me using the terms 'therapy' and 'therapist'. They read this case study in isolation. Where I have said the online groups felt somewhat like group therapy sessions, they would have talked about providing a safer environment for discussion or mediating feelings. The idea of therapy is often associated with a medical or pathological approach (see Lesson 3), and by taking for myself the descriptor 'therapist', they worried that I was erroneously describing myself as a medical professional and inviting critique. I am qualified as a therapist, and worked as one for many years and am not concerned about describing myself or my work that way; but they knew me as a researcher. Throughout this project, and largely due to the context and timing of it in relation to COVID-19, I was very aware of using my therapeutic skills and knowledge to boundary and establish a secure relational field or hold the space for the participants. This was much more evident when I was working with research students than with the collaborative autoethnography group. The collaborative autoethnography meetings had a feeling of process work and peer therapy where I was also a peer. Even within this egalitarian structure, I held responsibility for keeping boundaries of time and content. Working closely with Jen H, I led on the research outputs that resulted from our work. In this way our collaborative autoethnography was somewhat different from those more common in social sciences where the responsibilities of leading research (from analysis to dissemination) would also be held collaboratively and equally.

Due to time differences and the unexpectedly larger numbers, every month I organised two meetings, inviting everyone to join whichever session fitted their work calendar best. Initially I had tried to divide everyone into two separate groups so that people would get to know each other, building trust and rapport. The unpredictable nature of academic work and the pressures of COVID-19 meant that people needed to have the flexibility to switch when they required, and it did not take long before everyone had met everyone else. The shared experiences of being an independent researcher in the same field, being marginalised at the very least due to the gender imbalance in chemistry, and being brave enough to try something completely different meant that the whole group quickly bonded, even though the occasions when everyone was present in the same online meeting were relatively rare. My role was to facilitate the sessions by organising the meetings, taking notes, asking questions, ensuring everyone had a turn, and bringing in data or findings from other WISC research with the research groups or from surveys. The group was a site of peer support primarily, and I was a participant as much as anyone else, sharing my own experiences and gaining support and friendship. This model of peer support is one that has been championed for and by women in STEM before. Ellen Daniell wrote about her support group that met every two weeks in *Every Other Thursday* (Daniell 2006). Daniell's group used a system of active listening and 'work' to allow peers to share and gain support and advice. Ours was not so regimented, but in every session everyone (me included) had the opportunity to talk, process, and gain guidance from each other if needed.

The nature and terms of our group meant that the publications that resulted from the project were to be co-authored. Sue Rosser (1988, 2004,

2012, 2017) and Mary Ann Mason (2013; Mason and Ekman 2007) have written and researched around women in science. Rita Colwell wrote an autobiographical account of her own journey as a successful woman in science (Colwell and Bertsch McGrayne 2020), and Vivian Gornick wrote a retrospective including many such women (Gornick 2009). What is notable about these books is that they focus on women who are at the pinnacle or end of their career, or who have left science altogether. They had nothing to lose by sharing their stories. In contrast, the women in the collaborative autoethnography were all active researchers who were either early or mid-career and who were still striving to progress and succeed. The work was not my research *on* them, it was research *with* them. It was this, and the danger to their careers if they were to be accused of whistleblowing (Bjørkelo 2013) in any dissemination, that led to my use of fiction as a research method (Leavy 2016). While I led on the research analysis and dissemination, the decisions on what or how to present our work were not mine alone, and my drafts were edited in response to group discussions.

When I was working with the research students my role was somewhat different. In these sessions I was not an equal participant in the way I was in the collaborative autoethnography. I had a duty of care towards them that was much more explicit than the boundary holding needed for the collaborative autoethnography group. My intention was to benefit each research group as a whole, and the research students as individuals. The research groups were not where I went to get support or advice. My role here was to support the students as part of my work with their group leaders. I aimed to guide them through a process designed to contribute to their wellbeing, develop their self-awareness and the skills they would need for their research and to progress their careers. The development of academic identity can be somewhat challenging (Fanghanel 2012). While much has been written about the process of developing as an academic and surviving a PhD, particularly from the perspective of those who are marginalised (Shelton et al 2018; Van Galen and Sablan 2021), there is little that is specific to those in science.[1] I was much more aware of needing to try to establish a relational field to contain emotions, and of my role in guiding and supporting them as they reflected and shared their experiences in response questions and prompts I had given them. Whereas the collaborative autoethnography group topics and themes arose from the members, the prompts and questions for the research group were created from a combination of what came up naturally and what

[1] The board members of WISC have a book contracted to address this gap – a toolkit to surviving in science aimed at lab-based scientists from postgraduate students to those embarking on their independent career, to be published as part of the *Insider Guides to Success* series from Routledge and edited by Helen Kara and Pat Thompson.

I knew from their PIs were issues the group could do with considering. There were power dynamics in play in a way absent from the collaborative autoethnography. The research students were not equals and would not be co-authors on publications. They were co-researchers in the sense that the approach I used was participative and collaborative, but this was limited to the process of data gathering and did not formally extend to include analysis and dissemination, although I shared the draft fictional vignettes with them and they suggested edits to reflect their experiences more clearly.

Work with the research groups felt somewhat more stilted than the collaborative autoethnography meetings. Conversation was more likely to be *to* me and *in response to* me than a free-flowing rounded discussion as a group. A large factor of this was the online nature of the meetings. Online therapeutic work is not the same as in-person therapeutic work, whether it is peer, individual, or group work. It is harder to establish a secure relational field. A meeting can be interrupted at any moment by a technological fault, time delays can inhibit free-flowing conversation, and it is harder to establish an embodied rapport and connection. Relationships have to be negotiated through a lens of technology and cameras. Linda Finlay specifically addressed how a therapist should adapt their practice to work online:

- Attend to eye contact. Clients need to feel you looking at them so try to look into the camera, rather than at the screen. Note that sitting further away helps give the impression of eye contact and has the advantage of allowing the client to see more of your body particularly relevant if you're doing body work.
- Turn-taking needs to be more deliberate online. This means that we need to be more explicit and careful, making sure the client is equally on board. It's advisable to avoid the encouraging noises we often make in in-person therapy (like 'Uh, huh') as they interfere with speech clarity. Instead use non-verbal signals such as nodding. Keep (hand) gestures to a minimum as they can be distracting.
- Be attentive to the possibility of interruptions (including turning off notification/alert noises on devices). Therapists and clients alike may be tempted to check text messages during the session, disrupting presence, trust, and connection (Russell 2020).
- Consider adjusting your time boundaries to compensate for any technological failures (simultaneously holding clear boundaries) – something to negotiate on a client-to-client basis. (Finlay 2022: 98)

Finlay also warned:

> Experiences online can feel more casual and result in feeling more self-conscious, and can result in people disclosing more than they would

> in person –'the disinhibition effect' is usually seen when there is an absence of in-person cues. … Work with a client may go deeper or it may become more superficial. (Finlay 2022: 102).

I experienced both sides of this while working with WISC. With the research student groups I found a variation in how willing participants were to engage with and be authentic and honest about the questions or topic asked. Particularly at the beginning, there was a reluctance to be open with me and in front of their peers. Over time this dissipated, and it was often led by one student allowing themselves to be seen as vulnerable that allowed and encouraged the others to engage with the same amount of depth. Although these sessions were not my peer support, I always set the tone of what I was expecting from them by sharing my own experiences, my own vulnerability, and being honest about the topic. That is not to say that I was not careful about how much I shared and how, because I was. I used my vulnerability as a route to achieve a level of intimacy and trust with the students, which they then shared with me.

My work with the UK group was not limited to online sessions. Once the pandemic restrictions were lifted, I was able to spend time in the lab, meeting and talking to the students in person as well as undertaking some filming for the public engagement project and as part of the rhythmanalysis. The group were able to get to know me and build a relationship with me outside of the confines of the online meetings. The filming process was an aspect of my method to engage with and build relationship with the students, as well as the footage being a tool for research (Harris 2016). We were also able to hold some meetings in person, including presentation practice sessions and a collage-making activity. We did this around the multi-layered idea of success and what it looks like and feels like in the context of academia and wider life (see Figure 21). Conceptualising and celebrating success in academia can be knotty and complex (Balena et al 2012). Supporting reflection around what success meant to them personally was a way to avoid ruminating on failure (Joireman et al 2002) and to draw attention to, and hopefully guard against, the unhealthy academic behaviours of overwork and hyperproductivity that lead to burn-out and ill health (Gill 2016; Rolle et al 2021).

I could not, of course, meet the international group in person and work with them in the same way. However, at the time of writing these words I am sitting in the back row of a 500-person lecture theatre at an international chemistry conference. Earlier today two of the students from the group introduced themselves to me. It was lovely to see them in person (although it is always surprising to realise that people are different in height from how I had imagined them – in an online meeting everyone is more or less at the same level so having to look up is not needed!). In my time working with them, as well as asking the individual students to reflect on where

Figure 21: What success feels like and looks like

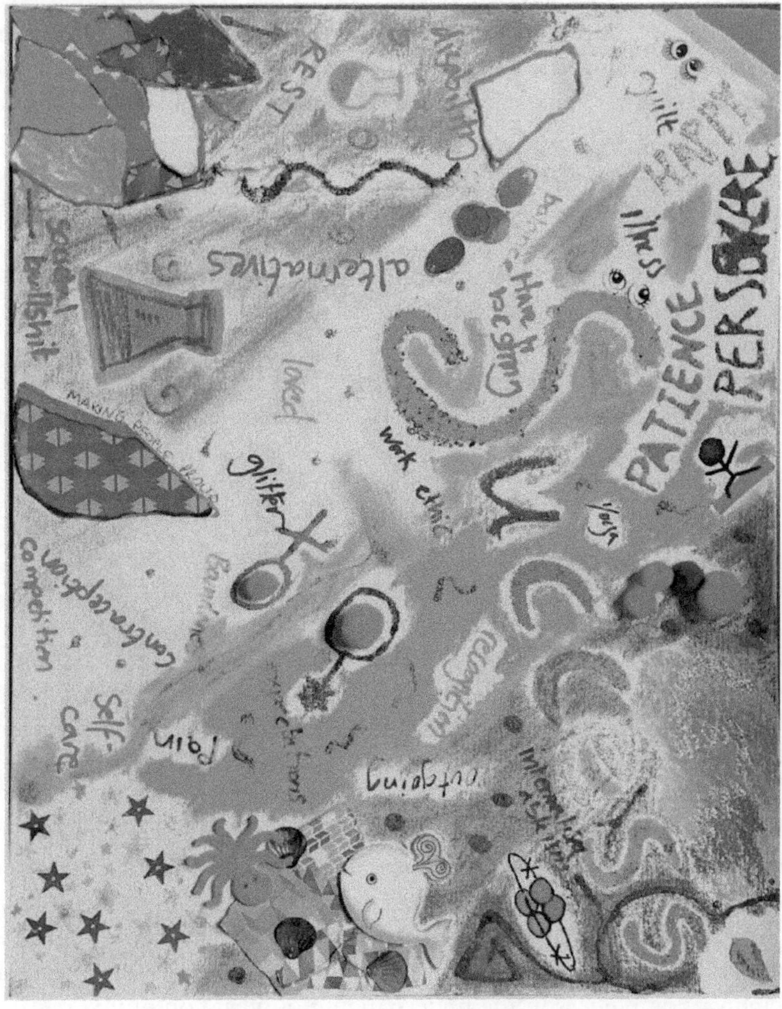

they were, what they wanted to achieve, and how they might develop the skills or attributes they would need to achieve their goals, I devoted a lot to aspects that emphasised the group dynamics, group culture, and group communication. This involved working closely with the PI and bringing into consciousness the unspoken tensions between the expectations of her students and herself when it came to her role and the purpose of the group. Over the year and a half that I worked with the group they were able to tell me how the culture had changed for the better, and to enculturate new members of the group into more positive ways of working rather than unconsciously re-enacting the negative and unproductive ways of the past. As a result, the group's productivity increased, and on an individual level the members gained confidence (Leigh et al 2024). Moving forward I would like to continue working with research students, though I intend to use the more structured approach developed for the DTP to encourage reflection, self-awareness, and positive ways of working and communication to encourage group dynamics to function well.

Border with science

Pushing the boundaries of qualitative research has been incredibly rewarding – though I will not deny that it has also been frustrating at times – for both me and the chemists. One of the challenges of working with WISC was that we were attempting to research using transdisciplinary approaches that pushed the boundaries of what was considered normal in terms of scientific research and dissemination:

> Interdisciplinarity can be defined in terms of task, process, product, or usage (Porter and Chubin 1985). Universities, though historically structured into disciplinary schools or departments, are increasingly favouring multi-disciplinary groups or structures (Friedman and Worden 2016; Hall et al. 2008). Multi-disciplinarity implies that teams from different disciplines collaborate to work on a single project; inter- or trans-disciplinary implies work between individuals or teams that cross disciplinary boundaries. (Leigh and Brown 2021b: 421)

When I conducted a post-hoc study exploring the experiences of researchers in the interdisciplinary project *Imagining Autism* (see Case Study 2), I noticed that some of the main points of tension between the disciplinary camps were the practical and logistical issues of carrying out field work, issues with communication and understanding of terminology between the teams, and disciplinary differences in the understanding of what constituted research. *Imagining Autism* was interdisciplinary in that it brought together two separate teams (psychologists/evaluators and drama practitioners/researchers) to research the effectiveness of an 'intervention'. I reflected on the process of interdisciplinary research:

> Challenges of interdisciplinarity include the tacit norms that prevent interaction between disciplines, and challenges of interaction—that is communicating across disciplines. Communication can prove challenging, both during a project and throughout its dissemination (Gewin 2014; Jeffrey 2003; Massey et al. 2006; Moti 1997). Such difficulties are inherent in any collaborative exercise, but with interdisciplinary projects, the fundamental epistemological beliefs of the

> collaborators—the understandings that they hold true about knowledge and the ways to increase that knowledge may be in opposition (Klein 1990). Jeffrey (2003) argues that interdisciplinary work cannot merely be 'bolted on' to existing research paradigms, but requires substantial and rigorous preparation and training and consequently, appropriate allocation of resources. The allocation of time and money to the development of interdisciplinary research is also a factor discussed in Lingard et al. (2007). They stated that for an interdisciplinary team and group identities to develop effectively, individual members must be socialised into their community of practice accordingly, a process that ultimately requires time and money (Lingard et al. 2007). Massey et al. (2006) and O'Cathain, Murphy and Nicholl (2008) report on mixed-methods research and highlight the implications for methodological decisions and team working. What becomes clear in both reports is the necessity for clear communication and a deep commitment to the research cause in order to overcome superficiality and fragmentation that seem to underpin interdisciplinary research work. As a consequence, it makes sense to allow time and space within any interdisciplinary research design to allow for the ongoing communication necessary for successful research, and any evaluation of interdisciplinary research should look for such a measure. Further to this, we wonder whether reflection and reflexivity are the keys to achieving this, as reflexivity within teams has a positive impact (see Hedman-Phillips and Barge 2017; Robinson 2008; Tesler et al. 2018) and allows for adaptability, change, and resolution of problems. (Leigh and Brown 2021b: 428)

My work with WISC was transdisciplinary because I, as a social scientist, was working together with the chemists (scientists) to cross disciplinary boundaries. When designing the research, I deliberately embedded time within the project for reflection for everyone involved – indeed the research approach foregrounded reflection and reflexivity through the use of collaborative autoethnography as a method. It is undoubtable that this allowed us to work together and to achieve successful outcomes. However, it did not eliminate the challenges in cross-disciplinary interactions and communications outlined above. My background and training as a chemist definitely contributed positively to our ability to work together. The chemists saw me as somewhat of an insider, though through a lot of the work I still *felt* like an outsider (Dwyer and Buckle 2009). My insider privilege granted me their trust.

A chemistry education does not traditionally include reflection or arts-based or creative research methods. Knowledge is known, truth is evidenced, and measured through experiment. When sharing the Lessons from science,

I reflected how science likes to believe that it is objective and meritocratic, and yet this is not reflected within the makeup of the scientific community. WISC's aim to address the lack of diversity and equality in science pushed against this idea that science is inherently meritocratic. To set out the history around gender imbalance in science I wrote:

> Women have historically been thought of as lesser, (Shildrick 1997) from Aristotle who wrote on women's general intellectual inferiority (Aristotle n.d.) to Galen who described female embryos as polluted (Galen 1968). In the Victorian period, prevailing biological and medical ideas reinforced the inferior status of women, making it more difficult for them to have a career in science (Fara 2018). Unfortunately, this attitude persisted well into the 20th (if not 21st) century. (Leigh et al 2022c: 57)

As part of research for a retrospective of women in science, Vivian Gornick interviewed an eminent male scientist: 'He confided in me that it was simply a matter of the nervous system… "Women may go into science, and they will do well enough, but they will never do great science"' (Gornick 2009: 26). Similarly, there are other assertions from male scientists that there is no unconscious bias in science: 'We don't do that… Science is objective. We only hire the best, and we know it when we see it' (Colwell and Bertsch McGrayne 2020: 184). While objectivity is seen as the scientific ideal, there is a vested interest in maintaining the idea that scientists are free from personal bias. However, it is easy to demonstrate that science is not as meritocratic as it claims. One senior scientist at a chemistry conference I was at called this out, saying that if he had two students of equal worth, and one was female, Brown, and from the Global South while the other was male, white, and from a Western country it should come as no surprise that only the latter received job offers. Discrimination of women and other marginalised groups is well described despite an abundance of measures to address discrimination and bias (Leigh et al 2022c). My work with WISC is part of a mission to combat this, to take action, and make the scientific world a better place; pushing back on the scientific assumption of meritocracy.

The scientific belief in objectivity had impact on my work in the fact that the chemists in WISC initially had a preference for working with numerical or quantitative data. They were more comfortable measuring, evaluating, and establishing an argument through demonstrating its truth than reflecting, sharing subjective experiences, or using creative approaches to evoke responses from an audience. When it came to analysing qualitative data, they were more drawn towards methods of discourse analysis (Grant 2018) than Reflexive Thematic Analysis (Braun and Clarke 2019). That said, it did not take long for them to experience and realise the power of a more embodied and creative approach. Beyond the pleasure and support they gained as individuals from being part of the collaborative autoethnography, as soon as we began disseminating work from WISC to a scientific audience it was clear that using fiction and creative methods had a lot of power to evoke a response. When I am talking to a scientific audience, I need to be careful and mindful of the scientific preference for objective truth; carefully introducing and framing the qualitative methods, data, and analysis. I have to present it in a way that allows them to connect with it rather than dismissing it out of hand as not rigorous or valid. One of the challenges in publishing in scientific journals has been to proactively address potential criticisms of qualitative methods, including its lack of generalisability (qualitative research does not have the same aim to be generalisable as quantitative research). We try to include some numbers in our publications – even if these are purely descriptive statistics – and triangulate data from different sources to create a sense that we are not 'just' being subjective. I also need to ensure that I frame and explain what I mean when using concepts that I or other social scientists might take for granted, such as those around social justice, privilege, and the like, as they can trigger defensiveness without proper and careful introduction. One of the most powerful ways we have been able to connect scientists to the work we are doing is by sharing the fictional narratives or vignettes created for the book, such as reading them aloud at conferences as part of a presentation in which we have first shared the hard numbers, data, and facts. I introduce the vignettes as being *true* but not *real*. Every time I have done this, I have had comments from the audience about how unusual it is, but how much they have enjoyed it. Each time people come up to me and other members of WISC and tell us about how they recognised themselves in the vignettes, or how they had never realised what the impact of being marginalised might feel like – which is exactly why they were written. These 'story times with Jen' sessions at conferences can be hard for the members of the collaborative autoethnography group to witness though, as they can see their own *real* stories in the fictionalised truths we are sharing.

Sixth vignette Phyllis, 63, Senior researcher

It was different in my day. There just weren't enough women about to have any sense of a community. I can see the difference it makes for the younger ones coming through to have enough of a critical mass to make a difference to each other. It felt very lonely back then – still does in a way. I think choices were starker – you either had to decide career over family, or career after family although that could mean that you just never progressed as far as your male colleagues. I don't have children. I've had relationships, but never met a man that could cope with me prioritising my career in the way I had to.

There have been so many women and men doing work to change things. It does make me wonder why young women are still facing the same barrier and having to make the same choices we did 30 years ago, but I suppose at least there are more of them making them. I do think there's a real willingness to learn and to do things differently though. I mean, I can count the number of times I *haven't* heard some version of 'you only got that because you're a woman' when I've shared funding or publication success, or when I was made a Fellow. I think the more of us who are senior can stand up and shout and lend our names and support to the ones coming through the better. I mentor where I can – both officially and unofficially. What makes me so proud is that I see my male colleagues doing the same. Really championing young women.

I know we need to address all kinds of diversity in chemistry – goodness knows we don't have enough range of skin colour – but I am hopeful. I appreciate that they recognise the hard work we all put in – by doing our best to change things and in some ways just by being here and achieving what we have achieved.

At least they have role models of a sort – more than I ever did. I want to be hopeful. I see all these brilliant young women, and I see them not dropping out, not leaving to a different profession, but staying, and having families, and getting the grants, and getting the papers out. One showed me a mug the other day that her wife had bought her – what did it say now? Oh yes – 'Girls just want to have funding for scientific research!' I thought that was a hoot! I am sometimes amazed by how bold this new generation are, how brave for calling out behaviour they will not put up with. I'm not sure that I could have back then – it felt much too risky. A lot more was just accepted as well.

If you asked me what I want for this new generation? I would say I want them to keep on being brilliant, to keep on being bold, to have ideas and to challenge us old dinosaurs. I love the way they smile and wave and get us all on side. It makes us want to work with them, and it keeps us on our toes as well! I want them to have opportunities – for scientific research, to have families, to have a life, and to have fun. I want them to remember that academia won't love you as much as the people in your life will. That it won't necessarily reward their long hours or dedication. It will take and take and take. I've heard it described as a 'consensual abusive relationship' and that hit home a bit! I want those coming through to have healthy, meaningful relationships with their work and the rest of their lives. I want them to keep fighting for themselves and for each other and to really change the culture of chemistry and science so that no one is marginalised anymore, and so that what really matters is the science. (Leigh et al 2022c: 122)

Weaving in

This final section of the book is a bit like the final bits of a textile art piece. The creative impulse is spent, the form is there, and now you need to sew it together, tidy up all the loose ends, weave them in, and finish it off. I have to admit this is my least favourite part of any project. I might not create so much artistic textiles these days, but I finished a jumper recently and for some reason chose stripes, which meant there were *a lot* of ends to weave in. My next project is a jumper worked from the neck down purely so there will be less to finish off. My intention here is to reflect on the value of taking space to consider my ontological perspective and how it has shaped my research, and bring together threads of how qualitative research, and particularly embodied and creative qualitative research, can border onto therapy, education, art, and science. The kind of research I have illustrated in this book has many positives; it captures and generates rich data and gives voice to those who are less often heard or who cannot easily express their stories in words alone. It allows us to find and express the rhythms inherent in our bodies, the bodies of our participants, and the world around us. It gives depth and richness when used alongside conventional research methods, and provides opportunities for engagement and dissemination that can have more impact with those outside of academia or our home discipline. However, this type of research can be challenging to negotiate, as techniques that intentionally open up the researcher and participant to the emotional content of stories mean that there is also the potential for risk, and to inadvertently wander over a boundary into uncharted territory.

Borders

The first border of qualitative research I considered is the one shared with therapeutic approaches designed to allow people to process their emotions and experiences. While researchers may receive training on methods, it is not common for them to receive the same kind of training and support on how to deal with people and their stories that therapists do. Researchers often choose to study emotional or difficult areas such as sexual or physical violence, mental health, poverty, or exclusion because of their own lived experiences. In my work supporting early career academics, I heard many stories about researchers who become burned out; unable to hear anymore, unable to process the stories they are told, and as a consequence leaving the field or changing their research area. It is common to hear from groups that feel exploited by interactions with researchers who left them feeling vulnerable and unsupported after an interview or research encounter triggered an emotional response or memories. People can be placed in vulnerable situations and potentially emotionally harmed if the researcher is inexperienced. Therapeutic training helps safeguard the person the therapist is working with, as well as themselves. It brings transference, countertransference, empathy, fatigue, and burn-out, to the fore, and allows the therapist to learn how to process and handle others' sensitive and emotional and often heart-rending stories (Rogers 1967; Leigh 1998).

Because of their usefulness in capturing the voices of those less able to speak, creative methods are most likely to be used with vulnerable groups, who are in turn most at risk of being exploited or harmed. Creative and embodied methods elicit emotional stories and evocative experiences in the form of words, images, artefacts, and models that go beyond the surface-level responses participants and researchers might expect to be shared in more conventional interviews (Brown and Leigh 2018a). As a consequence, they can encourage a wary researcher to tread close to the border with therapy. Without guidance, researchers may find themselves and their participants in uncomfortable situations. As an academic working with postgraduate students developing research projects, I am often struck by the conflicting desires of wanting to 'help' their participants while researching them; to go beyond capturing data and move toward an almost therapeutic interaction or encounter. Similar conflicts could be seen in Case Study 1, where educational research was taken and used with therapeutic intent by some of the participants, and in Case Study 2 where the artistic research using improvised drama sessions was intended to have a therapeutic effect and 'help' or ameliorate 'symptoms'; yet were theorised as 'just' drama. Wanting to help others is a powerful motivation for researchers, therapists, artists, educators, and scientists alike.

The second border is where qualitative research meets education. Research interventions and projects often have participants (or researchers) learning or taking part in something. Action Research projects (Hall 1996) are common in education settings, and these specifically cross the boundary between what is research and what is education. Education, in turn, can border with therapy and art. It is vital that we identify our intentions for a given project from the start. If the intention is to educate, then we as educators want our students to learn or to gain something from an interaction. Ideally, we hold the space for our students so they can be safe and flourish (Brighouse 2005). Depending on the age or vulnerability of those we are teaching, we might act *in loco parentis*. As such, we should put our students' safety and wellbeing first and foremost. Teachers have been accused of having to take an almost therapeutic responsibility for their students' happiness (Ecclestone and Hayes 2009). Researchers are not held to the same standards. In ethical application forms we are often asked about perceived benefit to participants, but is this comparable to a student having a positive outcome following an interaction with a teacher? If we are in a situation acting as both educator and researcher, we have to know which takes precedence; the need to collect or gather participant data, or the wellbeing of our students.

The third border is where qualitative research meets art. As research becomes more creative (see, for example, Barrett and Bolt 2010; Kara 2015; Leigh 2020a) with participants creating or co-creating artefacts, patterns, models, and images with and for researchers; and with researchers creating the same in response to their participants' stories as part of their analytic process or Practice-as-Research, where are the lines between art and research? Arts-based research is *not* the same as artistic research or Practice-as-Research, and using arts-based methods does not necessarily make a researcher into an artist. An object can be data and it can also be art. Just as with therapy, there is a difference in intention, knowledge, and training. There is a difference in intention between creating art as part of therapy, education, or research, and that intention impacts on how it should be analysed and handled. In addition, there has to be a consideration of how to disseminate the outputs of research: as data, where they may be buried in a book or research journal, or as part of an exhibit in person or online? If the latter, then there has to be clarity over who owns it, whether that is the author or creator if they are not the same. Some of these questions particularly revolve around participatory research and co-created artefacts, which is appropriate as these methods are commonly used in creative studies. Case Study 3 explored some of these issues, as well as how artistic or research work can border onto therapeutic territory. Attributing ownership can affect anonymity, and there are complex ethical issues around the use of creative methods that are not covered by many research ethics frameworks (Kara 2018).

The final border is that between science and qualitative research. While hard science and creative and embodied qualitative research may not immediately be easy bedfellows, in Case Study 4 I drew on ongoing work within a community aiming to address retention and progression of marginalised groups to demonstrate how they can nestle closely. This project intentionally introduced creative and reflective methods into academic scientific and laboratory spaces to create community and connection, to increase moments of inspiration, and improve group dynamics. Even years into this work, we have discussions on how 'scientific' qualitative research is, particularly the embodied and creative qualitative research we use. It is seen as more valid if it is triangulated with 'proper' data (that is, numbers), and ways to make it more representative or less subjective. In terms of assessments of research quality, including quantitative and measurable aspects might indicate that it has more rigour than purely qualitative work. I believe that the scientists I work with would now agree that a definitive hierarchy placing one over the other is unnecessary. There is a place for qualitative research within science; it can highlight lived experiences, impact us emotionally, and help us to understand the need for change that other modes may not.

Lessons learned

In order to address the potential for unintentional harm to either the researcher or participant, I have suggested developing an understanding of the self through reflection and awareness, and of relationships to and with others. Reflective practice and reflexivity should be essential components of education, therapy, art, science, and research. Reflection is most effective when it is grounded in embodied self-awareness. I view my body as the embodiment of me. The physical expression of me within this world. As such I can train, exercise, express, and create with it and through it. Although, my own perception and understanding of my body is actually at odds with that last sentence, as by terming my body an 'it' I am objectifying a part of myself. The practice I have developed and which informs my perceptions and understandings is an embodied reflexive practice (Leigh and Bailey 2013). I use the information from my senses (touch, smell, kinaesthesia, proprioception, sight, imagination, hearing, imagery, and internal awareness) to feed into a reflective and reflexive process of understanding myself, the world that surrounds me, and others that move within the world. My reflexive process is 'rooted in experiences of … [my] … kinetic/tactile-kinesthetic …[body]' (Sheets-Johnstone 2010a: 112). The exactness of language, and the nature of that language, can express the experience of my embodied self forms a part of the practice itself. As a child I had to find an explanation for the inevitable 'what is that?' when I answered 'osteopath' to the question of what my parents did. As I grew up, the idea that our bodies and the way that our bodies move and carry us through the world as we relate to others was integrated with a holistic view of our health and the ways in which we understood the world with our minds. It was never a question, it was a given. As I said in the very first chapter, I am a star child born of hippies. I appreciate that my view and experience of the world is not hegemonic, but it does appear to be becoming more prevalent.

Learning embodied self-awareness is easiest in a context where there is no competition with peers. This encourages the formation of a more positive relationship with the body based on experiences, rather than being informed by cultural or societal norms and becoming dissociated from it. However, it can be challenging to establish a non-competitive atmosphere. Linda Hartley placed great importance on a facilitator's role to reflect back experiences of the body, and the intention of touch to support a developing sense of self. Hartley recognised the ways in which educational somatics 'does touch upon deep emotional and psychological processes' (Hartley 2004: 28), and could enable a therapeutic process. This highlights the border between education and therapeutic work and the ways it is often necessary to hold space for both. Alan Fogel defined eight stages in the therapeutic treatment of lost embodied self-awareness: resources, slowing down, co-regulation, verbalisation, links and boundaries, self-regulation, re-engagement, and letting go (Fogel 2009: 23–24). Aspects of these can be seen in the projects described in the four case studies, and are explicitly identified in my work with child M (Case Study 1). Hartley used Authentic Movement (Adler 2002) to develop the idea of 'therapeutic presence', where 'the therapist's perceptions can be offered to a client, but owned for what they are – her own interpretations, judgements and projections' (Hartley 2004: 30). In my experience, some of the best ways to facilitate the development of embodied self-awareness is by using stillness and movement, and encouraging reflection.

I cannot emphasise enough that if a researcher, artist, or educator wants to investigate or use a material or a tool that takes people to the edge of what might be therapeutic, they pay attention to the relationships they construct with them. It is essential that they can hold the space necessary for that work (research, art, or education) to be done safely. In order to do this they need to be reflexive and have access to support, otherwise it is possible to become 'lost' in the process (Bainbridge-Cohen 1993). The boundaries between the therapeutic, educational, and artistic content and context of research can easily overlap (Nichols 2008). Individuals process information about themselves, their bodies, and their sense of embodiment differently, and will utilise the same content in different ways. Some might incorporate it into their bodies and learn (education), others might use it to begin a process of transformation and growth (therapy), while others use it to facilitate expression (art). As a facilitator it is possible to intentionally guide people toward one side of this continuum, but not control how they might take and use material. In my work with academics around embodied identity (Case Study 3), the relationships where trust was established most securely was evident with those who shared Authentic Movement as a practice. The ritual and form allowed them to trust that boundaries would be held, and they felt freer to enter into a space where they could process (Leigh 2019a). My doctoral research sessions were intended to be educational, and yet Case Study 1 illustrated how the relationships formed with the students meant that some were able to take the content and use it therapeutically. This was most evident with the older children. Whatever age group I worked with, I ensured that each session incorporated time for individual exploration and reflections as well as time for any issues that arose to be contained and 'held' (Rogers 1967). This recognised that although they were educational sessions, some children still needed therapeutic holding. The secure relational field I established and the trust that built up over time meant that the children felt safe enough to express deep feelings and emotions. They knew me and I knew them. If I asked them to do something, whether that was being still, recognising their own and others' achievements, or trying something new, they trusted me. The same is true in the creative work with scientists in Case Study 4 who were so brave to try a new way of working and researching with me. The relationships I established with them meant they trusted me in my role to hold the boundaries to keep them as safe as possible. Wherever research, education, or art has the potential for therapeutic content, it is vital that there are secure relationships and trust.

I am passionate about embedding embodiment and embodied methods into research (Ellingson 2017; Leigh and Brown 2021a; Spatz 2020). I am just as passionate about embedding embodiment and embodied reflection into education (Bresler 2004), therapy (Fischman 2009; Sheets-Johnstone 2010a; Finlay 2022), art (Chodrow 2009; Phalen 2015; Guillaumier 2016; Petsilas et al 2019b), and science (Aikenhead and Ogawa 2007; Leigh et al 2022c). I often use autoethnographic and participatory methods and produce outputs which can be received as artistic, scientific, educational, and therapeutic. As a researcher it is crucial to have an ongoing conversation with oneself and others engaged in the research and reflect on where learning and/or processing is happening and what needs to be in place to take care and safeguard everyone involved. In participatory research, it is also essential to have ongoing conversations around the mores of ownership and authorship. If we include art within an analysis, we have to be reflective about how we go about analysis and avoid judgement. This requires self-awareness and, in the words of Venus Evans-Winters demands that I as a researcher '[exhibit] reciprocity and vulnerability in the research process' and 'show how data analysis can also be soul work that serves to heal thyself' (Evans-Winters 2019: 7). As I have illustrated in this book, creative and embodied methods are incredibly valuable both to facilitate reflexivity in a researcher and to capture, generate, and disseminate data. As I continue with my own process and research journey, I want to continue exploring how embodied and creative research methods can feed into different research questions and approaches, deepening and widening the applicability and impact of science, art, education, and therapy.

The paths along these borders are not always clear, and though we might take hold of threads to guide us, they can become tangled. As researchers we need to be aware of how the porosity of these boundaries changes at different points during the process of research, and take paths appropriate to our project, our experience, our time, our participants, and our audience. We need to be aware of our intentions and where we tread.

References

Abbott, A. (2021), 'COVID's Mental-Health Toll: How Scientists Are Tracking a Surge in Depression', *Nature*, 3 February.

Acker, S. and C. Armenti (2004), 'Sleepless in Academia', *Gender and Education*, 16 (1): 3–24.

Adele Kentel, J. and T. M. Dobson (2007), 'Beyond Myopic Visions of Education: Revisiting Movement Literacy', *Physical Education and Sport Pedagogy*, 12 (2): 145–62.

Adler, J. (2002), *Offering from the Conscious Body: The Discipline of Authentic Movement*, Rochester, VT: Inner Traditions.

Adler, J. (2022), *Intimacy in Emptiness: An Evolution of Embodied Consciousness*, edited by B. Morrissey and P. Sager, Rochester, VT: Inner Traditions.

Advance-HE (2022), 'UK Professional Standards Framework'. Available online: www.advance-he.ac.uk/teaching-and-learning/psf#the-framework (accessed 26 July 2022).

Ahmed, S. (2017), *Living a Feminist Life*, Durham, NC: Duke University Press.

Aikenhead, G. S. and M. Ogawa (2007), 'Indigenous Knowledge and Science Revisited', *Cultural Studies of Science Education*, 2 (3): 539–620.

Alerby, E. (2003), '"During the Break We Have Fun": A Study Concerning Pupils' Experience of School', *Educational Research*, 45 (1): 17–28.

Alexander, F. M. (1932), *The Use of the Self: Its Conscious Direction in Relation to Diagnosis, Function, and the Control of Reaction*, New York: Dutton.

Alexis-Martin, B. (2019), *Disarming Doomsday: The Human Impact of Nuclear Weapons since Hiroshima*, London: Pluto Press.

Allain, P. (2009), *Grotowski's Empty Room: A Challenge to the Theatre (Enactments)*, Kolkata: Seagull Books.

Allen, J. M., G. A. Muragishi, J. L. Smith, D. B. Thoman and E. R. Brown (2015), 'To Grab and to Hold: Cultivating Communal Goals to Overcome Cultural and Structural Barriers in First Generation College Students' Science Interest', *Translational Issues in Psychological Science*, 1 (4): 331–41.

American Psychiatric Association (2022), *Diagnostic and Statistical Manual of Mental Disorders, Fifth Edition, Text Revision (DSM-5-TR™)*, Washington, DC: American Psychiatric Association.

Archibong, I., A. Bassey and D. Effiom (2010), 'Occupational Stress Sources among University Academic Staff', *European Journal of Educational Studies*, 2 (3): 217–25.

Aristotle (n.d.), *De Natura Animalium, De Partibus Animalium, De Generatione Animalium*, edited and translated by Theodorus Gaza, Venice.

Aston, J. (1995), 'Three Perceptions and One Compulsion', in D. H. Johnson (ed), *Bone, Breath and Gesture: Practices of Embodiment*, 207–18, Berkeley, CA: North Atlantic Books.

Aveline, M. (1990), 'The Training and Supervision of Individual Therapists', in W. Dryden (ed), *Individual Therapy: A Handbook*, 313–39, Buckingham: Open University Press.

Ayres, Z. (2022), *Managing Your Mental Health during Your PhD*, Chaim: Springer.

Back, L. (2007), *The Art of Listening*, Oxford: Berg.

Back, L. (2016), *Academic Diary: Or Why Higher Education Still Matters*, London: Goldsmiths Press.

Bacon, J. (2010), 'The Voice of Her Body: Somatic Practices as a Basis for Creative Research Methodology', *Journal of Dance & Somatic Practices*, 2 (1): 63–74.

Bacon, J. (2015), 'Authentic Movement as Well-Being Practice', in V. Karkou, S. Lycouris and S. Oliver (eds), *Oxford Handbook for Dance and Well-Being*, 149–64, Oxford: Oxford University Press.

BACP (n.d.), 'Ethical Framework for the Counselling Professions'. Available online: www.bacp.co.uk/events-and-resources/ethics-and-standards/ethical-framework-for-the-counselling-professions/ (accessed 4 September 2023).

Bailey, R. (2001), 'Overcoming Veriphobia: Learning to Love Truth Again', *British Journal of Educational Studies*, 49 (2): 159–72.

Bailey, R. (2002), 'Playing Social Chess: Children's Play and Social Intelligence', *Early Years*, 22 (2): 163–73.

Bailey, R. (2006), 'Science, Normal Science and Science Education: Thomas Kuhn and Education', *Learning for Democracy*, 2 (2): 7–20.

Bailey, R. (2009), 'Wellbeing, Happiness and Education', *British Journal of Sociology of Education*, 30 (6): 795–802.

Bailey, R. P. (2010), 'Indoctrination', in R. P. Bailey, D. Carr, R. Barrow and C. McCarthy (eds), *Handbook of the Philosophy of Education*, 269–82, London: Sage.

Bailey, R. (2012), 'What Is Developmentally Appropriate Sport?', *The Leisure Review*, 19 (2): 21–24.

Bailey, R. (2019), 'Being There: Exploring an Embodied-Relational Approach to Understanding Children's Physical Activity', in J. Leigh (ed), *Conversations on Embodiment across Higher Education: Teaching, Practice and Research*, 211–24, Abingdon: Routledge.

Bailey, R. and H. Dismore (2004), *SpinEd: The Role of Physical Education and Sport in Education*, Canterbury: Canterbury Christ Church University College.

Bailey, R. and M. Toms (2010), 'Youth Talent Development in Sport: Rethinking Luck and Justice', in A. Hardman and R. Jones (eds), *The Ethics of Sports Coaching*, 149–64, London: Routledge.

Bailey, R., K. Armour, D. Kirk, J. Mike, I. Pickup, R. Sandford and B. P. Group (2009), 'The Educational Benefits Claimed for Physical Education and School Sport: An Academic Review', *Research Papers in Education*, 24 (1): 1–27.

Bain, L. (1987), 'Modern Sports and the Eastern Tradition of Physical Culture: Emphasizing Nishida's Theory of the Body', *Journal of the Philosophy of Sport*, XIV: 44–47.

Bain, L. (1995), 'Mindfulness and Subjective Knowledge', *Quest*, 47: 238–53.

Bainbridge-Cohen, B. (1993), *Sensing, Feeling and Action*, Northampton, MA: Contact Editions.

Balen, B. van, P. van Arensbergen, I. van der Weijden and P. van den Besselaar (2012), 'Determinants of Success in Academic Careers', *Higher Education Policy*, 25: 313–34.

Barad, K. (2007), *Meeting the Universe Halfway: Quantum Physics and the Entanglement of Matter and Meaning*, Durham, NC: Duke University Press.

Barrett, E. and B. Bolt (2010), *Practice as Research: Approaches to Creative Arts Enquiry*, London: I.B. Tauris.

Barrow, R. (1980), *Happiness*, Oxford: Martin Robinson.

Barrow, R. (2008), 'Education and the Body: Prolegomena', *British Journal of Educational Studies*, 56 (3): 272–85.

Baxter, P. and S. Jack (2008), 'Qualitative Case Study Methodology: Study Design and Implementation for Novice Researchers', *The Qualitative Report*, 13: 554–59.

Beadle-Brown, J., J. Leigh, B. Whelton, L. Richardson, J. Beecham, T. Baumker and J. Bradshaw (2016), 'Quality of Life and Quality of Support for People with Severe Intellectual Disability and Complex Needs', *Journal of Applied Research in Intellectual Disabilities: JARID*, 29 (5): 409–21.

Beadle-Brown, J., D. Wilkinson, L. Richardson, N. Shaughnessy, M. Trimingham, J. Leigh, B. Whelton and J. Himmerich (2018), 'Imagining Autism: Feasibility of a Drama-Based Intervention on the Social, Communicative and Imaginative Behaviour of Children with Autism', *Autism*, 22 (8): 915–27.

Beringer, E. (1988), 'Interview with Ilse Middendorf', *Somatics*, 15: 17.

Bersin, D. (1983), 'Interview with Gerda Alexander', *Somatics*, 4: 10.

Best, D. (1978), *Philosophy and Human Movement*, London: Unwin Education Books.

Biesta, G. (1994), 'Education as Practical Intersubjectivity: Towards a Critical-Pragmatic Understanding of Education', *Educational Theory*, 44 (3): 299–317.

Bjørkelo, B. (2013), 'Workplace Bullying after Whistleblowing: Future Research and Implications', *Journal of Managerial Psychology*, 28 (3): 306–23.

Bleakley, A. (1999), 'From Reflective Practice to Holistic Reflexivity', *Studies in Higher Education*, 24 (3): 315–30.

Bloch, C. (2012), *Passion and Paranoia: Emotions and the Culture of Emotion in Academia*, Farnham: Ashgate Publishing.

Bloom, L. (1993), *The Transition from Infancy to Language: Acquiring the Power of Expression*, Cambridge: Cambridge University Press.

Bochner, A. and C. Ellis (2016), *Evocative Autoethnography: Writing Lives and Telling Stories*, London: Routledge.

Bordo, S. (1986), 'The Cartesian Masculinization of Thought', *Signs*, 11 (3): 439–56.

Bott, D. and P. Howard (2012), *The Therapeutic Encounter: A Cross Modality Approach*, London: Sage.

Bourdieu, P. (1990), *The Logic of Practice*, Stanford, CA: Stanford University Press.

Bourdieu, P. (1998), *On Television*, New York: The New Press.

Bourner, T. (2003), 'Assessing Reflective Learning', *Education and Training*, 45 (5): 267–72.

Bowman, P. (2019), 'Embodiment as Embodiment Of', in J. S. Leigh (ed), *Conversations on Embodiment across Higher Education: Teaching, Practice and Research*, 11–24, Abingdon: Routledge.

Boynton, P. (2020), *Being Well in Academia*, Abingdon: Routledge.

BPS (2010), 'Supervision Guidance'. Available online: https://explore.bps.org.uk/content/report-guideline/bpsrep.2017.inf115/chapter/bpsrep.2017.inf115.3#ch01lev1sec5 (accessed 4 February 2021).

Bradley, J. (2020), 'Ethnography, Arts Production and Performance: Meaning-Making in and for the Street', in T. Lähdesmäki, V. Ceginskas, E. Koskinen-Koivisto and A.-K. Koistinen (eds), *Challenges and Solutions in Ethnographic Research: Ethnography with a Twist*, 197–212, Abingdon: Routledge.

Bradshaw, J., J. Beadle-Brown, L. Richardson, B. Whelton and J. Leigh (2018), 'Managers' Views of Skilled Support', *Journal of Applied Research in Intellectual Disabilities*, 31 (5): 873–84.

Braun, V. and V. Clarke (2013), *Successful Qualitative Research: A Practical Guide for Beginners*, London: Sage.

Braun, V. and V. Clarke (2016), '(Mis)Conceptualising Themes, Thematic Analysis, and Other Problems with Fugard and Potts' (2015) Sample-Size Tool for Thematic Analysis', *International Journal of Social Research Methodology*, 19 (6): 739–43.

Braun, V. and V. Clarke (2019), 'Reflecting on Reflexive Thematic Analysis', *Qualitative Research in Sport, Exercise and Health*, 11 (4): 589–97.

Braun, V. and V. Clarke (2021a), 'To Saturate or Not to Saturate? Questioning Data Saturation as a Useful Concept for Thematic Analysis and Sample-Size Rationales', *Qualitative Research in Sport, Exercise and Health*, 13 (2): 201–16.

Braun, V. and V. Clarke (2021b), 'One Size Fits All? What Counts as Quality Practice in (Reflexive) Thematic Analysis?', *Qualitative Research in Psychology*, 18 (3): 328–52.

Braun, V., V. Clarke and H. Cooper (2012), 'Thematic Analysis', in H. Cooper, P. M. Camic, D. L. Long, A. T. Panter, D. Rindskopf, and K. J. Sher (eds), *APA Handbook of Research Methods in Psychology, Vol 2: Research Designs: Quantitative, Qualitative, Neuropsychological, and Biological*, 57–71, Washington, DC: American Psychological Association.

Braun, V., V. Clarke, G. Terry, N. Hayfield and P. Liamputtong (2019), 'Thematic Analysis', in P. Liamputtong (ed), *Handbook of Research Methods in Health and Social Sciences*, Singapore: Springer.

Bresler, L., ed (2004), *Knowing Bodies, Knowing Minds: Towards Embodied Teaching and Learning*, Norwell, MA: Kluwer Academic.

Brighouse, H. (2005), *On Education (Thinking in Action)*, Abingdon: Routledge.

Brinkmann, S. and S. Kvale (2014), *InterViews: Learning the Craft of Qualitative Research Interviewing*, Thousand Oaks: SAGE Publications Ltd.

BA (2021), 'British Academy APEX Awards', *The British Academy*. Available online: www.thebritishacademy.ac.uk/funding/apex-awards/ (accessed 24 July 2021).

Bromley, J., D. Hare, K. Davison and E. Emerson (2004), 'Mothers Supporting Children with Autistic Spectrum Disorders: Social Support, Mental Health Status and Satisfaction with Services', *Autism*, 8: 409–23.

Brook, A. (n.d.), *From Conception to Crawling*, Lafayette, CO: Ann Brook Publisher.

Brookfield, S. (1995), *Becoming a Critically Reflective Teacher*, San-Francisco, CA: Jossey-Bass.

Brown, K. and R. Ryan (2003), 'The Benefits of Being Present: Mindfulness and Its Role in Psychological Well-Being', *Journal of Personality and Social Psychology*, 84 (4): 822–48.

Brown, N. and J. Leigh (2018a), 'Creativity and Playfulness in HE Research', in J. Huisman and M. Tight (eds), *Theory and Method in Higher Education Research*, 49–66, Bingley: Emerald.

Brown, N. and J. Leigh (2018b), 'Ableism in Academia: Where Are the Disabled and Ill Academics?', *Disability and Society*, 33 (6): 985–89.

Brown, N. and J. Leigh, eds (2020), *Ableism in Academia: Theorising Experiences of Disabilities and Chronic Illnesses in Higher Education*, London: UCL Press.

Brown, T., R. Bennett, L. Ward and P. Payne (2009), 'The Context of Movement and Its Social Ecology', *International Conference of the Australian Association for Research in Education 2009 – Canberra, Australia*.

Buckingham, D. (2009), '"Creative" Visual Methods in Media Research: Possibilities, Problems and Proposals', *Media, Culture & Society*, 31 (4): 633–52.

Budd, K., S. Mckeever, T. Postings and H. Price (2020), *A Student's Guide to Therapeutic Counselling*, London: Sage.

Buddhananda, S. (1978), *Moola Bandha: The Master Key*, Munger, India: Yoga Publications Trust.

Buote, V., A. E. Wilson, E. J. Strahan, S. B. Gazzola and F. Papps (2011), 'Setting the Bar: Divergent Sociocultural Norms for Women's and Men's Ideal Appearance in Real-World Contexts', *Body Image*, 8 (4): 322–34.

Butler, J. (2015), *Senses of the Subject*, New York: Fordham University Press.

Caine, V., D. J. Clandinin and S. Lessard (2022), *Narrative Inquiry: Philosophical Roots*, London: Bloomsbury.

Calderhead, J. (1989), 'Reflective Teaching and Teacher Education', *Teaching and Teacher Education*, 5 (1): 43–51.

Caltagirone, C., E. Draper, M. Hardie, C. Haynes, J. Hiscock, K. Jolliffe, M. Kieffer, J. Leigh and A. McConnell (2021a), 'Calling in Support', *Chemistry World*, March.

Caltagirone, C., E. Draper, C. Haynes, M. Hardie, J. Hiscock, K. Jolliffe, M. Kieffer, A. McConnell and J. Leigh (2021b), 'An Area Specific, International Community-Led Approach to Understanding and Addressing EDI Issues within Supramolecular Chemistry', *Angewandte Chemie International Edition*, 60 (21): 11572–79.

Carbonneau, N., R. Vallerand and S. Massicotte (2010), 'Is the Practice of Yoga Invariably Associated with Positive Outcomes? The Role of Passion', *The Journal of Positive Psychology*, 5 (6): 452–65.

Carman, T. (1999), 'The Body in Husserl and Merleau-Ponty', *Philosophical Topics*, 27 (2): 205–26.

Cech, E. A. (2022), 'The Intersectional Privilege of White Able-Bodied Heterosexual Men in STEM', *Science Advances*, 8 (24): eabo1558.

Chaiklin, S. (2009), 'We Dance from the Moment Our Feet Touch the Earth', in S. Chaiklin and H. Wengrower (eds), *The Art and Science of Dance/Movement Therapy*, 3–11, Hove: Routledge.

Chang, H., F. Ngunjiri and K.-A. Hernandez (2016), *Collaborative Autoethnography*, Abingdon: Routledge.

Chilton, G. and P. Leavy (2014), 'Arts-Based Research Practice: Merging Social Research and the Creative Arts', in P. Leavy (ed), *The Oxford Handbook of Qualitative Research*, 403–22, New York: Oxford University Press.

Chodrow, J. (2009), 'Dance Therapy, Motion and Emotion', in S. Chaiklin and H. Wengrow (eds), *The Art and Science of Dance/Movement Therapy*, 55–73, Hove: Routledge.

Clark, A. (2005), 'Listening to and Involving Young Children: A Review of Research and Practice', *Early Child Development and Care*, 175 (6): 489–505.

Clark, A. and P. Moss (2005), *Spaces to Play: More Listening to Young Children Using the Mosaic Approach*, London: National Children's Bureau.

Clark, A. and B. Sousa (2018), *How to Be a Happy Academic*, London: Sage.

Clark, H. and E. Clark (1977), *Psychology and Language: An Introduction to Psycholinguistics*, New York: Harcourt Brace Jovanovich.

Clarke, V. (2021), 'As So Many People Are Announcing Their Promotions… I Am Pleased to Announce That I Haven't Been Promoted to Professor', *Twitter*. Available online: https://twitter.com/drvicclarke/status/1410275377927307272 (accessed 30 July 2022).

Clarke, V. and V. Braun (2019), 'Feminist Qualitative Methods and Methodologies in Psychology: A Review and Reflection', *Psychology of Women and Equalities Review*, 2 (1): 13–28.

Clarkeburn, H. and K. Kettula (2012), 'Fairness and Using Reflective Journals in Assessment', *Teaching in Higher Education*, 17 (4): 439–52.

Clegg, S., J. Tan and S. Saedid (2002), 'Reflecting or Acting? Reflective Practice and Continuing Professional Development in Higher Education', *Reflective Practice*, 3 (1): 131–46.

Clough, P. (2002), *Narratives and Fictions in Educational Research*, Maidenhead: Open University Press.

Coffey, A. (1999), *The Ethnographic Self*, London: Sage.

Cole, M. (2000), 'Learning through Reflective Practice: A Professional Approach to Effective Continuing Professional Development among Healthcare Professionals', *Research in Post-Compulsory Education*, 5 (1): 23–37.

Colwell, R. and S. Bertsch McGrayne (2020), *A Lab of One's Own: One Woman's Personal Journey through Sexism in Science*, New York: Simon & Schuster.

Cordingley, P. (1999), 'Constructing and Critiquing Reflective Practice', *Educational Action Research*, 7 (2): 183–91.

Cote, J. and J. Hay (2002), 'Children's Involvement in Sport: A Developmental Framework for the Acquisition of Expertise in Team Sports', in J. Silva and D. Stevens (eds), *Psychological Foundations of Sport*, 484–502, Boston, MA: Merrill.

Cox, M. (1988), *Structuring the Therapeutic Process: Compromise with Chaos*, London: Jessica Kingsley Publishers.

Cox, M. (2020), 'Show Me Your Papers: When Racism and Sexism Trump Credibility', in E. McGee and W. H. Robinson (eds), *Diversifying STEM: Multidisciplinary Perspectives on Race and Gender 2*, 53–66, New Brunswick, NJ: Rutgers University Press.

CRAC (2020), 'Qualitative Research on Barriers to Progression of Disabled Scientists', London: Careers Research & Advisory Centre.

Crenshaw, K. (1989), 'Demarginalizing the Intersection of Race and Sex: A Black Feminist Critique of Antidiscrimination Doctrine, Feminist Theory, and Antiracist Politics', *University of Chicago Legal Forum*, 1989 (1): 139–67.

Cresswell, J. W. (2003), *Research Design*, London: Sage.

Cresswell, J. W. and D. Miller (2000), 'Determining Validity in Qualitative Inquiry', *Theory into Practice*, 39 (3): 124–30.

Cromby, J. (2011), 'Affecting Qualitative Health Psychology', *Health Psychology Review*, 5 (1): 79–96.

Crossley, N. (2006), *Reflexive Embodiment in Contemporary Society*, Berkshire: Open University Press.

Csordas, T. (2002), *Body/Meaning/Healing*, Basingstoke: Palgrave Macmillan.

Cullen, L. and J. Barlow (2003), 'A Training and Support Programme for Caregivers of Children with Disabilities: An Exploratory Study', *Patient Education and Counseling*, 55: 203–09.

Cullen, L., J. Barlow and D. Cushway (2005), 'Positive Touch, the Implications for Parents and Their Children with Autism: An Exploratory Study', *Complementary Therapies in Clinical Practice*, 11: 182–89.

'Dance Your PhD' (n.d.), *Science*. Available online: www.science.org/content/page/announcing-annual-dance-your-ph-d-contest (accessed 30 August 2023).

Daniell, E. (2006), *Every Other Thursday: Stories and Strategies from Successful Women Scientists*, New Haven, CT: Yale University Press.

Danto, A. (2013), *What Art Is*, New Haven, CT: Yale University Press.

Davies, N. (2018), 'Giving Disadvantaged Students a Helping Hand', *Education in Chemistry*, 29 November.

de Botton, A. and J. Armstrong (2013), *Art as Therapy*, London: Phaidon Press.

Dean, J. (2017), *Doing Reflexivity*, Bristol: Policy Press.

Delamont, S. (2006), 'The Smell of Sweat and Rum: Teacher Authority in Capoeira Classes', *Ethnography and Education*, 1 (2): 161–75.

Denzin, N. (1997), *Interpretive Ethnography: Ethnographic Practices for the 21st Century*, Thousand Oaks: Sage.

Denzin, N. (2010), *The Qualitative Manifesto*, Abingdon: Routledge.

Derrida, J. (1987), *Of Spirit: Heidegger and the Question*, London: University of Chicago Press.

Devereux, G. (1998), *Dynamic Yoga*, London: Thorsons.

Dewey, J. (1933), *How We Think: A Restatement of the Relation of Reflective Thinking to the Educative Process*, Boston, MA: D.C. Heath.

Dingwall, R. (2016), 'The Social Costs of Ethics Regulation', in W. van den Hoonard and A. Hamilton (eds), *The Ethics Rupture: Exploring Alternatives to Formal Research Ethics Review*, 25–42, Toronto: University of Toronto Press.

Dismore, H. and R. Bailey (2010), 'Fun and Enjoyment in Physical Education: Young People's Attitudes', *Research Papers in Education*, 1: 18.

Dodge, R., A. Daly, J. Huyton and L. Sanders (2012), 'The Challenge of Defining Wellbeing', *International Journal of Wellbeing*, 2 (3): 222–35.

Donnelly, M. (1983), *Managing the Mind*, London: Tavistock.

Dreyfus, H. and P. Rabinow (1982), *Michel Foucault: Beyond Structuralism and Hermeneutics*, Hemel Hempstead: The Harvester Press.

Driessnack, M. (2005), 'Children's Drawings as Facilitators of Communication: A Meta-Analysis', *Journal of Pediatric Nursing*, 20 (6): 415–23.

Dryden, W., ed (1990), *Individual Therapy: A Handbook*, Buckingham: Open University Press.

Dryden, W. and J. Rowan, eds (1988), *Innovative Therapy in Britain*, Milton Keynes: Open University Press.

Dubois Baber, L. (2020), 'Color-Blind Liberalism in Postsecondary STEM Education', in E. McGee and W. Robinson (eds), *Diversifying STEM: Multidisciplinary Perspectives on Race and Gender*, 19–35, New Brunswick, NJ: Rutgers University Press.

Duncan, M. C. (2007), 'Bodies in Motion: The Sociology of Physical Activity', *Quest*, 59: 55–66.

Dwyer, S. C. and J. L. Buckle (2009), 'The Space Between: On Being an Insider-Outsider in Qualitative Research', *International Journal of Qualitative Methods*, 8 (1): 54–63.

Dychtwald, K. (1977), *Bodymind*, New York: Pantheon Books.

Dyck, N. and E. Archetti, eds (2003), *Sport, Dance and Embodied Identities*, Oxford: Berg.

Ecclestone, K. and D. Hayes (2009), *The Dangerous Rise of Therapeutic Education*, Abingdon: Routledge.

Edwards, S. (2001), 'The Phenomenology of Intervention', *The Indo-Pacific Journal of Phenomenology*, 1: 1–8.

Egambaram, O., K. Hilton, J. Leigh, R. Richardson, J. Sarju, A. Slater and B. Turner (2022), 'The Future of Laboratory Chemistry Learning and Teaching Must Be Accessible', *Journal of Chemical Education*, 99 (12): 3814–21.

Einarsdottir, J. (2007), 'Research with Children: Methodological and Ethical Challenges', *European Early Childhood Education Research Journal*, 15 (2): 197–211.

Ellingson, L. (2017), *Embodiment in Qualitative Research*, Abingdon: Routledge.

Ellis, C. (2009), 'Fighting Back or Moving On: An Autoethnographic Response to Critics', *International Review of Qualitative Research*, 2 (3): 371–78.

Escalona, A., T. Field, R. Singer-Strunck, C. Cullen and K. Hartshorn (2001), 'Brief Report: Improvements in the Behaviour of Children with Autism Following Massage Therapy', *Journal of Autism and Developmental Disorders*, 31 (5): 513–16.

Evans, E. and C. Grant, eds (2008), *Mama PhD: Women Write about Motherhood and Academic Life*, Piscataway, NJ: Rutgers University Press.

Evans, J., B. Davies and J. Wright, eds (2004), *Body Knowledge and Control: Studies in the Sociology of Physical Education and Health*, Abingdon: Routledge.

Evans-Winters, V. (2019), *Black Feminism in Qualitative Inquiry*, Abingdon: Routledge.

Fanghanel, J. (2012), *Being an Academic*, Abingdon: Routledge.

Fara, P. (2018), *A Lab of One's Own: Science and Suffrage in the First World War*, Oxford: Oxford University Press.

Fargas-Malet, M., D. McSherry, E. Larkin and C. Robinson (2010), 'Research with Children: Methodological Issues and Innovative Techniques', *Journal of Early Childhood Research*, 8 (2): 175–92.

Farhi, D. (2000), *Yoga Mind, Body & Spirit: A Return to Wholeness*, Dublin: Newleaf.

Feagin, J., A. Orum and G. Sjoberg, eds (1991), *A Case for Case Study*, Chapel Hill, NC: University of North Carolina Press.

Feitis, R. (1978), *Ida Rolf Talks about Rolfing and Physical Reality*, New York: Harper & Row.

Feldenkrais, M. (1981), *The Elusive Obvious*, Capitola, CA: Meta Publications.

Ferraro, J. (2000), 'Reflective Practice and Professional Development', *ERIC Digest*. Available online: https://files.eric.ed.gov/fulltext/ED449120.pdf (accessed 4 September 2023).

Field-Springer, K. (2020), 'Reflexive Embodied Ethnography with Applied Sensibilities: Methodological Reflections on Involved Qualitative Fieldwork', *Qualitative Research*, 20 (2): 194–212.

Finesilver, C., J. Leigh and N. Brown (2020), 'Invisible Disability, Unacknowledged Diversity', in N. Brown and J. Leigh (eds), *Ableism in Academia: Theorising Experiences of Disabilities and Chronic Illnesses in Higher Education*, 143–60, London: UCL Press.

Finlay, L. (2022), *The Therapeutic Use of Self in Counselling and Psychotherapy*, London: Sage.

Fischman, D. (2009), 'Therapeutic Relationships and Kinesthetic Empathy', in S. Chaiklin and H. Wengrower (eds), *The Art and Science of Dance/Movement Therapy*, 33–53, Hove: Routledge.

Fitzgerald, T., J. White and H. Gunter (2012), *Hard Labour? Academic Work and the Changing Landscape of Higher Education*, Bingley: Emerald Group.

Flaherty, C. (2020), 'No Room of One's Own', *Inside Higher Ed*. Available online: www.insidehighered.com/news/2020/04/21/early-journal-submission-data-suggest-covid-19-tanking-womens-research-productivity (accessed 10 November 2020).

Flyvbjerg, B. (2006), 'Social Science that Matters', *Foresight Europe*, October 2005–March 2006: 38–42.

Fogel, A. (2009), *The Psychophysiology of Self-Awareness*, London: Norton.

Ford, P., D. Collins, R. Bailey, A. MacNamara, G. Pearce and M. Toms (2012), 'Participant Development in Sport, Exercise and Physical Activity: The Impact of Biological Maturation', *European Journal of Sport Science*, 12 (6): 515–26.

Fortin, S., A. Viera and M. Tremblay (2009), 'The Experience of Discourses in Dance and Somatics', *Journal of Dance & Somatic Practices*, 1 (1): 47–64.

Foucault, M. (1963), *La Naissance de la Clinique*, Paris: Presses Universitaires de France.

Frank, A. (2012), 'Science: It's Really, Really Hard, and That's Something to Celebrate', *Cosmos & Culture*, February.

Freedman, D. and M. Stoddard Holmes (2003), *The Teacher's Body: Embodiment, Authority, and Identity in the Academy*, New York: State University of New York.

Friedman, J. and E. A. Worden (2016), 'Creating Interdisciplinary Space on Campus: Lessons from US Area Studies Centers', *Higher Education Research and Development*, 35 (1): 129–41.

Gabster, B. P., K. van Daalen, R. Dhatt and M. Barry (2020), 'Challenges for the Female Academic during the COVID-19 Pandemic', *Lancet (London, England)*, 395 (10242): 1968–70.

Galen (1968), *De Usu Partium*, edited and translated by Margaret Tallmadge May, Ithaca, NY: Cornell University Press.

Gandhi, M. (1929), *The Gita According to Gandhi*, Ahmedabad: Navajivan Publ. House.

Gatens, E. (1988), *Towards a Feminist Philosophy of the Body*, Sydney: Allen & Unwin.

Gaunt, H. (2016), 'Introduction to Special Issue on the Reflective Conservatoire', *Arts & Humanities in Higher Education*, 15 (3–4): 269–75.

Gauntlett, D. (2007), *Creative Explorations: New Approaches to Identities and Audiences*, Abingdon: Routledge.

Gauntlett, D. and P. Holzwarth (2006), 'Creative and Visual Methods for Exploring Identities', *Visual Studies*, 21 (1): 82–91.

Geller, S. and L. Greenberg (2002), 'Therapeutic Presence: Therapists' Experience of Presence in the Psychotherapy Encounter', *Person-Centred and Experiential Psychotherapies*, 1 (1–2): 71–86.

General Teaching Council for Scotland (n.d.), 'Professional Values'. Available online: https://www.gtcs.org.uk/professional-standards/key-cross-cutting-themes/professional-values/#:~:text=The%20professional%20values%20of%20social,core%20of%20the%20Professional%20Standards (accessed 26 July 2022).

Gewin, V. (2014), 'Interdisciplinary Research: Break Out', *Nature*, 511: 371–73.

Gill, R. (2016), 'Breaking the Silence: The Hidden Injuries of Neo-Liberal Academia', *Feministische Studien*, 34 (1): 39–55.

Gindler, E. (1986), 'Gymnastic for Everyman', *Somatics*, 35: 39.

Gindler, E. (1995), 'Gymnastik for People Whose Lives Are Full of Activity', in D. H. Johnson (ed), *Bone, Breath & Gesture: Practices of Embodiment*, 5–14, San Francisco, CA: North Atlantic Books.

Goldstein, S. (2020), 'Hear Us! Seven Women Diagnosed with Borderline Personality Disorder Describe What They Need from Their Therapy Relationships', *Qualitative Psychology*, 7 (2): 132–52.

Gornick, V. (2009), *Women in Science: Then and Now*, New York: The Feminist Press.

Grant, A. (2018), *Doing Excellent Social Research with Documents*, Abingdon: Routledge.

Grant, A., S. Jones, K. Williams, J. Leigh and A. Brown (2022), 'Autistic Women's Views and Experiences of Infant Feeding: A Systematic Review of Qualitative Evidence', *Autism*, 26 (6): 1341–52.

Gray, A. (1994), *An Introduction to the Therapeutic Frame*, London: Routledge.
Gray, J., L. Larson, M. Fernandez, L. Duffy, J. Sturts, G. Powell and K. Roberts (2019), 'The Academic Job Search: Steps for Success', *SCHOLE: A Journal of Leisure Studies and Recreation Education*, 34 (1): 16–28.
Green, J. (1999), 'Somatic Authority and the Myth of the Ideal Body in Education', *Dance Research Journal*, 31 (2): 80–100.
Greene, M. J. (2014), 'On the Inside Looking In: Methodological Insights and Challenges in Conducting Qualitative Insider Research', *The Qualitative Report*, 19 (29): 1–13.
Gregory, S. and J. Verdouw (2005), 'Therapeutic Touch: Its Application for Residents in Aged Care', *Australian Nursing Journal*, 12 (7): 1–3.
Greider, C. W., J. M. Sheltzer, N. C. Cantalupo, W. B. Copeland, N. Dasgupta, N. Hopkins, et al (2019), 'Increasing Gender Diversity in the STEM Research Workforce', *Science*, 366 (6466): 692–95.
Greig, A. and J. Taylor (1999), *Doing Research with Children*, London: Sage.
Griffin, J. (1996), *Well-Being*, Oxford: Clarendon Press.
Grotowski, J. (1975), *Towards a Poor Theatre*, 2nd revised edition, edited by E. Barba, London: Methuen Drama.
Guillaumier, C. (2016), 'Reflection as Creative Process: Perspectives, Challenges and Practice', *Arts & Humanities in Higher Education*, 15 (3–4): 353–63.
Guy, J. (1987), *The Personal Life of a Psychotherapist*, New York: Wiley.
Hall, K., D. Stokols, R. Moser, B. Taylor, M. Thornquist, L. Nebeling and R. Jeffrey (2008), 'The Collaboration Readiness of Transdisciplinary Research Teams and Centers: Findings from the National Cancer Institute's TREC Year-One Evaluation Study', *American Journal of Preventative Medicine*, 35 (2S): 161–72.
Hall, S. (1996), 'Reflexivity in Emancipatory Action Research: Illustrating the Researcher's Constitutiveness', in O. Zuber-Skerritt (ed), *New Directions in Action Research*, 28–48, London: Falmer Press.
Hammersly, M. (2006), 'Ethnography: Problems and Prospects', *Ethnography and Education*, 1 (1): 3–14.
Hanna, T. (1981), 'Interview with Carola Spreads', *Somatics*, 10: 13.
Hanna, T. (1985), 'Interview with Mia Segal', *Somatics*, 8: 6.
Hanna, T. (1988), *Somatics*, Lebanon, IN: Da Capo Press.
Hanna, T. (1990), *Clinical Somatic Education: A New Discipline in the Field of Health Care*, Northampton, MA: Somatic Systems Institute.
Hardy, J. (1996), *A Psychology with a Soul: Psychosynthesis in Evolutionary Context*, London: Woodgrange Press.
Harris, A. (2016), *Video as Method: Understanding Qualitative Research*, Oxford: Oxford University Press.
Hartley, L. (1989), *Wisdom of the Body Moving*, Berkeley, CA: North Atlantic Books.

Hartley, L. (2001), *Servants of the Sacred Dream: Rebirthing the Deep Feminine Psycho-Spiritual Crisis and Healing*, Saffron Walden: Elmdon.

Hartley, L. (2004), *Somatic Psychology: Body, Mind and Meaning*, London: Whurr Publishers.

Hartley, L. (2005), 'Seeking a Sense of Self'. Available online: www.lindahartley.co.uk/article_seeking-a-sense-of-self.html#:~:text=It%20is%20the%20failure%20to,intuitive%20choice%20for%20such%20people (accessed 4 September 2023).

Hatton, N. and D. Smith (1995), 'Reflection in Teacher Education: Towards Definition and Implementation', *Teaching and Teacher Education*, 11 (1): 33–49.

Hawkins, P. and R. Shohet (1989), *Supervision in the Helping Professions*, Buckingham: Open University Press.

Hay, D. and S. Pichford (2016), 'Curating Blood: How Students' and Researchers' Drawings Bring Potential Phenomena to Light', *International Journal of Science Education*, 38 (17): 2596–620.

Hayes, A. (2009), *UKCP Code of Ethics*. Available online: www.psychotherapy.org.uk/media/bkjdm33f/ukcp-code-of-ethics-and-professional-practice-2019.pdf (accessed 4 September 2023).

Hedman-Phillips, E. and J. K. Barge (2017), 'Facilitating Team Reflexivity about Communication', *Small Group Research*, 48 (3): 255–87.

Hefferon, K. and S. Ollis (2006), '"Just Clicks": An Interpretative Phenomenological Analysis of Professional Dancers' Experience of Flow', *Research in Dance Education*, 7 (2): 141–59.

Hickson, H. (2011), 'Critical Reflection: Reflecting on Learning to Be Reflective', *Reflective Practice: International and Multidisciplinary Perspectives*, 12 (6): 829–39.

Hofstadter, D. R. and D. C. Dennett (1981), *The Mind's I*, London: Penguin Books.

Hutchinson, L. (1999), 'Evaluating and Researching the Effectiveness of Educational Interventions', *British Medical Journal*, 318: 1267–69.

Hycner, R. and L. Jacobs (1995), *The Healing Relationship in Gestalt Therapy: A Dialogic/Self Psychology Approach*, Highland, NY: Gestalt Journal Press.

Irwin, L. and J. Johnson (2006), 'Interviewing Young Children: Explicating Our Practices and Dilemmas', *Qualitative Health Research*, 15 (6): 821–31.

Ixer, G. (1999), 'There's No Such Thing as Reflection', *British Journal of Social Work*, 29: 513–27.

Iyengar, B. K. (1966), *Light on Yoga*, London: HarperCollins.

Iyengar, B. K. (1993), *Light on the Yoga Sutras of Patanjali*, Glasgow: Caledonian I.B.M. Ltd.

Jago, R. and R. Bailey (2001), 'Ethics and Paediatric Exercise Science: Issues and Making a Submission to a Local Ethics and Research Committee', *Journal of Sports Sciences*, 19 (7): 527–35.

Jagodzinski, J. and J. Wallin (2013), *Arts-Based Research: A Critique and a Proposal*, Rotterdam: Sense.

Jay, J. and K. Johnson (2002), 'Capturing Complexity: A Typology of Reflective Practice for Teacher Education', *Teaching and Teacher Education*, 18: 73–85.

Jeffrey, P. (2003), 'Smoothing the Waters: Observations on the Process of Cross-Disciplinary Research Collaboration', *Social Studies of Science*, 33 (4): 539–62.

Jewitt, C., J. Bezemer and K. O'Halloran (2016), *Introducing Multimodality*, Abingdon: Routledge.

Johns, D., C. Flynn, M. Hall, C. Spivakovsky and S. Turner (2022), *Co-Production and Criminal Justice*, Abingdon: Routledge.

Johnson, D. H. (1995), *Bone, Breath and Gesture: Practices of Embodiment*, Berkeley, CA: North Atlantic Books.

Joireman, J., L. Parrott III and J. Hammersla (2002), 'Empathy and the Self-Absorption Paradox: Support for the Distinction between Self-Rumination and Self-Reflection', *Self and Identity*, 1: 53–65.

Jonas, H. (2001), *The Phenomenon of Life*, Evanston, IL: Northwestern University Press.

Jones, G. (2012), 'Reflections on the Evolution of Higher Education as a Field of Study in Canada', *Higher Education Research & Development*, 31 (5): 711–22.

Juhan, D. (1987), *Job's Body*, Barrytown, NY: Station Hill Press.

Jung, C. (1957), *The Undiscovered Self*, Princeton, NJ: Princeton University Press.

Junker, J., C. Oberwittler, D. Jackson and K. Berger (2004), 'Utilization and Perceived Effectiveness of Complementary and Alternative Medicine in Patients with Dystonia', *Movement Disorders*, 19 (2): 158–61.

kamila_k_benova (2015), 'Athena Forum', *GenPORT*. Available online: www.genderportal.eu/organisations/athena-forum (accessed 17 January 2023).

Kara, H. (2015), *Creative Research Methods in the Social Sciences: A Practical Guide*, Bristol: Policy Press.

Kara, H. (2018), *Research Ethics in the Real World: Euro-Western and Indigenous Perspectives*, Bristol: Policy Press.

Kara, H. (2022), *Qualitative Research for Quantitative Researchers*, London: SAGE Publications Ltd.

Kennelly, R. and C. McCormack (2015), 'Creating More "Elbow Room" for Collaborative Reflective Practice in the Competitive, Performance Culture of Today's University', *Higher Education Research & Development*, 34 (5): 942–56.

Kern, J., M. Trivedi, C. Garver, B. Grannemann, A. Andrews and J. Savla (2006), 'The Pattern of Sensory Processing Abnormalities in Autism', *Autism*, 10: 480–94.

Keys, C. and R. Bailey (2006), *Theory of Mind and Blindness In Young Children: Towards Testable Hypotheses* (unpublished manuscript).

Kirschenbaum, H. and V. Henderson, eds (1990), *The Carl Rogers Reader*, London: Constable.

Klein, J. (1990), *Interdisciplinarity: History, Theory, and Practice*, Detroit, MI: Wayne University State Press.

Kozlov, M. (2023), '"Disruptive" Science Has Declined – and No One Knows Why', *Nature*, 613 (7943): 225.

Krishnamurti, J. (2002), 'No Title', in R. Rosen (ed), *The Yoga of Breath*, 280, London: Shambhala.

Kuhn, T. (1962), *The Structure of Scientific Revolutions*, Chicago, IL: University of Chicago Press.

Kyburz-Graber, R. (2004), 'Does Case-Study Methodology Lack Rigour? The Need for Quality Criteria for Sound Case-Study Research, as Illustrated by a Recent Case in Secondary and Higher Education', *Environmental Education Research*, 10 (1): 53–65.

Kyriacou, C. (1998), *Essential Teaching Skills*, Cheltenham: Nelson Thornes.

Kyvik, S. and D. Aksnes (2015), 'Explaining the Increase in Publication Productivity among Academic Staff: A Generational Perspective', *Studies in Higher Education*, 40 (8): 1438–53.

Lakoff, G. and M. Johnson (2003), *Metaphors We Live By*, Chicago, IL: University of Chicago Press.

Lamarque, P. and S. Haugom Olsen (2019), *Aesthetics and the Philosophy of Art: The Analytic Tradition, an Anthology*, Hoboken, NJ: John Wiley & Sons, Ltd.

Lambie, J. and A. Marcel (2002), 'Consciousness and the Varieties of Emotion Experience', *Psychological Review*, 109 (2): 219–59.

Langer, E. (1989), *Mindfulness*, Reading, MA: Perseus Books.

Langer, E. (2000), 'The Construct of Mindfulness', *Journal of Social Issues*, 56 (1): 1–9.

Lapum, J., P. Ruttonsha, K. Church, T. Yau and A. M. David (2011), 'Employing the Arts in Research as an Analytical Tool and Dissemination Method: Interpreting Experience through the Aesthetic', *Qualitative Inquiry*, 18 (1): 100–15.

Larkin, M., S. Watts and E. Clifton (2006), 'Giving Voice and Making Sense in Interpretative Phenomenological Analysis', *Qualitative Research in Psychology*, 3: 102–20.

Latour, B. (1999), *Pandora's Hope: Essays on the Realities of Science Studies*, Cambridge, MA: Harvard University Press.

Leavy, P. (2015), *Method Meets Art: Arts-Based Research Practice*, New York: Guildford.

Leavy, P. (2016), *Fiction as Research Practice: Short Stories, Novellas, and Novels*, Abingdon: Routledge.

Leboyer, F. (1974), *Birth Without Violence*, Norwich: Fletcher & Son.

Leder, D. (1990), *The Absent Body*, Chicago, IL: University of Chicago Press.

Leigh, A. (1998), *Referral and Termination Issues for Counsellors*, London: Sage.

Leigh, J. (2012), 'Somatic Movement and Education: A Phenomenological Study of Young Children's Perceptions, Expressions and Reflections of Embodiment through Movement', PhD thesis, University of Birmingham.

Leigh, J. (2016), 'An Embodied Perspective on Judgements of Written Reflective Practice for Professional Development in Higher Education', *Reflective Practice: International and Multidisciplinary Perspectives*, 17 (1): 72–85.

Leigh, J. (2017), 'Experiencing Emotion: Children's Perceptions, Reflections and Self-Regulation', *Body, Movement and Dance in Psychotherapy*, 12 (2): 128–44.

Leigh, J. (2019a), *Conversations on Embodiment across Higher Education: Research, Teaching and Practice*, Abingdon: Routledge.

Leigh, J. (2019b), 'An Embodied Approach in a Cognitive Discipline', *Educational Futures and Fractures*, London: Palgrave.

Leigh, J. (2019c), 'Embodied Practice and Embodied Academic Identity', in J. Leigh (ed), *Conversations on Embodiment across Higher Education: Teaching, Practice and Research*, 151–70, Abingdon: Routledge.

Leigh, J. (2019d), 'Exploring Multiple Identities: An Embodied Perspective on Academic Development and Higher Education Research', *Journal of Dance & Somatic Practices*, 11 (1).

Leigh, J. (2020a), 'Using Creative Research Methods and Movement to Encourage Reflection in Children', *Journal of Early Childhood Research*, 18 (2): 130–42.

Leigh, J. (2020b), 'What Would a Longitudinal Rhythmanalysis of a Qualitative Researcher's Life Look Like?', in B. Clift, J. Gore, S. Gustafsson, S. Bekker, I. Costas Batlle, and J. Hatchard (eds), Chapter 4, *Temporality in Qualitative Inquiry: Theory, Methods, and Practices*, Abingdon: Routledge.

Leigh, J. (2021), 'Embodiment and Authenticity', in N. Brown (ed), *Lived Experiences of Ableism in Academia: Strategies for Inclusion in Higher Education*, Chapter 3, Bristol: Policy Press.

Leigh, J. (2023), 'Leeches' (unpublished).

Leigh, J. and R. Bailey (2013), 'Reflection, Reflective Practice and Embodied Reflective Practice', *Body, Movement and Dance in Psychotherapy*, 8 (3): 160–71.

Leigh, J. and C. A. Blackburn (2017), *Exploring Embodied Academic Identity through Creative Research Methods* (film). https://vimeo.com/245602322

Leigh, J. and N. Brown (2020), 'Internalised Ableism: Of the Political and the Personal', in N. Brown and J. Leigh (eds), *Ableism in Academia: Theorising Experiences of Disabilities and Chronic Illnesses in Higher Education*, 164–81, London: UCL Press.

Leigh, J. and N. Brown (2021a), *Embodied Inquiry: Research Methods*, London: Bloomsbury.

Leigh, J. and N. Brown (2021b), 'Researcher Experiences in Practice-Based Interdisciplinary Research', *Research Evaluation*, 30 (4): 421–30.

Leigh, J. S., N. Busschaert, C. J. E. Haynes, J. R. Hiscock, K. M. Hutchins, L. K. S. von Krbek, et al (2022a), 'Planning a Family', *Nature Reviews Chemistry*, 6 (10): 673–75.

Leigh, J. S., J. R. Hiscock, S. Koops, A. J. McConnell, C. J. E. Haynes, C. Caltagirone, et al (2022b), 'Managing Research throughout COVID-19: Lived Experiences of Supramolecular Chemists', *CHEM*, 8: 299–311.

Leigh, J., J. Hiscock, A. McConnell, M. Kieffer, E. Draper, K. Hutchins, et al (2022c), *Women in Supramolecular Chemistry: Collectively Crafting the Rhythms of Our Work and Lives in STEM*, Bristol: Policy Press.

Leigh, J., D. Smith, B. Blight, G. Lloyd, C. McTernan and E. Draper (2022d), 'Listening to Fathers in STEM', *Nature Reviews Chemistry*, 7: 67–68.

Leigh, J., J. Hiscock, A. McConnell, C. Haynes, C. Caltagirone, M. Kieffer, et al (2023), 'Women in Supramolecular Chemistry: Narratives of Resilience and Community Building in a Gender-Constrained Field', in M. Ronksley-Pavla, M. Neumann, J. Manakil and K. Pickard-Smith (eds), *Academic Women: Voicing Narratives of Gendered Experiences*, Chapter 10, London: Bloomsbury.

Leigh, J., J. Sarju and A. Slater (2024a), 'Can Science Be Inclusive? Belonging and Identity When You Are Disabled, Chronically Ill, or Neurodivergent', in C. Kandiko-Smith (ed), *Belonging in STEM*, Chapter 14, London: UCL Press.

Leigh, J., J. Hiscock, S. Koops, A. McConnell, C. Haynes, C. Caltagirone, et al (2024b), 'Analysing Creative Multi-Modal Data for a Scientific Audience', in H. Kara, D. Mannay and A. Roy (eds), *Creative Data Analysis Handbook*, Bristol: Policy Press.

Linden, P. (1994), 'Somatic Literacy: Bringing Somatic Education into Physical Education', *Journal of Physical Education, Recreation & Dance*, 65 (7): 15–21.

Linden, P. (2007), *Embodied Peacemaking: Body Awareness, Self-Regulation and Conflict Resolution,* Columbus, OH: CCMS Publications.

Lingard, L., C. Schryer, M. Spafford and S. Campbell (2007), 'Negotiating the Politics of Identity in an Interdisciplinary Research Team', *Qualitative Research*, 7: 501–19.

Lischetzke, T. and M. Eid (2003), 'Is Attention to Feelings Beneficial or Detrimental to Affective Well-Being? Mood Regulation as a Moderator Variable', *Emotion*, 3 (4): 361–77.

Longhurst, R. (1997), '(Dis)Embodied Geographies', *Progress in Human Geography*, 21 (4): 486–501.

Lu, C., J. M. Tito and J. A. Kentel (2009), 'Eastern Movement Disciplines (EMDs) and Mindfulness: A New Path to Subjective Knowledge in Western Physical Education', *Quest*, 61 (3): 353–70.

Lyon, D. (2016), 'Researching Young People's Orientations to the Future: The Methodological Challenges of Using Arts Practice', *Qualitative Research*, 16 (4): 430–45.

Lyon, D. (2019), *What Is Rhythmanalysis?*, London: Bloomsbury.

Lyon, D. and L. Back (2012), 'Fishmongers in a Global Economy: Craft and Social Relations on a London Market', *Sociological Research Online*, 17 (2): 1–11.

Macfarlane, B. and L. Gourlay (2009), 'Points of Departure', *Teaching in Higher Education*, 14 (4): 455–59.

Mainland, P. (1998), *A Yoga Parade of Animals*, Shaftesbury: Element Children's Books.

Makgoba, M. (2020), 'Black Scientists Matter', *Science*, 369 (6506): 884.

Mallipeddi, N. and R. VanDaalen (2022), 'Intersectionality Within Critical Autism Studies: A Narrative Review', *Autism in Adulthood*, 4 (4): 281–89.

Maloney, P. (2018), *The Britannia Panopticon Music Hall and Cosmopolitan Entertainment Culture*, Palgrave Studies in Theatre and Performance History, London: Palgrave Macmillan.

Mandell, D. S., L. D. Wiggins, L. A. Carpenter, J. Daniels, C. DiGuiseppi, M. S. Durkin, et al (2009), 'Racial/Ethnic Disparities in the Identification of Children with Autism Spectrum Disorders', *American Journal of Public Health*, 99 (3): 493–98.

Mannay, D., E. Staples and V. Edwards (2017), 'Visual Methodologies, Sand and Psychoanalysis: Employing Creative Participatory Techniques to Explore the Educational Experiences of Mature Students and Children in Care', *Visual Studies*, 32 (4): 345–58.

Manning, E. (2016), *The Minor Gesture*, Durham, NC: Duke University Press.

Mansell, J. and J. Beadle-Brown (2012), *Active Support: Enabling and Empowering People with Intellectual Disabilities*, Philadelphia, PA: Jessica Kingsley Publishers.

Marcel, G. (2011), *The Mystery of Being*, Toronto: University of Toronto Libraries.

Markula, P. and R. Pringle (2006), *Foucault, Sport and Exercise*, Oxon: Routledge.

Mårtensson, P., U. Fors, S. B. Wallin, U. Zander and G. H. Nilsson (2016), 'Evaluating Research: A Multidisciplinary Approach to Assessing Research Practice and Quality', *Research Policy*, 45 (3): 593–603.

Martin, B. (2011), 'The Research Excellence Framework and the "Impact Agenda": Are We Creating a Frankenstein Monster', *Research Evaluation*, 20 (3): 247–54.

Maslow, A. H. (1959), 'Cognition of Being in the Peak Experiences', *The Journal of Genetic Psychology: Research and Theory on Human Development*, 94: 43–66.

Mason, M. A. (2013), 'In the Ivory Tower, Men Only: For Men, Having Children Is a Career Advantage. For Women, It's a Career Killer', *Slate*, June.

Mason, M. A. and E. M. Ekman (2007), *Mothers on the Fast Track: How a New Generation Can Balance Family and Careers*, Oxford: Oxford University Press.

Massey, C., F. Alpass, R. Flett, K. Lewis, S. Morriss and F. Sligo (2006), 'Crossing Fields: The Case of a Multi-Disciplinary Research Team', *Qualitative Research*, 6 (2): 131–49.

Matthew, R. and J. Pritchard (2010), 'Hard and Soft – A Useful Way of Thinking about Disciplines? Reflections from Engineering Education on Disciplinary Identities', in C. Kreber (ed), *The University and Its Disciplines: Teaching and Learning within and beyond Disciplinary Boundaries*, Chapter 5, Abingdon: Routledge.

Mauthner, M. (1997), 'Methodological Aspects of Collecting Data from Children: Lessons from Three Research Projects', *Children and Society*, 11: 16–28.

May, R. with G. Parkes (1989), *Heidegger's Hidden Sources*, London: Routledge.

Mayland, E. (1991), *The Rosen Method*, published privately.

McCormack, D. (2013), *Refrains for Moving Bodies: Experience and Experiment in Affective Spaces*, Durham, NC: Duke University Press.

McGee, E. and W. Robinson, eds (2020), *Diversifying STEM: Multidisciplinary Perspectives on Race and Gender*, New Brunswick, NJ: Rutgers University Press.

McMillan, M. (2015), 'Pedagogy of the Workshop: An "Expert-Intuitive" Practice', in K. Hatton (ed), *Towards an Inclusive Arts Education*, 78–96, London: Trentham.

McNamee, M. and R. Bailey (2010), 'Physical Education', *Handbook of the Philosophy of Education*, 467–80, London: Sage.

Mearns, D. and B. Thorne (1998), *Person-Centred Counselling in Action*, London: Sage.

Merleau-Ponty, M. (2002), *Phenomenology of Perception*, translated by C. Smith, Oxon: Routledge.

Merton, R. (1996), *On Social Structure and Science*, Chicago, IL: University of Chicago Press.

Middendorf, I. (1990), *The Perceptible Breath: A Breathing Science*, Paderborn: Junferman Verlag.

Miles, A. (2011), 'The Reflective Coach', in I. Stafford (ed), *Coaching Children in Sport*, 109–20, Abingdon: Routledge.

Millar, R. (1991), 'Why Is Science Hard to Learn?', *Journal of Computer Assisted Learning*, 7 (2): 66–74.

Mindell, A. (1995), 'Moving the Dreambody: Movement Work in Process Orientated Psychology', *Contact Quarterly*, 56: 62.

Mipham, S. (2013), *Running with the Mind of Meditation: Lessons for Training Body and Mind*, Reprint edition, New York: Harmony Books.

Mitchell, L. (2016), *Creativity as Co-Therapists: The Practitioner's Guide to the Art of Psychotherapy*, New York: Routledge.

Moen, T. (2006), 'Reflections on the Narrative Research Approach', *International Journal of Qualitative Methods*, 5 (4): 56–69.

Moffat, A., M. Ryan and G. Barton (2016), 'Reflexivity and Self-Care for Creative Facilitators: Stepping Outside the Circle', *Studies in Continuing Education*, 38 (1): 29–46.

Monosson, E., ed (2008), *Motherhood, the Elephant in the Laboratory: Women Scientists Speak Out*, Ithaca, NY: Cornell University.

Montagu, A. (1971), *Touching: The Human Significance of Skin*, London: Harper & Row.

Moon, J. (2007), 'Getting the Measure of Reflection: Considering Matters of Definition and Depth', *Journal of Radiotherapy in Practice*, 6 (4): 191–200.

Morgan, W. J. (2006), 'Philosophy and Physical Education', in D. Kirk, D. Macdonald and M. O'Sullivan (eds), *Handbook of Physical Education*, 97–108, London: SAGE Publications Ltd.

Morley, D., R. Bailey, J. Tan and B. Cooke (2005), 'Inclusive Physical Education: Teachers' Views of Including Pupils with Special Educational Needs and/or Disabilities in Physical Education', *European Physical Education Review*, 11 (1): 84–107.

Morowitz, H. J. (1981), 'Rediscovering the Mind', in D. R. Hofstadter and D. C. Dennett (eds), *The Mind's I*, 34–42, London: Penguin Books.

Moti, N. (1997), 'Ten Cheers for Interdisciplinarity: The Case for Interdisciplinary Knowledge and Research', *Social Science Journal*, 34 (2): 201–17.

Moustakas, C. (1994), *Phenomenological Research Methods*, London: SAGE.

Mujtaba, T., R. Sheldrake and M. Reiss (2020), 'Chemistry for All: Reducing Inequalities in Chemistry Aspirations and Attitudes', London: Royal Society of Chemistry.

Myers, N. (2015), *Rendering Life Molecular: Models, Modelers, and Excitable Matter*, Durham, NC: Duke University Press.

Navarro, T. (2017), 'But Some of Us Are Broke: Race, Gender, and the Neoliberalization of the Academy', *American Anthropologist*, 119 (3): 506–17.

Newton, B., Z. Rothlingova, R. Gutteridge, K. LeMarchand and J. Raphael (2011), 'No Room for Reflexivity? Critical Reflections Following a Systematic Review of Qualitative Research', *Journal of Health Psychology*, 0 (0): 1–20.

Nguyen, T.-H. and B. M. D. Nguyen (2018), 'Is the "First-Generation Student" Term Useful for Understanding Inequality? The Role of Intersectionality in Illuminating the Implications of an Accepted – Yet Unchallenged – Term', *Review of Research in Education*, 42 (1): 146–76.

NHS (n.d.), 'Dramatherapist'. Online: www.healthcareers.nhs.uk/explore-roles/allied-health-professionals/roles-allied-health-professions/dramatherapist (accessed 17 August 2022).

Nichols, B. (2008), *Somatic Psychotherapy and Somatic Education: Designing and Developing the Interface between Education and Therapy; Utilizing the Autonomic Nervous System as a Primary Design Element for Transformative and Therapeutic Learning Curriculum*, Santa Barbara, CA: Santa Barbara Graduate Institute.

Nolen-Hoeksema, S., E. Stice, E. Wade and C. Bohon (2007), 'Reciprocal Relations between Rumination and Bulimic, Substance Abuse, and Depressive Symptoms in Female Adolescents', *Journal of Abnormal Psychology*, 116 (1): 198–207.

Nussbaum, M. (2000), *Women and Human Development: The Capabilities Approach*, Cambridge: Cambridge University Press.

Oakley, A. (1981), 'Interviewing Women: A Contradiction in Terms', in H. Roberts (ed), *Doing Feminist Research*, 30–61, London: Routledge.

O'Cathain, A., E. Murphy and J. Nicholl (2008), 'Multidisciplinary, Interdisciplinary or Dysfunctional? Team Working in Mixed-Methods Research', *Qualitative Research*, 18: 1574–85.

OECD (2018), 'Equity in Education: Breaking down Barriers to Social Mobility', Paris: OECD Publishing, Paris.

Oliver, K. and R. Lalik (2001), 'The Body as Curriculum: Learning with Adolescent Girls', *Journal of Curriculum Studies*, 33 (3): 303–33.

Oliver, M. (2013), 'The Social Model of Disability: Thirty Years On', *Disability & Society*, 28 (7): 1024–26.

O'Loughlin, M. (2006), *Embodiment and Education: Exploring Creatural Existence*, Dordrecht: Springer.

Olsen, A. (1998), *Body Stories: A Guide to Experiential Anatomy*, Lebanon, NH: University Press of New England.

Osterman, K. and P. Kottkamp (1993), *Reflective Practice for Educators: Improving Schooling through Professional Development*, Newbury Park, CA: Corwin Press, Inc.

Parfit, D. (1984), *Reasons and Persons*, Oxford: Clarendon Press.

Pattabhi Jois, S. K. (1999), *Yoga Mala*, New York: North Point Press.

Pavlov, B. (2010), 'Conditioned Reflexes: An Investigation of the Physiological Activity of the Cerebral Cortex', *Annals of Neurosciences*, 17 (3): 136–41.

Peabody, M. A. and S. Noyes (2017), 'Reflective Boot Camp: Adapting LEGO® SERIOUS PLAY in Higher Education', *Reflective Practice*, 18: 232–43.

Pearce, G. and R. P. Bailey (2010), 'Football Pitches and Barbie Dolls: Young Childrens' Perceptions of Their School Playground', *Early Child Development and Care*, 181 (10): 1361–79.

Pereira, M. (1999), 'My Reflective Practice as Research', *Teaching in Higher Education*, 4 (3): 339–54.

Pert, C. B. (1999), *Molecules of Emotion*, London: Pocket Books Simon & Schuster.

Petsilas, P., J. Leigh, N. Brown and C. Blackburn (2019a), 'Embodied Reflection: Exploring Creative Routes to Teaching Reflective Practice within Dance Training', *Journal of Dance & Somatic Practices*, 11 (2): 177–95.

Petsilas, P., J. Leigh, N. Brown and C. Blackburn (2019b), 'Creative and Embodied Methods to Teach Reflections and Support Students' Learning', *Research in Dance Education*, 20 (1): 19–35.

Phalen, S. (2015), 'Making Music as Embodied Dialogue', *Qualitative Inquiry*, 21 (9): 787–97.

Philips, R. and H. Kara (2021), *Creative Writing for Social Research: A Practical Guide*, Bristol: Bristol University Press.

Phillips, D. (1971), *Knowledge from What? Theories and Methods in Social Research*, Chicago, IL: Rand McNally.

Phillips, K. (2001), *The Spirit of Yoga*, London: Cassell & Co.

Phillips, K. and M. Stewart (1992), *Yoga for Children*, New York: Simon & Schuster.

Piaget, J. (1928), *The Child's Conception of the World*, London: Routledge and Kegan Paul.

Piaget, J. (1976), *The Grasp of Consciousness: Action and Concept in the Young Child*, translated by S. Wedgwood, Cambridge, MA: Harvard University Press.

Pickard, A. (2007), 'Girls, Bodies and Pain: Negotiating the Body in Ballet', in I. Wellard (ed), *Rethinking Gender and Youth Sport*, 8–50, London: Routledge.

Pickard, A. (2019), 'Under This Weight: Embodiment in Dance Choreography', in J. Leigh (ed), *Conversations on Embodiment across Higher Education: Teaching, Practice and Research*, 98–108, Abingdon: Routledge.

Pickard, A. and R. Bailey (2009), 'Crystallising Experiences among Young Elite Dancers', *Sport, Education and Society*, 14 (2): 165–81.

Pilgrim, D. (1990), 'British Psychotherapy in Context', in W. Dryden (ed), *Individual Therapy: A Handbook*, 1–17, Buckingham: Open University Press.

Pink, S. (2007), *Doing Visual Ethnography*, second edition, London: Sage.

Pink, S. (2009), *Doing Sensory Ethnography*, London: Sage.

Piper, H. (2003), '"Touch" in Educational and Child Care Settings: Dilemmas and Responses', *British Educational Research Journal*, 29 (6): 879–94.

Piper, H. and I. Stronach (2008), *Don't Touch: The Educational Story of a Panic*, Abingdon: Routledge.

Poltorak, M. (2019), 'Embodied Reflexivity: Sharing and Transformation in Teaching Visual Anthropology', in J. Leigh (ed), *Conversations on Embodiment across Higher Education: Teaching, Practice and Research*, 192–208, Abingdon: Routledge.

Popper, K. (1959), *The Logic of Scientific Discovery*, London: Routledge & Kegan Paul.

Porter, D. and A. Chubin (1985), 'An Indicator of Cross-Disciplinary Research', *Scientometrics*, 8 (3–4): 161–76.

Postma, M. and P. Crawford (2006), *Reflecting Visual Ethnography: Using the Camera in Anthropological Research*, Michigan: CNWS Publications.

Powell, K. (2021), 'The Parenting Penalties Faced by Scientist Mothers', *Nature*, 595: 611–13.

Powell, L., J. Barlow and A. Cheshire (2006), 'The Training and Support Programme for Parents of Children with Cerebral Palsy: A Process Evaluation', *Complementary Therapies in Clinical Practice*, 12 (3): 192–99.

Prichard, I. T. (2007), 'Relations among Exercise Type, Self-Objectification, and Body Image in the Fitness Centre Environment: The Role of Reasons for Exercise', *Psychology of Sport and Exercise*, 9 (6): 855–66.

Prideaux, E. (2021), 'When the Pandemic Is Over, How Should We Process the Memories of What Happened? Ed Prideaux Discovers Counter-Intuitive Answers from the Science of Trauma', *BBC Future*, February.

Prondzynski, F. von (2014), 'A University Blog: A Diary of Life and Strategy inside and Outside the University'. Available online: https://universitydiary.wordpress.com (accessed 4 September 2023).

Prosser, J., ed (1998), *Image-Based Research: A Sourcebook for Qualitative Researchers*, London: Falmer Press.

Punch, S. (2002), 'Research with Children: The Same or Different from Research with Adults?', *Childhood*, 9 (3): 321–41.

Robertson, C., C. Childs and E. Marsden (2000), 'Equality and the Inclusion of Pupils with Special Educational Needs in Physical Education', in S. Capel and S. Piotrowski (eds), *Issues in Physical Education*, 47–63, London: Routledge.

Robinson, J. (2008), 'Being Undisciplined: Transgressions and Intersections in Academia and Beyond', *Futures*, 40: 70–86.

Rogers, C. A. (1967), *A Therapist's View of Psychotherapy*, London: Constable.

Rolle, T., Z. Vue, S. A. Murray, S. A. Shareef, H. D. Shuler, H. K. Beasley, et al (2021), 'Toxic Stress and Burnout: John Henryism and Social Dominance in the Laboratory and STEM Workforce', *Pathogens and Disease*, 79 (7): ftab041.

Rosa, H. (2010), 'Full Speed Burnout? From the Pleasures of the Motorcycle to the Bleakness of the Treadmill: The Dual Face of Social Acceleration', *International Journal of Motorcycle Studies*, 6 (1).

Rose, G. (2007), *Visual Methodologies: An Introduction to the Interpretation of Visual Materials*, London: Sage.

Rosen, M. and H. Oxenbury (illus) (1989), *We're Going on a Bear Hunt*, London: Walker Books.

Ross, J. (2014), 'Performing the Reflective Self: Awareness in High-Stakes Reflection', *Studies in Higher Education*, 39: 219–32.

Rosser, S. (1988), *Feminism within the Science and Health Care Professions: Overcoming Resistance*, Oxford: Pergamon Press Ltd.

Rosser, S. (2004), *The Science Glass Ceiling: Academic Women Scientists and the Struggle to Succeed*, New York: Routledge.

Rosser, S. (2012), *Breaking into the Lab: Engineering Progress for Women in Science*, New York: New York University Press.

Rosser, S. (2017), *Academic Women in STEM Faculty*, Basingstoke: Palgrave Macmillan.

Rowan, J. (1993), *The Transpersonal Spirituality in Psychotherapy and Counseling*, London: Routledge.

Royal Society (2021), 'Ethnicity in STEM Academic Communities', London: Royal Society.

Royal Society of Chemistry (2018), *Diversity Landscape of the Chemical Sciences*, London: Royal Society of Chemistry.

Royal Society of Chemistry (2019a), *Breaking the Barriers: Women's Retention and Progression in the Chemical Sciences*, London: Royal Society of Chemistry.

Royal Society of Chemistry (2019b), 'Is Publishing in the Chemical Sciences Gender Biased? Driving Change in Research Culture', London: Royal Society of Chemistry.

Royal Society of Chemistry (2022a), 'Written Evidence to the Parliamentary Committee on Diversity in Science and Technology: Submitted by the Royal Society of Chemistry (DIV0032)', London: UK Parliament.

Royal Society of Chemistry (2022b), 'Missing Elements: Racial and Ethnic Inequalities in the Chemical Sciences', London: Royal Society of Chemistry.

Rubenfeld, I. (1977), 'Interview with Irmgard Bertenieff', *Somatics*, 9: 13.

Ruby, J. (1980), 'Exposing Yourself: Reflexivity, Anthropology and Film', *Semiotics*, 30 (1/2): 153–79.

Russell, B. (1946), *A History of Western Philosophy*, London: Unwin Hyman.

Russell, G. (2020), 'Remote Working during the Pandemic: A Q&A with Gillian Isaacs Russell: Questions from the Editor and Editorial Board of the BJP', *British Journal of Psychotherapy*, 3 (3): 364–74.

Russell, T. (2005), 'Can Reflective Practice Be Taught?', *Reflective Practice: International and Multidisciplinary Perspectives*, 6 (2): 199–204.

Salmon, P. (2020), *Mindful Movement in Psychotherapy*, New York: Guildford.

Sartre, J.-P. (1969), *Being and Nothingness*, Northampton: John Dickens and Co.

Scaffidi, A. K. and J. E. Berman (2011), 'A Positive Postdoctoral Experience Is Related to Quality Supervision and Career Mentoring, Collaborations, Networking and a Nurturing Research Environment', *Higher Education*, 62: 685–98.

Schick, J. (1987), 'Interview with Charlotte', *The Sensory Awareness Foundation Newsletter*.

Schiffmann, E. (1996), *Yoga: The Spirit and Practice of Moving into Stillness*, New York: Pocket Books.

Schirle, J. (1987), 'A Conversation with Marjory Barlow', *Somatics*, 22: 25.

Schön, D. (1987), *Educating the Reflective Practitioner: Toward a New Design for Teaching and Learning in the Professions*, San Francisco, CA: Jossey-Bass.

Science Buddies (n.d.), 'What Is the Scientific Method?', *Science Buddies*. Available online: www.sciencebuddies.org/science-fair-projects/science-fair/steps-of-the-scientific-method (accessed 26 July 2022).

Scull, A. (1977), *Decarceration*, Englewood Cliffs, NJ: Prentice Hall.

Sen, A. (1999), *Commodities and Capabilities*, New Delhi: OUP India.

Shahjahan, R. (2019), 'On "Being for Others": Time and Shame in the Neoliberal Academy', *Journal of Education Policy*, 35 (6): 785–811.

Shakespeare, P., D. Atkinson and S. French, eds (1993), *Reflecting on Research Practice: Issues in Health and Social Welfare*, Buckingham: Open University Press.

Shapiro, S. and L. Carlsom (2009), *The Art and Science of Mindfulness*, Washington, DC: American Psychological Association.

Shaughnessy, N. (2017), 'Do You See What I See? Arts, Science and Evidence in Autism Research', in N. Rowe and M. Reason (eds), *Applied Practice: Evidence and Impact in Theatre, Music and Art*, 80–94, London: Bloomsbury Methuen Drama

Shaughnessy, N. and M. Trimingham (2016), *Autism in the Wild: Bridging the Gap between Experiment and Experience*, in P. Garratt (ed), The Cognitive Humanities: Embodied Mind in Literature and Culture, 191–211, London: Palgrave Macmillan.

Sheets-Johnstone, M. (2009), *The Corporeal Turn: An Interdisciplinary Reader*, London: Imprint Academic.

Sheets-Johnstone, M. (2010a), 'Why Is Movement Therapeutic?', *American Journal of Dance Therapy*, 32: 2–15.

Sheets-Johnstone, M. (2010b), 'Kinesthetic Experience: Understanding Movement Inside and Out', *Body, Movement and Dance in Psychotherapy*, 5 (2): 111–27.

Sheets-Johnstone, M. (2015), 'Embodiment on Trial: A Phenomenological Investigation', *Continental Philosophy Review*, 48: 23–39.

Shelton, S. A., J. E. Flynn and T. J. Grosland, eds (2018), *Feminism and Intersectionality in Academia: Women's Narratives and Experiences in Higher Education*, Basingstoke: Palgrave Macmillan.

Shepherd, M., ed (1982), *Psychiatrists on Psychiatry*, Cambridge: Cambridge University Press.

Shildrick, M. (1997), *Leaky Bodies and Boundaries: Feminism, Postmodernism and (Bio)Ethics*, Abingdon: Routledge.

Shilling, C. (2005), *The Body in Culture, Technology and Society*, London: Sage.

Shilling, C. (2008), *Changing Bodies: Habit, Crisis and Creativity*, London: Sage.

Shilling, C. (2012), *The Body and Social Theory*, London: Sage.

Sidebottom, K. and D. Ball (2018), 'Art as a "Thing That Does": Creative Assemblages, Expressive Lines of Flight, and Becoming Cosmic-Artisan in Teacher Education', in K. Strom, T. Mills and A. Ovens (eds), *Decentering the Researcher in Intimate Scholarship (Advances in Research on Teaching, Vol. 31)*, 153–65, Bingley: Emerald Publishing Limited.

Sills, M. (2000), 'Inner Processes of the Practitioner', CSTA AGM, 6–11.

Silvia, P. (2002), 'Self-Awareness and the Regulation of Emotional Intensity', *Self and Identity*, 1 (1): 3–10.

Skinner, B. (1948), *Verbal Behaviour*, Cambridge, MA: Harvard University Press.

Slater, A. G., C. Caltagirone, E. Draper, N. Busschaert, K. M. Hutchins and J. Leigh (2022), 'Pregnancy in the Lab', *Nature Reviews Chemistry*, 6: 163–64.

Sleater, A. and J. Scheiner (2022), 'Impact of the Therapist's "Use of Self"', *The European Journal of Counselling Psychology*, 8 (1): 118–43.

Slowe, S., J. Leigh and J. Caplehorne (2023), 'Ableism and Exclusion: Challenging Academic Cultural Norms in Research Communication', *Journal of Research Management and Administration*, 2 (1): 030220232.

Smears, E. (2009), 'Breaking Old Habits: Professional Development through an Embodied Approach to Reflective Practice', *Journal of Dance & Somatic Practices*, 1 (1): 99–110.

Smith, D. K. (2020), 'The Race to the Bottom and the Route to the Top', *Nature Chemistry*, 12: 101–03.

Smith, E. (2011), 'Teaching Critical Reflection', *Teaching in Higher Education*, 16 (2): 211–23.

Sokolowski, R. (2000), *Introduction to Phenomenology*, Cambridge: Cambridge University Press.

Sparkes, A. and B. Smith (2002), 'Sport, Spinal Cord Injury, Embodied Masculinities, and the Dilemmas of Narrative Identity', *Men and Masculinities*, 4 (3): 258–85.

Spatz, B. (2015), *What a Body Can Do: Technique as Knowledge, Practice as Research*, Abingdon: Routledge.

Spatz, B. (2020), *Blue Sky Body: Thresholds for Embodied Research*, Abingdon: Routledge.

Spatz, B. (n.d.), *Making a Laboratory: Dynamic Configurations with Transversal Video*, Brooklyn, NY: Punctum Books.

Spreads, C. (1986), *Ways to Better Breathing*, Great Neck, NY: Felix Morrow.

Sprenger, Julian and Jan Sprenger (2020), 'Scientific Objectivity', in E. Zalta (ed), *The Stanford Encyclopedia of Philosophy*.

Stanfield, J. H. I. (2006), 'The Possible Restorative Justice Functions of Qualitative Research', *International Journal of Qualitative Studies in Education*, 19 (6): 673–84.

Stephens, C. (2011), 'Narrative Analysis in Health Psychology Research: Personal, Dialogical and Social Stories of Health', *Health Psychology Review*, 5 (1): 62–78.

Stevens, J. (2001), *Budo Secrets*, London: Shambhala.

Stinson, S. W. (2004), 'My Body/Myself: Lessons from Dance Education', in L. Bresler (ed), *Knowing Bodies, Moving Minds: Towards Embodied Teaching and Learning*, 153–67, Norwell, MA: Kluwer Academic Publishers.

Straus, L. (1935/1963), *The Primary World of the Senses*, translated by J. Needleman, Glencoe, IL: Free Press.

Stronach, I., D. Garatt, C. Pearce and H. Piper (2007), 'Reflexivity: The Picturing of Selves, the Forging of Method', *Qualitative Inquiry*, 13 (2): 179–203.

Sumar, S. (2007), *Yoga for the Special Child: A Therapeutic Approach for Infants and Children with Downs Syndrome, Cerebral Palsy and Learning Disabilities*, Sarasota, FL: Special Yoga Publications.

Tesler, R., S. Mohammed, K. Hamilton, V. Mancuso and M. McNeese (2018), 'Mirror, Mirror: Guided Storytelling and Team Reflexivity's Influence on Team Mental Models', *Small Group Research*, 49 (3): 267–305.

Thomson, P. (2008), 'Children and Young People: Voices in Visual Research', in P. Thomson (ed), *Doing Visual Research with Children and Young People*, 1–19, London: Routledge.

Thorburn, M. (2008), 'Articulating a Merleau-Pontian Phenomenology of Physical Education: The Quest for Active Student Engagement and Authentic Assessment in High-Stakes Examination Awards', *European Physical Education Review*, 14 (2): 263–80.

Tobin, J. (2004), 'The Disappearance of the Body in Early Childhood Education', in L. Bresler (ed), *Knowing Bodies, Moving Minds: Towards Embodied Teaching and Learning*, 111–25, Norwell, MA: Kluwer Academic Publishers.

Totton, N. (2003), *Body Psychotherapy: An Introduction*, Maidenhead: Open University Press.

Totton, N. (2009), 'Body Psychotherapy and Social Theory', *Body, Movement and Dance in Psychotherapy*, 4 (3): 187–200.

Tremmel, R. (1993), 'Zen and the Art of Reflective Practice in Teacher Education', *Harvard Educational Review*, 63 (4): 434–58.

Trimingham, M. (2002), 'A Methodology for Practice as Research', *Studies in Theatre Performance*, 22 (1): 54–60.

Trimingham, M. (2010), *The Theatre of the Bauhaus: The Modern and Postmodern Stage of Oskar Schlemmer* (Routledge Advances in Theatre & Performance Studies), Abingdon: Routledge.

Trimingham, M. and N. Shaughnessy (2016), 'Material Voices: Intermediality and Autism', *Research in Drama Education: The Journal of Applied Theatre and Performance*, 21 (3): 293–308.

Trippany, R., V. White Kress and S. Wilcoxon (2011), 'Preventing Vicarious Trauma: What Counselors Should Know When Working with Trauma Survivors', *Journal of Counselling and Development*, 82 (1): 31–37.

Uche, A. R. (2015), 'The Retention of First-Generation College Students in STEM: An Extension of Tinto's Longitudinal Model', PhD thesis, The University of North Carolina at Charlotte.

UKAHPP (2009), 'Membership Categories'. Available online: http://ahpp.org/join/memcats.htm (accessed 30 August 2023).

UK National Account of Well-being (2012), 'What Is Well-being?'. Available online: www.nationalaccountsofwellbeing.org/learn/what-is-well-being.html the page is 'what is wellbeing' (accessed 30 August 2023).

Urbina-Garcia, A. (2020), 'What Do We Know about University Academics' Mental Health? A Systematic Literature Review', *Stress & Health*, 36 (5): 563–85.

Van Galen, J. and J. Sablan, eds (2021), *Amplified Voices, Intersecting Identities: Volume 1: First-Gen PhDs Navigating Institutional Power*, Boston, MA: Brill Sense.

Varela, F., E. Thompson and E. Rosch (1993), *The Embodied Mind: Cognitive Science and Human Experience*, Cambridge, MA: MIT Press.

Vaughan, M. (2006), *Summerhill and A.S, Neill*, Maidenhead: Open University Press.

Vickerman, P. (2007), 'Training Physical Education Teachers to Include Children with Special Educational Needs: Perspectives from Physical Education Initial Teacher Training Providers', *European Physical Education Review*, 13 (3): 385–402.

Vishnu-devanander, S. (1997), *Hatha Yoga Pradipika*, New York: Om Lotus.

Vostal, F. (2016), *Accelerating Academia: The Changing Structure of Academic Time*, Basingstoke: Palgrave Macmillan.

Vygotsky, L. S. (1987), *The Collected Works of L. S. Vygotsky*, Soviet Psychology.

Wacquant, L. (2004), *Body and Soul: Ethnographic Notebooks of an Apprentice-Boxer*, New York: Oxford University Press.

Watson, B. and J. Leigh (2021), 'Using Photo Diaries as an Inclusive Method to Explore Information Experiences in Higher Education', in X. Cao and E. Henderson (eds), *Exploring Diary Methods in Higher Education Research Opportunities, Choices and Challenges*, Abingdon: Routledge.

Watts, A. (1957), *The Way of Zen*, New York: Vintage Books.

Weir, L. (2018), *Pina Bausch's Dance Theatre: Tracing the Evolution of Tanztheater* (Edinburgh Critical Studies in Modernism, Drama and Performance), Edinburgh: Edinburgh University Press.

Weiss, H. (2009), 'The Use of Mindfulness in Psychodynamic and Body Orientated Psychotherapy', *Body, Movement and Dance in Psychotherapy*, 4 (1): 5–16.

Wellard, I. (2006), 'Able Bodies and Sport Participation: Social Constructions of Physical Ability for Gendered and Sexually Identified Bodies', *Sport, Education and Society*, 11 (2): 105–19.

Wellard, I. (2010), 'Body Reflexive Pleasures: Exploring Bodily Experiences within the Context of Sport and Physical Activity', *Sport, Education and Society*, 17 (1): 21–33.

Wellard, I. (2015), *Researching Embodied Sport: Exploring Movement Cultures*, London: Routledge.

Wellard, I. (2019a), 'Ian Wellard in Conversation with Jennifer Leigh', in J. Leigh (ed), *Conversations on Embodiment across Higher Education: Teaching, Practice and Research*, 171–72, Abingdon: Routledge.

Wellard, I. (2019b), 'Researching Embodied Sport and Movement Cultures: Theoretical and Methodological Considerations', in J. Leigh (ed), *Conversations on Embodiment across Higher Education: Teaching, Practice and Research*, 139–50, Abingdon: Routledge.

Wellcome (2020), 'What Researchers Think about the Culture They Work In' (report), London: Wellcome.

Wengrower, H. (2009), 'The Creative-Artistic Processes in Dance/Movement Therapy', in S. Chaiklin and H. Wengrower (eds), *The Art and Science of Dance/Movement Therapy*, 13–32, Hove: Routledge.

Wengrower, H. and S. Chaiklin (2020), *Dance and Creativity within Dance Movement Therapy: International Perspectives*, Abingdon: Routledge.

Westland, G. (2011), 'Physical Touch in Psychotherapy: Why Are We Not Touching More?', *Body, Movement and Dance in Psychotherapy*, 6 (1): 17–19.

Whewell, C. (2005), 'Translating Policy into Practice: Reflective Practice'. Paper presented at the *Partnership for Professional Enquiry Seminar*, Stirling, June.

Whitehouse, M. (1995), 'The Tao of the Body', in D. H. Johnson (ed), *Bone, Breath, and Gesture: Practices of Embodiment*, 239–51, Berkeley, CA: North Atlantic Books.

Wilber, K. (2006), *Integral Spirituality*, London: Integral Books.

Williams, D. (2003), *Exposure Anxiety: The Invisible Cage*, London: Jessica Kingsley.

Williams, J. (2013), *Consuming Higher Education: Why Education Can't Be Bought*, London: Bloomsbury.

Wilson, S. (2008), *Research Is Ceremony: Indigenous Research Methods*, Halifax and Winnipeg: Fernwood Publishing.

Wilson, S. (2018), 'Haunting and the Knowing and Showing of Qualitative Research', *The Sociological Review*, 66 (6): 1209–25.

WISC (2020), 'WISC: Women in Suprachem'. Available online: www.womeninsuprachem.com/ (accessed 13 October 2020).

Wittgenstein, L. (1963), *Philosophical Investigations*, translated by G. Anscombe, Oxford: Basil Blackwell.

Wood, E. (1959), *Yoga*, Middlesex: Penguin.

World Health Organization (2022), *The International Classification of Diseases 11th Revision*, Geneva: World Health Organization.

Woronchak, M. and G. Comeau (2016), 'The Value of Reflective Journalling with Advanced Piano Students', *Reflective Practice*, 17 (6): 792–805.

Yee, R. and N. Zolotow (2002), *Yoga: The Poetry of the Body*, New York: Thomas Dunne Books.

Young, I. (1980), 'Throwing Like a Girl: A Phenomenology of Feminine Body Comportment Motility and Spatiality', *Human Studies*, 3: 137–56.

Zalaquett, C. P. (1999), 'Do Students of Noncollege-Educated Parents Achieve Less Academically than Students of College-Educated Parents?', *Psychological Reports*, 85 (2): 417–21.

Zaleski, K., D. Johnson and J. Klein (2016), 'Grounding Judith Herman's Trauma Theory within Interpersonal Neuroscience and Evidence-Based Practice Modalities for Trauma Treatment', *Smith College Studies in Social Work*, 86 (4): 377–93.

Zuesse, E. (1985), 'The Role of Intentionality in the Phenomenology of Religion', *Journal of the American Academy of Religion*, 53 (1): 51–73.

Index

C

D